ALSO BY JEFF GUINN

*The Vagabonds: The Story of Henry Ford and
Thomas Edison's Ten-Year Road Trip*

The Road to Jonestown: Jim Jones and Peoples Temple

Manson: The Life and Times of Charles Manson

*The Last Gunfight: The Real Story of the Shootout at the
O.K. Corral—And How It Changed the American West*

Go Down Together: The True, Untold Story of Bonnie and Clyde

WAR ON THE BORDER

Villa, Pershing, the Texas Rangers,
and an American Invasion

JEFF GUINN

Simon & Schuster

NEW YORK · LONDON · TORONTO
SYDNEY · NEW DELHI

Simon & Schuster
1230 Avenue of the Americas
New York, NY 10020

First Simon & Schuster hardcover edition May 2021

SIMON & SCHUSTER and colophon are registered trademarks
of Simon & Schuster, Inc.

For information about special discounts for bulk purchases,
please contact Simon & Schuster Special Sales at 1-866-506-1949
or business@simonandschuster.com.

The Simon & Schuster Speakers Bureau can bring authors to your
live event. For more information or to book an event, contact
the Simon & Schuster Speakers Bureau at 1-866-248-3049
or visit our website at www.simonspeakers.com.

Interior design by Paul Dippolito

Manufactured in the United States of America

1   3   5   7   9   10   8   6   4   2

Library of Congress Cataloging-in-Publication Data
Names: Guinn, Jeff, author.
Title: War on the border : Villa, Pershing, the Texas Rangers,
and an American invasion / by Jeff Guinn.
Description: First Simon & Schuster hardcover edition. | New York :
Simon & Schuster, 2021. | Includes bibliographical references and index.
Identifiers: LCCN 2020049279 | ISBN 9781982128869 (hardcover) |
ISBN 9781982128876 (trade paperback) | ISBN 9781982128883 (ebook)
Subjects: LCSH: Pershing, John J. (John Joseph), 1860–1948. | Villa, Pancho,
1878–1923. | United States. Army—History—Punitive Expedition into Mexico,
1916. | Texas Rangers—History—20th century. | Mexican-American Border
Region—History—20th century. | Mexico—History—Revolution, 1910–1920.
Classification: LCC F1234 .G928 | DDC 972.08/16—dc23
LC record available at https://lccn.loc.gov/2020049279

ISBN 978-1-9821-2886-9
ISBN 978-1-9821-2888-3 (ebook)

For Charles and Mary Rogers, friends of the heart

Contents

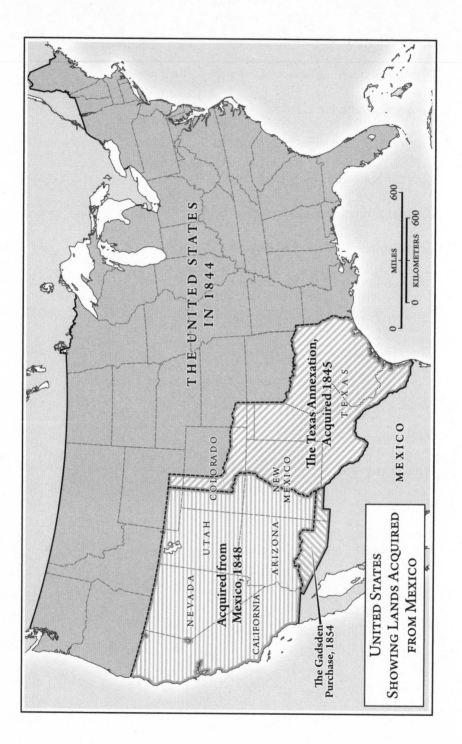

THE UNITED STATES
IN 1844

The Texas Annexation,
Acquired 1845

T E X A S

MEXICO

COLORADO

NEVADA

UTAH

NEW
MEXICO

ARIZONA

CALIFORNIA

Acquired from
Mexico, 1848

The Gadsden
Purchase, 1854

600

600

MILES

KILOMETERS

0

0

UNITED STATES
SHOWING LANDS ACQUIRED
FROM MEXICO

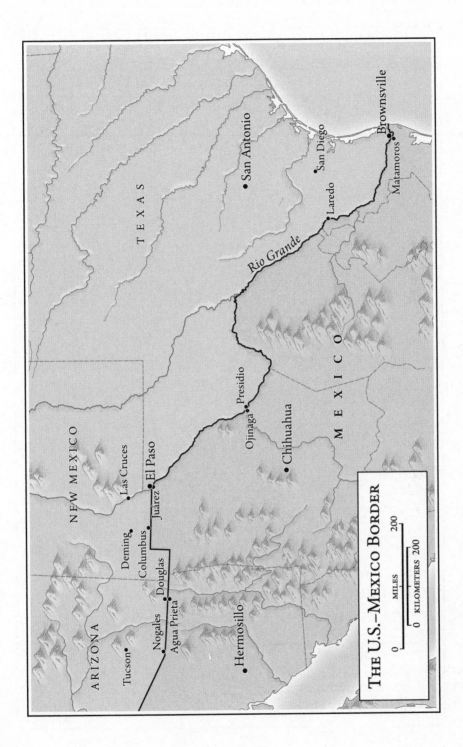

THE U.S.–MEXICO BORDER

MILES
0   200

KILOMETERS
0   200

ARIZONA
Tucson
Nogales
Agua Prieta
Douglas
Columbus
Deming
Las Cruces
El Paso
Juárez

NEW MEXICO

TEXAS

San Antonio
San Diego
Laredo
Brownsville
Matamoros

Rio Grande

Presidio
Ojinaga
Chihuahua

Hermosillo

MEXICO

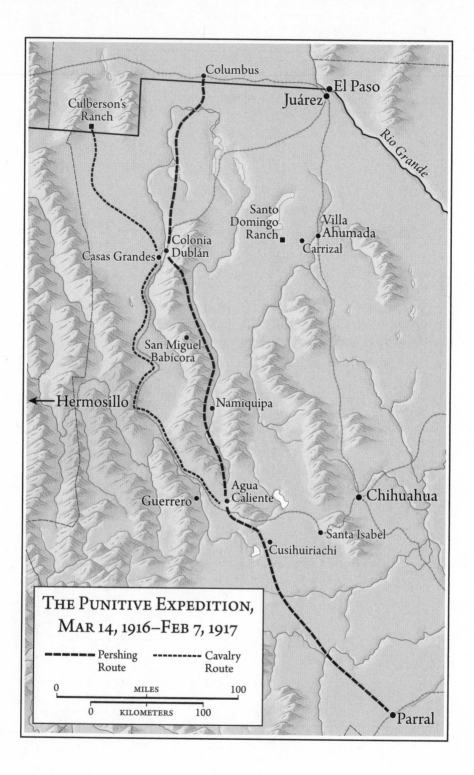

Columbus

Culberson's
Ranch

El Paso

Juárez

Rio Grande

Santo
Domingo
Ranch

Villa
Ahumada

Carrizal

Colonia
Dublán

Casas Grandes

San Miguel
Babícora

Hermosillo

Namiquipa

Agua
Caliente

Guerrero

Chihuahua

Santa Isabel

Cusihuiriachi

THE PUNITIVE EXPEDITION,
MAR 14, 1916–FEB 7, 1917

Pershing
Route

Cavalry
Route

0   MILES   100

0   KILOMETERS   100

Parral

WAR ON
THE
BORDER

Prologue

Columbus, New Mexico, March 8–9, 1916

On Wednesday afternoon, March 8, in 1916, thirty-seven-year-old Pancho Villa crouched on a low hill about a mile south of the U.S.-Mexican border. A morning dust storm had left him and his exhausted followers coated with sand, but during the last few hours the air cleared and so Villa had an excellent view as he trained his binoculars four miles to the northeast. For several long minutes, Mexico's most notorious rebel leader studied the American border town of Columbus, a desolate New Mexico hamlet described by one U.S. soldier stationed there as "a cluster of adobe houses, a hotel, a few stores, and streets knee-deep in sand, [which] combined with the cactus, mesquite and rattlesnakes of the surrounding desert were enough to present a picture horrible to the eyes." Columbus was home to perhaps five hundred hardscrabble civilians—approximately a fifty-fifty mix of Anglos and Hispanics—and a military camp whose officers and enlisted men faced daily the impossible task of guarding a sixty-five-mile stretch on the American side of the sievelike border against rustlers and other unwelcome interlopers. But to Villa, desperate after several overwhelming defeats against Mexican government forces and massive desertions reduced his once mighty army from about forty thousand to a few hundred, the unsightly little place represented opportunity.

Five months earlier, the U.S. had formally recognized the regime of patrician Venustiano Carranza, Villa's archenemy and the man whose forces decimated Villa's in battles throughout 1915, as the official government of Mexico. President Woodrow Wilson and his advisors made the decision despite their collective dislike of the prickly Carranza, a haughty Mexican nationalist who constantly criticized every American diplomatic and military effort to suppress danger to U.S. citizens from Mexico's apparently endless civil revolution. That fighting threatened not only American citizens along the northern side of the border, but also the property of many politically influential U.S. owners of sprawling ranches and flourishing factories and mines on Mexican soil. In contrast, Villa repeatedly proved himself to be a firm American friend, acting in 1914 as the sole voice among Mexican leadership in support of America's months-long occupation of Mexico's vital port city of Veracruz, protecting American-owned property in Mexico, and even withdrawing his troops from a border town battle against the Carrancistas when gawking American spectators from the U.S. side ventured too close and found themselves in danger from stray shots. But in October 1915, during Villa's own time of greatest need, Wilson recognized Carranza, going so far as to immediately ferry Carrancista reinforcements on U.S. trains to the border battle site of Agua Prieta, where Villa was decisively defeated. He and his few surviving followers fled into the mountains of northern Mexico, while Carranza crowed that his longtime antagonist was gone for good. In his rocky exile, Villa realized that, in his current, desperate circumstances, he could no longer hope to defeat Carranza by force of arms.

With all apparently lost, Villa recognized an opportunity to regain popular support by appealing to his countrymen's deep-seated animosity toward the United States of America. Though a 1900 census indicated that only 16 percent of the country's population could read and write, virtually every citizen resented America's remorseless acquisition of Mexican land. Through war, purchase, and outright coercion, over half of Mexico's original territory now belonged to the U.S. Even the potential for American soldiers crossing their border again enraged most Mexicans, especially the multitude of powerless poor who relied on a sense of national honor as their basis for self-esteem.

Villa began declaring that the *yanquis* were returning, this time with Carranza's blessing because, in return for U.S. diplomatic recognition, military assistance at Agua Prieta, and bribes, he'd already sold them Mexico's remaining northern states. The lie resonated with many Mexicans; all that was needed for them to fully believe, and to actively turn on Carranza, was for American soldiers to come again; then Villa would have Carranza neatly trapped. The American-anointed leader would have to demand that the invaders leave at once, even use Mexican troops in an attempt to force them out, or else grudgingly accept their presence. If he chose the former, his alliance with the U.S. would likely crumble, and with it any chance of receiving American bank loans and additional business investments that were badly needed to bolster the sagging Mexican economy. Yet if Carranza didn't immediately expel the American soldiers, he'd be perceived as a gringo lackey. Either way, Villa would make clear that while Carranza must in some way be complicit with this latest invasion—America picked *him* as Mexico's leader, after all—Villa hated the gringos just as much as every other proud Mexican did. Public outrage against Carranza and the U.S. could do for Villa what his once mighty forces could not.

On January 10, 1916, Villista fighters blocked a rail line and stopped a train outside Santa Ysabel in northern Mexico, forced a party of American passengers to disembark, and summarily executed all eighteen, leaving their stripped, mutilated bodies for the vultures. The U.S. was predictably outraged. President Wilson sent stern messages to Carranza, demanding that the Mexican head of state use all his resources to pursue, capture, and punish the murderers, and warning that if Carranza could not protect American citizens in Mexico, the United States would. But despite the massacre, American troops did not come.

Apparently, mass murder of their countrymen in Mexico wasn't enough to bait the *yanquis* in. Given his consuming hatred of the U.S., Villa was willing to attempt even bloodier provocation—slaughtering U.S. citizens on the American side of the border. It would be the ultimate insult. Surely the gringo soldiers would come south to avenge *that*. It was a matter of choosing the appropriate American border town, one sufficiently isolated so that the Villistas could enjoy a head start on pursuers, and certainly a location adjacent to Villa's own massive northern Mexican home state of Chihuahua—he and his men were familiar with every hiding place in its sprawling deserts and craggy mountains. In Chihuahua, they could elude pursuers indefinitely, while the Mexican people built up sufficient rage against *yanqui* invaders to renounce Carranza and flock to Villa, the newly resurrected hero who dared to stand up to America.

Columbus, New Mexico, thirty miles from any other U.S. town and just two miles north of the Mexican border crossing point of Palomas, seemed perfect. It had a bank to rob, stores to pillage, and Americans to kill. For two dreadful weeks, Villa led his followers there through mountain and desert, enduring anticipated swirling dust and unexpected torrential rain, subsisting mostly on corn and bits of dried beef, stumbling for hundreds of rugged miles. Villa suffered as much as his men—one witness recalled him barely able to ride, swaying glassy-eyed and openmouthed on the back of his plodding mount. About half of his 485 troops were reluctant conscripts, given a choice of joining or facing immediate execution. Villa's loyal followers kept watchful eyes on them, warning that if any deserted, Villa would "hang their families from the trees." The conscripts weren't told where they were going or what would happen when they got there. That information was closely held among Villa and his most trusted officers.

To better avoid discovery, the Villistas traveled mostly at night in several separate bands, but sometimes they encountered cowhands and ranchers. Mexicans were temporarily held prisoner, then released, but gringos were killed, with the exception of a white woman and a black cowboy, who were forced to come along. When the Villistas were a day or so away, Villa sent spies ahead to scout Columbus—Mexicans crossed the border to go there all the time, often on business, sometimes just to visit friends. The spies reported that Columbus was ripe for attack. There weren't many soldiers in town, fifty at most, perhaps even fewer, which suggested to Villa that the Columbus Army camp was a small border station rather than anything more militarily substantial. His force of nearly five hundred would overwhelm such paltry resistance. The spies even provided a rough Columbus town map, indicating the locations of the bank, railroad station, hotels, and various stores as well as the military barracks, stables, and other structures.

Yet on the afternoon of March 8, studying Columbus through his binoculars, Villa reconsidered his intended target. Almost everything he observed appeared ideal, especially the lack of guards on the town perimeter. Though the Villistas had done their best to maintain a stealthy approach, during the past several days they hadn't been able to capture everyone they'd encountered. Some riders eluded pursuit, and it was only logical that at least one or two had warned Mexican government officials at Palomas or even the *yanqui* soldiers in Columbus that an armed, aggressive band of rebels was in the vicinity. Between the hill where Villa and some of his officers crouched and Columbus were four miles of flat, slightly sloping valley, bisected approximately midway by a flimsy barbed wire fence marking the border and a rough road running north–south between Columbus and Palomas. Besides a thimble-like hill on the southwest edge of town, there was no cover for assailants to approach Columbus unseen if anyone was watching for them. Anticipating such lookouts, Villa already planned a night attack, though even then in the wide, flat space between him and his target, a single inadvertent whinny of a horse or clink of metal on rock would give away the Villistas' presence.

The lack of sentries was an unexpected advantage—unlikely as it seemed, the gringos apparently had no idea that Villa and his men were near. But Villa was troubled by another observation. His spies swore that only a few dozen *yanqui* soldiers were stationed in Columbus. But it appeared to the rebel leader that many more milled about in the Army camp on the southeast quadrant of town. How many, he couldn't tell, but Villa knew that his worn-out troops couldn't defeat a substantial U.S. force. Abruptly, he told his officers that the raid on Columbus was too risky. They would find some other American border town to attack, one with fewer soldiers. Columbus was not the Villistas' initial target. In late January, Villa had called off a similar attack across the border into Texas when he determined that the odds were not sufficiently in his favor.

Villa's subordinates rarely disputed their leader's decisions, but they argued about this one. The spies were certain about the limited number of soldiers in town; Columbus could be overrun and looted in a very short time, perhaps as little as two hours. Villa resisted for a while, then instructed some of his officers to ride closer and reconnoiter. When the riders returned, they swore the spies were right. There were very few soldiers, and victory was certain. After more discussion, Villa was persuaded. They would attack during the night after all, in the dark hours before dawn when the unsuspecting gringos were groggy with sleep.

About 10 p.m., Villa and his captains led their men north. At one point they halted when lights appeared, chugging toward Columbus from the east—it was a train from El Paso, which paused briefly at the town depot, apparently to disembark passengers, then rumbled away. Another halt was necessary when the Villistas reached the barbed wire border fence. Palomas, the designated Mexican crossing point guarded by a handful of government troops, lay about two miles east. The fence was meant more as a border indicator than a barrier. Villa's men clipped the wires, bent them to the side, and passed through, leaving a few of their number there to provide covering fire if rapid retreat became necessary.

Once beyond the fence, the Villistas turned east to the Columbus–Palomas road, easing their exhausted mounts along a deep, man-made ditch on the side rather than on the road itself. Although there were no clouds, a minimal quarter-moon left the night virtually pitch-black, and the temperature was cool but not cold. As they drew near to town, Villa whispered final instructions—the main body of men would divide into two columns, one striking the Army camp, the other racing into Columbus's modest business district. Both wings would loot, burn, and kill. At this time, ammunition was passed out to the conscripts. They'd previously carried unloaded guns, to discourage insubordination or desertion. Some men were selected to remain in place at the base of the stumpy promontory just west of town, holding some of the horses. Villa said he'd place himself there, too, along with a minimal bodyguard, so he could observe and issue additional orders if necessary. Columbus was silent, defenseless.

A clock hanging outside the train depot read a few minutes after 4 a.m. when Villa hissed, *"Vámanos, muchachos"*—"Let's go, boys"—and the assault began.

⇌•⟶•○•⟵•⇋

CHAPTER ONE

Mexico and America

The chain of events that included Pancho Villa's raid on Columbus began ninety-one years earlier in 1825, when the first envoys of the United States government arrived in Mexico City. Mexicans had won independence from Spain in 1821, but there were some early stumbles—for a short time Mexico was an empire ruled by an emperor before converting to a republic with an elected president. The appearance of U.S. envoys was interpreted by the fledgling Mexican government as a welcome sign of neighborly acceptance. The two similarly sized young nations (about 1.7 million square miles each) shared a 2,400-mile-long border beginning in what would eventually become the American state of Wyoming, and ending where the Sabine River emptied into the Gulf of Mexico and separated the Mexican colony of Texas from the American state of Louisiana. Since the U.S. had had a thirty-five-year head start—its constitution was adopted in 1789— Mexican leaders hoped that America could offer guidance through Mexico's inevitable growing pains. Their sprawling nation had virtually no infrastructure or economic stability, but great potential: deep deposits of minerals, sprawling expanses of fine land for grazing herds or growing crops, and lengthy coasts teeming with fish.

Mexico's national pride matched America's, which is why Mexican leaders were stunned when the newly arrived U.S. envoys delivered an offer from President John Quincy Adams to buy any or all of Mexico between its border with America and the Pacific Ocean. This seemed logical to the U.S., which had previously gained just over half of its current territory through purchase, 865,000 square miles from France in 1803 and 72,000 from Spain in 1819. Now America wanted more land and Mexico desperately needed money; it seemed to American officials that both nations would benefit. The U.S. envoys were surprised when Mexican leaders refused to sell even an inch. A newly formed Mexican government committee on foreign affairs predicted that, through purchase or other means, America's intention toward Mexico was to "overrun" its land. Soon, there was additional evidence.

Texas was Mexico's most promising colony. Its crops and herds provided desperately needed food and tax income. But it was problematic, too—its distance from Mexico City made Texas a hard place to properly administer. Many of its settlers were American; this was allowed in return for their pledge to live as loyal Mexican citizens and observe all national laws. But colonists from the U.S. chafed at these restrictions. In the late 1820s and early 1830s Mexico was rocked by a series of political upheavals that swept a half dozen presidents in and out of office. When General Antonio López de Santa Anna seized power and withdrew almost all Mexico's military from the frontier to Mexico City to consolidate control, colonists in Texas took advantage by declaring their independence. In early 1836 Santa Anna risked leaving his still volatile capital to quell this latest rebellion. After a few initial victories against the self-styled Texians, including at the Alamo, Santa Anna was defeated and captured at San Jacinto by rebel general Sam Houston; he bargained for his freedom by granting Texas independence. Within days, Mexico's congress removed him as president (Santa Anna soon regained power, which he held on and off through 1855) and repudiated the agreement—so far as the Mexican government was concerned, Texas remained its colony, and the rebellion would eventually be put down. Meanwhile, Texas proclaimed itself a republic, and acting as an independent nation began protracted negotiations to join the American union. Mexican leaders believed that the U.S. must have encouraged the Texian revolt for that very purpose. After Texas became America's twenty-eighth state in December 1845, Mexico broke off diplomatic relations with the U.S. and recalled its ambassador from Washington. But that wasn't the end of the dispute.

Since Mexico never acknowledged Texas's independence, there was never any formal agreement over the border between Mexico and Texas. Texas claimed the Rio Grande was the border; Mexico insisted it was the narrower Nueces River seventy-five miles farther north. The land in between, known as the Nueces Strip, was sun-blasted and desolate. Neither side particularly wanted it, but both coveted the meandering Rio Grande (called the Río Bravo by Mexico), with its potential to link far-flung towns and markets with the Gulf of Mexico. Mexicans believed the U.S. had effectively stolen Texas and now intended to snatch the Rio Grande. Americans considered control of the river as one more step toward fulfilling its "manifest destiny." That term was probably coined by journalist John L. O'Sullivan, who in the December 12, 1845, edition of the *New York Morning News* urged his country "to overspread and to possess the whole of the continent which Providence has given us." The *New York Herald* was more plain-spoken in an editorial: Mexico must "learn to love her ravishers." President James K. Polk offered $25 million for the Nueces Strip, plus New Mexico and Alta [Upper] California. Mexican leaders refused to consider the offer. After the rejection of his carrot, Polk brandished his stick, sending General Zachary Taylor and 3,500 troops through the Nueces Strip to the north bank of the Rio Grande. Mexico responded by placing soldiers on the south bank. There was a skirmish that predictably led to war. All of the major fighting took place on Mexican soil, and the better-equipped and -organized American forces prevailed. By the end of 1847, Mexico was forced to negotiate a peace settlement. In the Treaty of Guadalupe Hidalgo, America came away with almost one million square miles of new territory that included all or part of what would become the states of California, New Mexico, Oklahoma, Utah, Nevada, Arizona, Colorado, and Wyoming, plus the Nueces Strip, which remained so uninviting that General William T. Sherman subsequently suggested that "we should go to war again, to make them take it back."

In return for about half of its nation, Mexico received $15 million, plus the cancellation of another $3.25 million in American business claims. The country's leaders did what they could for Mexican nationals who suddenly found themselves living in the United States. Those who wanted to move back across the Rio Grande received 25 pesos per adult or 12 per child to help pay related expenses. But many others chose to become American citizens by remaining where they were, on land that in some cases had belonged to their families for generations—America promised to honor existing Mexican land grants in its newly acquired territory. But Mexicans-turned-Americans were immediately liable for U.S. property taxes, and those who couldn't pay were forced off their land. Others found themselves in American courts when land speculators and individual settlers rushed in to claim Mexican-held property for themselves. The U.S. set up a series of "land courts" to settle such cases. Many of the Mexicans, especially those with only rudimentary or no English-speaking ability, agreed to sell and resettle themselves south of the border, if it could ever be determined where the new U.S.-Mexican border was.

It was sixteen months after the peace treaty was signed before American and Mexican surveyors began work. Negotiators agreed that the Rio Grande would form the 1,200-mile border between Texas and Mexico, with many Washington officials assuming that it was a mighty river similar to the Mississippi, wide and deep and therefore a daunting natural barrier that would discourage unwanted crossings. In fact, the Rio Grande was often narrow or shallow in many long stretches, making it easy to wade. West of the Rio Grande, the treaty had few specifics. For six years, the surveyors trekked through deserts and up and down mountains, occasionally placing small border markers at irregular intervals, usually mounds of stones. Only in the early 1890s was there a concerted effort to mark the border more clearly, with 257 prominent monuments placed along the roughly 750 miles between the Rio Grande and the Pacific Ocean.

Settlements sprang up on both sides of the border, including adjacent towns that served as convenient, supervised crossing points for merchants, ranchers with livestock to trade or sell, and anyone else with legitimate business. Some of the more prominent towns included Brownsville (Texas) and Matamoros, Eagle Pass (Texas) and Piedras Negras, El Paso and Juárez, Douglas (Arizona) and Agua Prieta, Nogales, where Main Street was a portion of the Arizona-Mexico border, Calexico (California) and Mexicali, and San Diego and Tijuana. Customs officials for both countries straddled the borders in these towns and along other selected border points, collecting taxes on goods and money from international transactions. Many businessmen and ranchers resented this, and avoided paying by driving their herds or freighting their wares across isolated stretches of border, often through canyons or other areas where detection was virtually impossible. The U.S. government countered by hiring riders to patrol the border, but there were never enough to guard everywhere.

Lawlessness was pronounced on both sides of the border. Rustlers proliferated—Americans took Mexican cattle, and Mexicans reciprocated. Bandits of all stripes knew that to elude capture, they had only to reach the border ahead of any pursuers. Soldiers and lawmen were forbidden to cross without specific permission from the other government, which, due to distance and bureaucratic delay, was never immediate. Border tension between Mexico and America flared from the start and steadily escalated. Each nation claimed it was the other that not only tolerated, but encouraged, criminal incursions.

Twice, mercenary forces attempted to capture Mexican territory adjacent to the border and establish their own countries. Because Mexico continued suffering internal turmoil, with presidents passing in and out of office as revolts erupted (eighteen different administrations between 1836 and 1851 alone), its federal troops were kept busy around Mexico City. That left its side of the border relatively unguarded, and in 1851, José Carbajal, a Mexican educated in the U.S., claimed American merchants were being discriminated against by stiff Mexican tariffs. Carbajal recruited a troop of American volunteers, crossed back into Mexico, and announced he'd established the Republic of Sierra Madre. Mexican forces rushed north and defeated the interlopers in what became known as the Merchants War. Mexico resented the Americans who'd fought for Carbajal. Some of these captured *yanqui* invaders were summarily executed, which in turn outraged many U.S. citizens. A court in Brownsville tried Carbajal for violation of America's Neutrality Act, but the charge was eventually withdrawn.

During the summer of 1853, there was a more extended effort to wrest away part of Mexico's remaining territory. The Mexican government turned down a land grant request by American William Walker, who wanted to create a buffer colony between the U.S. and Mexico. Walker then recruited about fifty mercenaries, who easily captured the Baja California capital of La Paz—there was only a sparse Mexican population in the area, and even fewer soldiers. Walker named himself president of the new Republic of Lower California, then set out to take the much larger Mexican state of Sonora with the goal of annexing this expanded state into the U.S. in the same manner as Texas. But as Mexican forces approached, Walker fled to San Francisco, where, like Carbajal, he was tried for violation of the Neutrality Act. Much to Mexico's disgust, the American jury needed only eight minutes of deliberation to acquit Walker.

Late in 1853, America began pressing Mexico to sell more land. The U.S. wanted to build a rail line to the Pacific through its southwestern states and territories, but part of the existing border with

Mexico was miles north of the most suitable territory for construction. Additionally, the Treaty of Guadalupe Hidalgo in 1848 obligated America to prevent Indians from attacking the Mexican side of the border. That hadn't worked well—Apaches found the U.S. Army easy to elude, and Mexico's demands that Americans do better were tiresome. So the U.S. offered to purchase 29,670 more square miles that would extend America's Arizona and New Mexico territories south, and also terminate U.S. responsibility to fight off Indians on Mexico's behalf. U.S. ambassador to Mexico James Gadsden offered $15 million, and Mexican negotiators agreed. But when the U.S. Senate convened in early 1854 to officially ratify the agreement, it arbitrarily reduced the purchase price to $10 million—Mexico must accept the reduced amount or the deal was off. The Mexican congress perceived an unspoken threat that, should the sale fall through, the U.S. might very well send troops to the area and take it anyway. This latest insult to Mexican national pride was further compounded when America sent only $7 million as an initial payment. Though the U.S. insisted on taking immediate possession, the additional $3 million was paid only two years later when some ongoing border boundary surveys and disputes were concluded to America's satisfaction. The Mexican land acquired by the U.S. included the fertile Mesilla Valley and the town of Tucson, and this fresh insult inflamed already lingering resentment. In July 1859, a Mexican struck back.

Thirty-five-year-old Juan Cortina had fought for Mexico against the U.S., his patriotism fueled equally by national pride and the fact that his family lands extended on both sides of the Rio Grande. When the peace treaty of 1848 established some of that property as American rather than Mexican, Cortina was incensed, and his fury intensified when U.S. land courts awarded some of the Cortina holdings in South Texas to Americans. During the summer of 1859, Cortina intervened when he saw a former family employee being beaten by Robert Shears, a Brownsville city marshal. Shears told Cortina to mind his own business—an American officer of the law could do what he liked to Mexicans. Cortina shot him in the shoulder and rode away, explaining afterward that "I punished [Shears] for his insolence." This made Cortina a hero to other Mexicans, and a pariah to Americans. A Brownsville grand jury indicted him for attempted murder. Rather than surrender to the local law, Cortina recruited seventy followers and in September launched an attack on Brownsville. The assault was so successful that the Cortina troops temporarily occupied the town. When a civilian militia from Matamoros gathered on the south bank of the Rio Grande with the intention of driving Cortina out of Brownsville—the last thing the Mexican government wanted was for some local hothead to instigate another war with America—Cortina withdrew. For the next several months U.S. Army troops, Texas Rangers, and American civilians calling themselves the Brownsville Tigers pursued Cortina in Texas and in Mexico. There was hard fighting— Cortina's outspoken disrespect for Americans, whom he termed "flocks of vampires," attracted several hundred additional men to his cause. Eventually the combined U.S. forces were able to force Cortina's retreat deep into Mexico, eliminating him as an immediate threat. American officials were furious when Mexicans treated Cortina like a hero rather than a criminal. He became a general in the federal army, and later mayor of Matamoros. But the damage inflicted by Cortina went far beyond a few Anglo casualties. Americans living along the U.S.-Mexican border were uncomfortably reminded that they were greatly outnumbered by Hispanics—who could tell which ones might be contemplating violence? From the day that Brownsville was overrun, American border towns were periodically shaken by rumors that Juan Cortina, or some savage Mexican like him, was about to attack.

><+><-<>-<O><<>+><

For a time, both the U.S. and Mexico endured periods of extended civil war. In America, as the Confederacy was gradually worn down by the Union and faced inevitable defeat, Southern leaders suggested to Abraham Lincoln that a joint invasion of Mexico might reunite the warring factions. Lincoln declined, and another nation conquered Mexico instead.

Mexico was deeply in debt to several countries, and in October 1861 France, Britain, and Spain agreed to a joint demand for repayment. The threat was simple—Mexico must meet its financial obligations to all three nations or risk port blockades and even military action. This was a clear violation of America's long-standing Monroe Doctrine, a U.S. policy forbidding outside countries from threatening independent nations in the Americas. But foreign nations weren't obligated to respect this American-mandated rule, and now its own civil war distracted the U.S. from concern for Mexico's security.

Spain and Britain abandoned the coalition when it became obvious that France's actual intention was to seize part or all of Mexico for itself. This wasn't the first time; France had briefly occupied the port city of Veracruz in 1839, and withdrew only when the Mexican government settled some claims and promised future trade rights. Now France intended making Mexico a permanent French client state, serving as both a fresh foothold in the Americas and a buffer against further U.S. expansion. President Benito Juárez fled Mexico City and vowed resistance. The U.S. government continued recognizing Juárez as Mexico's official leader rather than the junta controlled by France. In July 1863, the junta declared Mexico once again to be an empire rather than a republic, and France supplied the new emperor. Maximilian I, younger brother of Austria's emperor, took the throne, apparently for a lengthy reign.

Juárez's forces couldn't beat the French in pitched battles, so they fought guerrilla-style and succeeded to the point that France sent twenty thousand additional soldiers to maintain control. For Mexican peasants caught in the crossfire, survival was paramount. Many fled across the border to America, in numbers that were uncounted but substantial. One exasperated U.S. official described frustration at having to deal with packs of "poor, deluded half-civilized creatures." Then in 1865 the American Civil War ended, and because of that the tide in Mexico turned.

Now, America was able to support Juárez and his forces with more than words. Juárez's representatives were permitted to sell Mexican government bonds in America, and these were purchased by pragmatic investors who understood the preference of an independent Mexico to a French client state on America's border. Juárez had money for munitions, and U.S. suppliers made them available. At the same time Mexican insurgents finally had sufficient guns and ammunition to make a more extensive fight, America did its own saber-rattling at France. Secretary of State William H. Seward declared that the U.S. was once again in position to enforce the Monroe Doctrine. By the end of 1867 France had withdrawn, Maximilian was executed, Mexico was again a republic, and Benito Juárez reoccupied the presidential palace. For the first time, Mexicans had reason to appreciate rather than resent the United States. Juárez suggested to American bankers and business leaders that Mexico offered attractive opportunities for investment, particularly mining, farming, and ranching in northern Mexican states. Response was immediate and positive. The U.S. government expressed full support; a new era of warmer relations between Mexico and America commenced. It lasted less than five years.

CHAPTER TWO

Border Fences and Revolution

Benito Juárez died of a heart attack in July 1872 and was succeeded by Sebastián Lerdo, chief justice of the Mexican Supreme Court. Unlike Juárez, Lerdo viewed American business magnates with suspicion. He thwarted plans for several *yanqui* companies to jointly build north–south rail lines between Mexico's interior and the U.S. border, first insisting that only Mexican firms must do the construction, then limiting foreign participation to a single U.S. entity. This alienated American financiers, who wanted the relatively unlimited investment opportunities previously offered by Juárez. At the same time, Lerdo attempted to strengthen Mexico's central government while lessening the authority of state officials. It earned him the enmity of powerful landowners outside the Mexico City area, who were accustomed to virtual autonomy. Porfirio Díaz, a general who fought gallantly against France, sensed opportunity. In 1875 he ran against Lerdo for the presidency and lost.

A few months later Díaz revolted; he made his initial base in Brownsville, Texas, where border-crossing restrictions placed him beyond Lerdo's reach. Díaz pledged that, as Mexico's president, he would unconditionally welcome American investors with the kind of generous terms that guaranteed hefty profits. Americans responded by providing Díaz with money for men and munitions; he enjoyed almost unlimited financial resources, and because of them could afford to keep well-equipped forces in the field against Lerdo's inadequately funded federal army. The result was inevitable. In November 1876 Lerdo fled into exile, and in early 1877 Porfirio Díaz assumed the Mexican presidency.

The Americans who'd given Díaz financial support expected their promised quid pro quo, and he delivered. Díaz met in New York City with U.S. business leaders (including former president Ulysses Grant); together they designed a massive program of American investment in Mexico, focusing first on railroads so that raw materials could easily be shipped to manufacturers in the U.S. Díaz didn't intend to sell out his countrymen in return for the presidency. American businessmen financed his successful rebellion; now he would use their Mexican investments to revitalize his country. American-owned mines, railroads, farms, and ranches would need Mexican workers. American-built infrastructure—rail lines, roads—would benefit Mexicans as well as *yanqui* investors. True, for the present Americans owned most of the minerals and oil extracted from Mexican soil. But sometime in the future Mexico would be in position to nationalize these businesses, and the American owners, having long since recouped their investments and made considerable profit, would have to accept new arrangements. In the meantime, they would pay taxes on their Mexican holdings, pumping more desperately needed financial lifeblood into their host country.

In 1880, Díaz's four-year presidential term was up. He relinquished office to a political crony, and spent the next four years controlling Mexico from behind the scenes. Then, at his direction, the constitution was amended to allow multiple presidential terms, and in 1884 Díaz was elected for the second time. He began aggressive land privatization by targeting the Catholic Church, which owned 48 percent of Mexican land and paid no taxes on it. Once most of that property was wrenched free, Díaz pounced on Mexico's numerous communally owned *pueblos*, using the courts to free up that land for sale. Every newly available acre was snapped up, often by American investors—William Randolph Hearst, delighted with his new, expan-sive ranch property, mused, "I don't see what is to prevent us from owning all of Mexico and running it to suit ourselves." The wealthiest Mexicans acquired the rest. Known as *hacendados*, they often lived in Mexico City and owned properties of a half-million acres or more out in the country. These men became Díaz's most dependable po-litical base. Under Díaz, *hacendados* and American investors eventually owned between them approximately 95 percent of Mexico's arable or grazing land. The Catholic Church retained a little, and individual peasants collectively owned 2 percent. Mexico's railroads were almost entirely American-owned, as were most mining operations. Outside investment in Mexico totaled $1.2 billion.

Díaz believed that these changes would bring about a national economic boom, and he was right. Mexico's gross national product began growing an average of 8 percent annually (half that would have been considered impressive). For the first time, income from Mexican exports sometimes outpaced money spent on imports. American inves-tors mined, farmed, ran railroads, and also, according to a report by the U.S. consul general, opened and operated "banks, water companies, electric light and power plants, gas and water works plants, telephone systems and similar industries." Díaz was well satisfied, so much so that after his second four-year term he chose to keep seeking reelection. His rigid control of the voting process resulted each time in Díaz victories by margins of 90 percent or more. American investors considered him their valued partner; the U.S. press couldn't laud him enough. In Feb-ruary 1902, when he had held the presidency for twenty-two years (not counting the break in 1880–1884), the *New York Times* credited Díaz "for the present eras of peace and prosperity in Mexico." But many Mexicans did not feel peaceful or prosperous at all.

The glittering economic successes disguised a contradiction. Mexico was richer but most Mexicans were worse off than they'd been before their country's supposed savior gained the presidency. Díaz's policy of turning over as much land as possible to wealthy investors was largely responsible. Denied small plots of land of their own, country peasants, comprising 80 percent of Mexico's population, had no option other than to work for the rich Mexican *hacendados* or American landowners, most often as field workers or herders. *Hacendados* paid low wages, the equivalent of $3–$4 a month, and American employers in Mexico, focused on profit, were pleased to follow the custom. Many also adopted the *hacendado* tradition of requiring workers to live on their employer's land and make all of their food and clothing purchases at the employer's store, where prices for staples like cornmeal, coffee, clothing, and shoes were inflated, in part to force workers to buy on credit, obligating them to stay indefinitely in their backbreaking jobs until they satisfied their debts—which, with their minimal pay, was impossible to do. The descriptive term later adopted by historians is *debt peonage*. In practice if not in name, these workers were slaves.

In the cities, Mexican employees of American-owned businesses found themselves gradually made redundant by technology. Every new-fangled machine brought in by gringo owners to power plants, water works, and construction eliminated the need for at least a few employees. Working conditions were also difficult. Hours were long and supervision onerous—the Americans had no tolerance for employees giving anything but all-out effort. The workers sometimes formed labor unions to protect their interests. The Díaz government, firmly on the side of management, shut down attempted strikes. These companies made profits, and the profits were taxed—this arrangement took precedence over workers' rights.

But rank-and-file Mexicans felt growing antipathy for Americans beyond the workplace. More *yanquis* arrived all the time, an average of about three thousand every year. Not all of them were investors or company bosses. In Mexico, middle-class Americans could afford land and big houses that they could never have aspired to in the U.S. Virtually all Americans moving to Mexico showed no interest in conforming with, or even learning much about, their new country's culture. Instead, they clustered together, refusing to learn Spanish or mingle with Mexicans. They showed no respect for Mexican customs and insisted on retaining their own. Most infuriating of all was the Americans' attitude that their presence was a favor to Mexicans; the same *New York Times* article in 1902 that praised Díaz included interviews with Americans living in Mexico. The reporter noted that it was difficult for them to feel comfortable in such a primitive land— "Bathrooms are seldom found in Mexican houses"—but that expatriates were comforted "by the notion that the influence of American customs upon those of the native people is beginning to be felt."

Mexicans living on the U.S. side of the border felt even more at odds with what some Spanish-language publications termed "blonds" or "the blond race." The number of arriving Mexicans was not yet being definitely counted, but historian Arnoldo de León estimates that sixty thousand annually crossed into El Paso alone. They came to work on the ranches and farms that sprang up along the border from the southern tip of Texas to the California coast, and they were badly needed. Mexicans provided cheap labor, working for perhaps a third of what Americans expected to be paid. But these workers could not overcome, or, in many cases, forgive, racial prejudice against them. This was evident since the conclusion of the U.S.-Mexican war, when American settlers began pouring into what had been Mexican territory, but it intensified in the mid-1860s. After the Civil War, Southerners dominated frontier settlement, all of them desperate to escape Reconstruction and many retaining the ingrained belief that people of color were inferior. Mexicans were not only "colored," but frequently a racial mix of Indian, Spanish, and, sometimes, African forebears. In the American southwest and, especially, along the border, Mexicans were often stigmatized as *greasers*, probably because, to newly arrived whites who'd had little or no interaction with Mexicans before, their various shades of brown skin resembled grease.

But along the border, American disdain for Mexicans remained tinged with fear. Anglos remembered the Alamo and Juan Cortina. Ongoing depredations on American ranches and travelers were real rather than rumored. The border was unsafe, and Mexican and Anglo criminals were equally culpable. Díaz didn't have sufficient military capacity to do much about it, so American forces took up the slack, including the Army, state rangers (especially in Texas), regional and town lawmen, and self-appointed civilian militias who hunted Mexican bandits and too frequently decided that any "greaser" would do. U.S. government officials were also concerned about Mexican criminal elements on and below the border. While Hearst and other American business titans assumed that at some point Mexico's northern states would surely be annexed by the U.S., political leaders in Washington, wearied by complaints about the border depredations, never considered it. They believed that annexation would burden America with too many undesirable new citizens.

Despite ongoing border-related tension, Díaz took every opportunity to remind Americans how grateful he and his people were to the U.S. In 1891 he granted a lengthy interview to a reporter from the *Buffalo* (New York) *Morning Express*, who dutifully quoted the Mexican president about how Mexican land could be purchased by Americans "at very attractive prices," and concluded his story with Díaz's promise that Mexico's goal remained becoming "day after day more worthy of being called a sister of the great model republic, the United States of America." By 1902, one American government survey indicated that 1,117 U.S. "companies, firms and individuals" had established business interests in Mexico. Porfirio Díaz, now seventy and in his fifth presidential term, seemed invulnerable and determined to remain in office for life.

The first real threat to Díaz initially seemed insubstantial. In August 1900 a young lawyer named Ricardo Flores Magón published *Regeneración*, an anti-Díaz newspaper. In 1902, Magón fled across the border and set up editorial shop in St. Louis, where he and his brother Enrique resumed publishing *Regeneración* and, with a few other expatriated dissidents, formed the Liberal Party of Mexico, which demanded eight-hour workdays and a minimum wage for all workers. The newspaper and fledgling political party gained support from U.S. labor unions and liberal firebrand Emma Goldman. The unions and Goldman were despised by the same American business elite that supported Díaz. They made their concerns known to U.S. authorities, and Magón was soon arrested on suspicion of committing seditious acts in violation of American neutrality laws. Temporarily free on bail, Magón escaped to Canada. He reemerged in El Paso a few years later, and *Regeneración* editorials called for armed rebellion against Díaz. But an amateurish attempt plotted by Magón to attack neighboring Juárez was easily thwarted. Magón avoided arrest and went to Los Angeles, where he was taken into custody and sent to U.S. prison for Neutrality Act violations. But articles Magón wrote and smuggled out of his cell inspired Mexicans who chafed under their president.

There was also a wobble in Díaz's support among American owners of vast ranching operations in Mexico. Tired of bandit raids and rustling, despairing of the Mexican government's inability to defend against them, some chose to protect their property with fences. Among the first was the 2.4-million-acre Wood Hagenbarth Ranch near Palomas, just below the border. In 1903, ranch management announced it would mark its northern boundary with a three-strand barbed wire fence extending from "18 miles west of El Paso to three miles into the Mexican state of Sonora," a distance of 140 miles. A barbed wire fence couldn't keep rustlers out, but it would make the process of driving stolen cattle away more difficult, increasing opportunities for successful pursuit. U.S. state and federal officials considered similar fences along the border itself. Through legitimate purchases as well as rustling, tick-fever-afflicted Mexican cattle were frequently passing the infection on to American stock. The U.S. Bureau of Animal Industry tried, and failed, to thoroughly monitor all possible border crossing points, legal or otherwise.

In 1909, the bureau proposed erecting a barbed wire fence along the 137-mile California–Baja California border, with construction due to begin in 1911. The September 5, 1910, edition of the *Boston Daily Globe* reported that the California–Baja California border might be extended by the American government into "the longest fence in the world and the oddest artificial boundary between two countries. . . . This fence will consist of stout posts, possibly of reinforced concrete, and 5-strand, steer-tight barbed wire. . . . The fence will be about 1000 miles long." Six weeks later, the October 25 edition of the *Los Angeles Herald* informed readers that "a fence along the border between Mexico and the United States seems assured. Surveyors are now in the field." But the massive fence never advanced beyond widespread speculation.

About the same time that the California–Baja California border fence was proposed, Díaz granted an interview to a writer from *Pearson's Magazine*. During the interview, the seventy-eight-year-old proclaimed Mexico finally ready for new leadership, and announced he would retire from the presidency when his current term ended in July 1910. Anyone who liked could run. A surprising candidate emerged—Francisco Madero, a scrawny, squeaky-voiced member of a prominent family. He wrote a book in 1908 titled *La sucesión presidencial en 1910* (*The Presidential Succession of 1910*), arguing that allowing one man to hold power indefinitely was wrong for Mexico. Madero's flowery campaign speeches lacked specific promises beyond pledging an incorruptible administration that would remain for only a single term, but they caused the aging incumbent president to reconsider. If Madero were elected, he might undo all of Díaz's accomplishments. Díaz announced he would run again after all.

Madero campaigned in villages, among the working class and poor; Díaz knew his own support lay elsewhere. He formally requested

William Howard Taft to meet with him in Mexico, which would be the first state visit by an incumbent American president to the country. A Díaz-Taft summit would remind *hacendados* that it was Díaz who made America their lucrative business partner, and perhaps impress the peasantry with their leader's lofty stature in the world. Taft was persuaded to participate by Henry Lane Wilson, the U.S. ambassador to Mexico and a firm supporter of Díaz's policies favoring American investors. The historic meeting took place in October 1909, with the two presidents exchanging formal visits between the twin cities of El Paso and Juárez. Díaz asked Taft for full U.S. endorsement in the coming election. Taft pressed for the renewal of several American military leases in Baja California. The American president left the historic summit certain that Díaz would not last much longer in office, probably through bloody revolution and with the almost inevitable consequence of America becoming involved to protect its border and Mexican investments. In a note to his wife immediately following his meeting with Díaz, Taft wrote, "I can only hope and pray that his demise does not come until I am out of office."

Madero's campaign gained momentum that astonished even the upstart's own family—his grandfather, himself one of the grand *hacendados*, compared it to "a microbe's challenge to an elephant." But the elephant sensed danger, and in June Díaz had his rival arrested on charges of fomenting revolution and disrespecting the president. Two weeks later, while Madero languished in jail, Díaz was elected to his eighth term, running against a nonentity who replaced Madero. Voting results released by the government indicated Díaz won almost unanimously.

Madero escaped custody in October 1910 and fled to San Antonio, Texas, where he declared the recent election invalid and announced an armed uprising against Díaz that would commence on November 20. It was Madero's belief that his countrymen would rise up in great numbers and overthrow the tyrant. On November 19, Madero crossed the Rio

Grande, expecting that the next day he'd greet at least five hundred revolutionaries. Fewer than a dozen showed up. Madero took this disappointment well, and moved his headquarters to El Paso. Throughout the winter and early spring, more revolutionary leaders emerged in separate rebellions against Díaz, notably Emiliano Zapata in the south and Pascual Orozco in the north. Orozco won victories against federal troops in the north, and Zapata kept steady pressure on Díaz from the south. Madero persuaded Orozco to join him, and, due in great part to Orozco's success in the field, Madero gained control over much of Chihuahua. He named his trusted subordinate Abraham González to be the state's provisional governor, and González in turn recruited to Madero's cause a young man calling himself Francisco Villa, whose background was questionable but whose fighting skills were exceptional.

By February 1911, Madero sent a formal letter to U.S. secretary of state Philander C. Knox. In it, Madero promised that, under his leadership, Mexico would remain America's friend: "At the proper time and in due form, [I will] take steps to secure just recognition from the Government of Your Excellency." Acknowledging America's most obvious concern, Madero added that "the interests . . . of your citizens [in Mexico] have been and will continue to be protected." Knox and Taft weren't convinced. With the fighting extending across the northern Mexican states, they believed a buffer was needed at the border. On March 7, Taft ordered twenty thousand U.S. troops—about a fourth of the entire American Army—to the border, where they would conduct "routine maneuvers" while being in place, if necessary, to "restore order to Mexico." Díaz was offended; this seemed a clear sign that the U.S. believed he might lose. Had Díaz known the extent of America's preparation, he would have been even more upset. The Office of Naval Intelligence sent spies to evaluate several Mexican seaports as potential landing sites for a U.S. invasion. Soon, Taft approved a projected first step—America would, if and when necessary, begin by landing in Veracruz and occupying the city.

In April, Madero gathered the bulk of his rebel forces and, with Orozco and Villa under his command, set out to take Juárez, which was defended by a much smaller federal force. Juárez was the border point where American shipments of guns and ammunition purchased by Díaz were brought in by rail. Rebel occupation would deny him these munitions, and perhaps make them available to Madero instead. Madero was a philosopher rather than a warrior. To the dismay of Orozco and Villa, he agreed to a temporary cease-fire with General Juan Navarro, leader of the federal forces in Juárez. For several days, Madero's generals chafed while he and Navarro engaged in long discussions about how Juárez might be surrendered with minimal bloodshed and loss of honor by the federals.

On May 8, while Madero and Navarro still negotiated, Orozco and Villa sent their troops to attack, then informed Madero that, through some miscommunication, the battle had begun and there was no way to stop it. After three days of fighting, Navarro surrendered. With the revolutionaries in firm control of Juárez, Díaz realized that his best remaining option was resigning the presidency. On May 25, 1911, two weeks after the fall of Juárez, he sailed off aboard the German steamer *Ypiranga* into European exile. On June 7, enthusiastic crowds jammed Mexico City streets as Francisco Madero made his triumphant return. That fall, Madero was legally elected president. As historian John S. D. Eisenhower wrote in his book *Intervention*, "The Mexican Revolution had thus far been a success." But success was fleeting.

CHAPTER THREE

><+<>+0+<>+<

The American Puppeteer

Prior to Porfirio Díaz, Mexican presidents were pressured or driven from office at a dizzying rate—forty administrations in fifty-five years, along with a junta from 1860 to 1864 and the doomed reign of Emperor Maximilian from 1864 to 1867—but never as the result of a protracted nationwide revolt. The fight against Díaz lasted eight months, during which Pascual Orozco, Francisco Villa, and Emiliano Zapata, all regional military powers in their own right, consented to work together under the leadership of Francisco Madero. He swept triumphantly into Mexico City on June 7, 1911, but almost immediately his coalition began disintegrating. The cause was Madero himself, who allowed Díaz's officials to remain in place and run the interim government. Zapata stormed back to Morelos, convinced that Madero was just one more *hacendado* who couldn't care less about the plight of Mexico's peasants. Orozco, already offended that Madero appointed Coahuila state governor Venustiano Carranza rather than himself to be minister of war, was appalled when Madero dismissed all revolutionary forces while retaining the federal army under command of Díaz-appointed officers. Villa, who'd grown to despise Orozco during the siege of Juárez, simply rode back to Chihuahua.

Even after Madero was elected president of Mexico in a landslide and formally assumed office in November, he took no definitive steps toward any reform. It was as though Madero believed that ridding

Mexico of Porfirio Díaz was all he was obligated to do. Less than three weeks after Madero's inauguration, Zapata publicly repudiated him. Madero sent federal troops to Morelos to put down his former ally, and these were led by Victoriano Huerta, a hard-bitten sixty-year-old Huichol Indian who'd previously served as Díaz's military enforcer. Zapata was a committed but geographically limited revolutionary. He cared solely about land reform, and never fought far from his beloved southern home state. But he enjoyed almost complete support in Morelos, and now he and his followers fought Huerta to a stalemate. Meanwhile, *hacendados* still resented Madero's anticipated land reforms, there were problems with some federal troops in far-flung states receiving their pay, and border depredations were increasing in frequency. Though Madero felt himself assaulted from all sides, he had yet to identify another threat, this one emanating from the U.S. embassy in Mexico City.

>━━◆◦◆━━<

Henry Lane Wilson was a lawyer and newspaper publisher prior to 1897, when President William McKinley named him minister to Chile. In his memoir, Wilson wrote that he entered diplomatic service "with a sympathetic understanding of racial psychology" regarding "Latins," no matter their individual countries of origin: "The Latin-American has in common his prejudices, his traditions, his habits of thought and living, and to these he stubbornly adheres in spite of the changing modes of life and thought created by inventive genius and the tremendous stride of Anglo-Saxon energy." He served in Chile for seven years, then accepted President Theodore Roosevelt's nomination to the same post in Belgium. President Taft, increasingly concerned about border security and protection of American investments, appointed Wilson to be ambassador to Mexico in December 1909.

Taft's faith in Wilson was such that the new U.S. minister in Mexico could, and occasionally did, ignore State Department chain of command and communicate directly with the president himself.

President Díaz felt that anything Wilson said or did directly reflected the wishes of President Taft, and Wilson was pleased to let him believe it. Wilson emphasized two areas of concern with Díaz: border security and protection of American investments in Mexico. So long as American business was happy with Díaz, then so was Wilson, and his reports to Washington reflected it. After Díaz's resignation, Wilson warned Secretary Knox in a memo marked "confidential" that Madero, certain to be elected Mexico's president in the fall, was "a dreamer of uncertain tendencies." Most Mexicans "are illiterate and wholly without the necessary training to fit them for the responsibilities of intelligent citizenship."

The Madero administration unhappily discovered that Mexico's money was in the hands of the *hacendados* rather than the government. Federal funds were too short to cover many basic expenses, including military salaries. Troops in Juárez, informed in January 1912 that their pay was delayed again, mutinied. They took over the border city and blocked U.S. shipments of goods and munitions to Mexico. Having defeated Díaz by capturing Juárez, Madero well understood its importance. He ordered Pascual Orozco to put down the mutiny and retake the city. It seemed a logical response—Orozco was from the north, knew the territory, and had conquered Juárez before. But upon arrival, instead of fighting the mutineers, he joined them, and to Madero's horror began successfully recruiting volunteers for a rebellion of his own. To quell this particularly dangerous uprising, Madero chose another battle-tested veteran who'd previous fought for him. Francisco Villa had retired to civilian life, operating several butcher shops in the state capital of Chihuahua City. Madero had some concern whether Villa would rally to his cause again or rebel himself—the man's current loyalties were as murky as his past.

Born in 1878 to sharecropper parents in the Mexican state of Durango, Doroteo Arango changed his name to Francisco Villa around 1902. He probably took his new surname from wealthy forebears—his father was a rich man's illegitimate son—but let others think he'd adopted the name of a well-known regional outlaw instead. The newly monickered Villa looked and acted the part of a dangerous man. Though he could read and write passably well, Villa frequently described himself as virtually illiterate. Enemies underestimated his intelligence, usually to their regret. Most Mexican officers of high rank, federal and rebel alike, wore neat, elegant caps and uniforms adorned with medals and braid. Villa was usually clad in the same nondescript sombrero, shirt, and pants worn by peasants. There was some calculation in this, adopting a wardrobe to complement his intended public image, but Villa also felt genuinely comfortable in these clothes. Top-heavy and sporting a bristling mustache, he lurched slightly when he walked, but was grace itself on horseback. Villa's mood could and frequently did change in an instant, from charming rogue to raging ogre and back again. Above all, he knew how to build support among the poor, for he could truthfully say he had lived as one of them. For a while Villa made a mostly honest living running work crews for foreign businesses in Chihuahua, supplementing his income as many others did with occasional rustling. But in 1910, Villa had a dispute with a member of the state governor's police and killed him; his temper was always a flaw. Now a fugitive, he was glad to accept recruitment by Madero ally Abraham González in the revolt against Díaz.

Villa's splendid service gained him rapid advancement, until he stood second only to Orozco in the rebels' military hierarchy. Orozco was threatened by Villa's rising reputation, and Villa always chafed under someone else's command. The two rebel officers developed mutual antipathy, and so when Orozco betrayed Madero, the president hoped that Villa would put aside his own disappointment with his administration and come out of retirement to fight Orozco for him. Villa agreed, but when he called for volunteers, he found that many potential recruits had already gone over to Orozco. Villa and the limited force he could muster still fought Orozco; though they lost most major battles, they occupied Orozco while Huerta gathered loyal federal troops to go north and fight. Madero wrote to Villa that "I shall see to it that you are rewarded for the services you have rendered to the republic."

Villa considered himself a temporary volunteer rather than a full-time federal officer. In June, he and another federal quarreled over ownership of a horse. Villa telegraphed Madero's General Huerta that he'd had enough—he and his men were done fighting for the government. Huerta announced that Villa was deserting to start his own uprising against Madero, and he captured the rebellious leader. Villa was promptly placed before a firing squad. In direct contrast to his public image as a fearless man, Villa groveled and cried, pleading for his life. There were many witnesses. At the very last moment—rifles were cocked—Villa was reprieved. President Madero had somehow learned of the imminent execution and sent orders for it to be stopped. But Madero could not entirely dismiss Huerta's charges against Villa. He needed Huerta too much, so most of Villa's volunteer troops were forcibly conscripted into the federal army and Villa himself was sent to prison. On Christmas Day 1912, he escaped and fled to El Paso. In the sure knowledge that Villa made a better ally than enemy, Madero sent word that in return for a promise not to rebel, he would be allowed to return home to Chihuahua. An agreement was reached, but before Villa was back across the border Madero's fortunes took their final, fatal turn.

While Villa was in prison, Huerta pounded at Orozco's forces until, in August 1912, the rebels broke and Orozco escaped over the border into the U.S. In recognition of this success, Madero named Huerta as commander of Mexico's armed forces. Madero believed the danger to his government was past. But on February 9, 1913, troops led by federal general Manuel Mondragón unexpectedly marched into Mexico City. Once arrived, they split into two separate forces and freed two prominent anti-Madero leaders, Bernardo Reyes and Félix Díaz, from the prisons where they were held. The rebels believed they would next take Madero captive, but soldiers remaining loyal to the president put up a stiff fight. About 1,800 took refuge in the massive Ciudada (Citadel) fortress. Huerta placed his government forces around the Ciudada. After a direct assault failed, Huerta ordered heavy bombardment. Stray explosions battered many parts of Mexico City, including neighborhoods mostly populated by Americans.

On February 12, Ambassador Wilson met with Madero, informing the beleaguered president that the U.S. demanded that the fighting stop. Wilson warned that American warships and marines were prepared, even poised, to intervene. Madero responded directly to President Taft. In a message transmitted to the White House, Madero wrote that "I have been informed that the Government over which Your Excellency worthily presides has ordered that war ships shall set out for Mexican coasts with troops to be disembarked to come to this capital to give protection to Americans." Any reports that Americans in Mexico City were in danger were exaggerated; all they had to do was "concentrate" in specific parts of the capital or in suburban towns, and Madero would guarantee they'd receive "every measure of protection." Madero acknowledged that "my country is passing at this moment through a terrible trial," but if, after receiving erroneous information, Taft intervened, "the United States would do a terrible wrong to a nation which has always been a loyal friend." Madero unwisely shared the letter with Wilson, who was offended and fired off a telegram to Washington claiming Madero was "misleading and inexact." The ambassador was further infuriated on February 16 when Taft replied directly to Madero that "perhaps Your Excellency was somewhat misinformed." The president assured his Mexican counterpart that America had no present intention of sending in troops. In closing, though, Taft wrote that he felt obligated "to add sincerely and without reserve that the course of events during the past two years culminating in the present most dangerous situation creates in this country extreme pessimism."

Mexico City was awash in rumors that Huerta and the troops serving under him either had or would soon join the rebels. On the night of the 17th, Ambassador Wilson notified Washington that he'd just received a private message from Huerta advising that Madero would be removed from power "at any moment," to which Secretary Knox responded only with the request that "no lives be taken beyond the due process of law." The ambassador did not alert Madero.

On Tuesday the 18th, Madero and Vice President José María Pino Suárez were arrested while conducting a cabinet meeting. Huerta sent a terse one-sentence message to Taft announcing that "I have overthrown this government, the forces are with me and from now on peace and prosperity will reign." Late that night, Wilson sent a telegram to Washington reporting that, at his invitation, Huerta and fellow rebel Félix Díaz, nephew of Porfirio Díaz, came to the American embassy "for the purpose of considering the question of preserving order in the city." But the ambassador realized "many other things had to be discussed first," including who would now head the Mexican government. Both men wanted the presidency, and Wilson bragged in the telegram that "after enormous difficulties I managed to get them to work in common on an understanding." With the American ambassador orchestrating, it was agreed that Huerta would become provisional president, Félix Díaz would appoint the new cabinet, and, when formal elections were set, Huerta would support Díaz for the presidency.

On February 19, Huerta had a question for Wilson: What should he do with former president Madero, place him in a lunatic asylum or exile him? The ambassador replied that Huerta "ought to do that which was best for the peace of the country." Huerta chose a third option. Shortly after taking the presidential oath, he ordered Madero and Suárez taken to a place away from the presidential palace where they would be safe "until public passions have subsided." On the way, their cars were engulfed in gunfire and both were killed. Huerta claimed the two men died when their supporters attempted a rescue and shot them by mistake. Taft and Secretary Knox were appalled, and ordered Wilson to investigate. Four days later the ambassador replied that "in spite of all the rumors that are afloat I am disposed to accept [Huerta's] version of the affair and consider it a closed incident." Wilson then badgered Taft and Knox to make America the first country to formally recognize the Huerta government. The ambassador was not pleased when Knox replied that "for the present no formal recognition is to be accorded those *de facto* in control." Taft had lost the November 1912 U.S. presidential election; he and Knox had only a few days remaining in office. Their successors would be sworn in on March 4. Let them sort out the mess in Mexico.

CHAPTER FOUR

"I Do Not Know What to Make of Mexico"

Woodrow Wilson was in many ways an unlikely candidate for the White House. He was a Southerner (born in Virginia, raised mostly in Georgia and South Carolina) in a time when post–Civil War grievances still divided the nation and Northerners dominated the national government. Though he had a law degree, Wilson's primary career was in education, first as a college professor and later as president of Princeton University. While an academic, he wrote extensively on the subject of American government—it wasn't enough, Wilson insisted, for government to maintain the status quo. Life for all could and must be made better by acting on rather than simply talking about noble principles, and by teaching the less fortunate how to improve themselves.

Wilson came to believe that his vision and leadership skills were stifled in academia, and sensed a better opportunity in politics. Democrats in New Jersey were regularly lambasted in state elections. But Wilson ran for governor in 1910 as a committed progressive on the Democratic ticket and won in a landslide. He swiftly revamped New Jersey's convoluted electoral system, enforced new statutes for workmen's compensation, and became a candidate for his party's presidential nomination in 1912. Getting the nomination wasn't easy. Several rivals, including former three-time Democratic nominee William Jennings Bryan, were far more skilled at political infighting, which Wilson disdained. No clear winner emerged through dozens of ballots at the Democrats' national convention. Bryan eventually realized that he wouldn't gain a fourth presidential nomination from his party, and announced he could never support Speaker of the House Champ Clark, his most detested rival. That opened the way for Wilson to win as a compromise candidate on the forty-sixth ballot. In the general election that fall, Wilson was lucky again. Former Republican president Theodore Roosevelt returned as an independent to challenge incumbent William Howard Taft, once Roosevelt's close friend and, in the 1908 election, his chosen successor. That split the Republican vote, and Wilson was elected.

Traditionally, new American presidents had focused on domestic legislation—foreign affairs were usually an afterthought. That changed in 1898 with the Spanish-American War. Previous U.S. wars had been fought against England (twice), Mexico, and itself in the Civil War, but always on American soil or, in the case of Mexico, in a nation immediately contiguous with America's southwestern border. America's quarrel with Spain involved Cuba's fight for independence from Spanish rule, threats to American business in Cuba because of it, and the mysterious sinking of the USS *Maine* in Havana Harbor. This time, Americans fought in Cuba and Puerto Rico (another Spanish fiefdom), and also in the Pacific, where Spain held the Philippines and Guam. The U.S. war with Spain was shockingly brief, lasting less than four months. Spain was no longer capable of maintaining a global empire, and its capitulation included turning over Cuba, Puerto Rico, Guam, and the Philippines to the U.S. in exchange for $20 million. Cuba was briefly a U.S. protectorate, then granted independence in 1902 (America was guaranteed a permanent lease on a base at Guantánamo Bay); Puerto Rico and Guam were declared and remain U.S. territories. Filipinos, already in revolt against Spain before Americans arrived, declared themselves independent as the First Philippines Republic, and fought the U.S. until 1902, when superior American firepower finally prevailed.

But these overseas holdings, along with Hawaii, annexed by the U.S. in 1898, meant that America now had its own far-flung empire, like England and Germany and France. There was also the Panama Canal, a fifty-one-mile work in progress that would allow greater shipping access between the Atlantic and Pacific Oceans. France tried and failed to build the canal, abandoning the project in 1841. America stepped up in 1904, and the canal was scheduled to open in 1914. For the first time, the U.S. had the trappings of an international superpower. Its new subjects (not yet citizens) were mostly people of color, living in cultures Americans considered unenlightened. Presidents McKinley and Roosevelt and Taft and their administrations adopted policies best described as condescending. Primitive peoples could be helped to live in more sanitary surroundings and, in a limited sense, govern themselves under strict American supervision, although they could never entirely overcome their inherent inferiority. Mexico's proximity and the potential of the Panama Canal meant that the U.S. must also exert its influence over as much of Central America as possible, and, by logical extension, at least some of South America and the Caribbean, too. Lurking foreign powers would be warned off as necessary—the Monroe Doctrine remained U.S. policy.

But in March 1914 the new U.S. president had a radically different approach in mind. At heart, Woodrow Wilson was a teacher—and, instead of benignly overseeing inferior races and cultures, he would teach America's lesser neighbors how to raise themselves up into proper democracies. Mexico was an excellent starting point. The idealistic Wilson saw things as entirely right or entirely wrong. Mexico's current president had gained power by murdering the duly-elected incumbent. This was wrong. Victoriano Huerta must surrender his office to a more acceptable Mexican leader, someone dedicated enough to his country's future to become the willing pupil of America's professorial president.

There were two immediate obstacles. Huerta had no intention of giving up Mexico's presidency, and the rival best positioned to replace him was Venustiano Carranza, an especially proud Mexican nationalist who considered America to be the inferior country and culture. It was easy for Woodrow Wilson to underestimate Huerta, who was renowned as a battlefield butcher. Huerta's lumpy cranium and perpetually grim expression gave his head the overall appearance of a clenched fist, an accurate representation of his character. It was an open secret among the international diplomats stationed in Mexico City that Huerta was a functioning alcoholic. He made many decisions while in a hungover daze. But by the standards of his country, Huerta was a very well-educated man; he had attended Mexico's military academy and excelled in math. Huerta was also a shrewd judge of character. When Woodrow Wilson took office and immediately began calling for Huerta to step down because of the means by which he gained the Mexican presidency, Huerta nicknamed him "the Puritan of the North." He publicly ignored Wilson, realizing that directly engaging the verbally adept American president would be disadvantageous.

Above all, having achieved Mexico's presidency, Huerta had no intention of serving on an interim basis. Félix Díaz soon realized that Huerta's pledge to support him in the next presidential election meant nothing. Aware of how Huerta would deal with him as a potential rival, Díaz instead accepted an assignment as a foreign ambassador and sailed overseas. Woodrow Wilson continued calling for Huerta's resignation, but at least for the moment, the American president's carping meant little to the burly Huichol Indian. His immediate attention was occupied by a northern revolutionary leader who, like Madero, seemed able to pull together disparate packs of rebels into a single menacing force. But Madero had been too scatterbrained to hold his ragtag coalition together for long. This man, apparently, was different.

Venustiano Carranza hailed from *hacendado* stock, and came late to the Madero revolution because he considered it to be philosophically misguided. To Carranza, Porfirio Díaz had to go because he sold out Mexican interests to foreign investors. The land distribution dear to Zapata and Villa was repugnant to Carranza, whose ideal Mexico was a country that vigorously defended its honor and treasures against outsiders, while offering equally rigorous protection to the great Mexican landowners whose prosperity was beneficial to all. When it became apparent Madero posed a real threat to Díaz, Carranza, governor of the northern state of Coahuila, joined the rebel cause just in time to be on hand when Díaz capitulated after the fall of Juárez. Madero, himself part of a landowning family, felt more comfortable with Carranza than with rougher-edged allies like Orozco, Villa, and Zapata. Madero named Carranza his minister of war and made him a confidant. Carranza believed presidents should be authoritarian, not weaklings. He quickly became disgusted with Madero's retention of many Díaz cronies and his inability to insulate Mexico from foreign influence. Carranza made his opinions known to Madero in hopes of stiffening the new president's spine. The effect was negative; the two men grew estranged.

It was no surprise to Carranza when Madero fell and Huerta snatched the presidency. He believed Huerta, like Porfirio Díaz, was wrong for Mexico. Back home in Coahuila, a safe distance from Mexico City while Huerta consolidated his hold there, Carranza sent telegrams to America's lame-duck president, urging Taft not to recognize Huerta's administration. Carranza called for Madero's former allies to join him in the north—once again, a tyrant must be overthrown. Some anti-Huerta forces rallied to him, but not enough. Zapata remained entrenched in Morelos, fighting Huerta from there. Orozco, returning from his U.S. exile, joined Huerta instead. Villa remained in El Paso, invited back to Mexico by Madero but certainly persona non grata to Huerta. Álvaro Obregón, who'd fought effectively for Madero, now battled Huerta while leading the revolutionary troops of his home state of Sonora, whose government refused to recognize the Huerta regime.

Carranza made the best of his precarious situation. He announced that his forces would be known as "Constitutionalists," offering a clear distinction from Huerta's conscripted, mostly reluctant forces, and designated himself not as general but the more modest-sounding First Chief (*Premier Jefe*). It was an apt title; at fifty-four, very late middle age in 1913 Mexico, Carranza was the antithesis of a warrior. According to John S. D. Eisenhower, Carranza's "movements were slow and ponderous, accentuated by his great height and his large potbelly. Because of his weak eyes he wore blue-tinted sunglasses, and he had the disconcerting habit of stroking his white beard when in thought." Carranza made no pretense that he was in rebellion on behalf of Mexico's peasantry. It wasn't that he disdained the common people, but rather that he didn't think much about them at all. In a properly governed Mexico, the rich and well educated would thrive, and in turn their affluence would lift up everyone else. In modern-day economic terms, Carranza was a proponent of the "trickle down" effect. As an intellectual rather than a military man, it was inconvenient for Carranza that he had to fight Huerta rather than politically maneuver his way to the presidency. Ideally, Carranza would have appointed a skilled, battle-tested general to lead the Constitutionalist troops, but since he had none the First Chief stepped up himself.

The results were disastrous—Carranza had no conception of battlefield strategy. He anticipated a specific flow of battle and was offended when the enemy didn't act exactly as expected. Huerta's forces won three consecutive battles against the Constitutionalists in Coahuila, and with the *federales* now firmly in control of the border state, Carranza fled west to Sonora with his remaining forces. Álvaro Obregón was entrenched there, so Huerta's troops chose not to immediately pursue. But Obregón was willing to serve as a military leader under Carranza's command. He was acceptable to the First Chief because he was respectful, well-spoken, and had demonstrated on the battlefield that he was an effective commander despite lacking formal military training. Obregón's leadership vastly upgraded the Constitutionalists' battlefield performances, and, about the same time, another formidable opponent took the field against Huerta.

> ⊷•○•⊶ ◄

Villa had become a popular local figure in El Paso. Reporters for local American newspapers couldn't write enough about him; almost daily their readers were treated to laudatory articles and photos of Villa enjoying ice cream cones or swimming in a city pool, apparently at complete ease on the northern side of the border. Though the man formerly known as Doroteo Arango had taken the name Francisco Villa, some of his closest friends affectionately called him "Pancho." That name seemed catchier to the American press, who repeated it in print until its use became near-universal. Villa had no objection; the informal nickname complemented his reputation as a man of the people.

Despite Madero's previously jailing him, Villa retained an almost idealistic loyalty to his former leader. It was through his service to Madero that Villa rose out of relative obscurity; that alone might have been enough for Villa to return to Mexico and fight Madero's murderer. Yet there was additional, even more burning incentive—Villa had a personal score to settle with Huerta, who'd sentenced him to a firing squad and had been the cause of many people witnessing Villa on his knees, sobbing and pleading for his life. Honor meant everything to Villa, and to some extent it was tarnished, in his own mind above all, by his craven behavior when facing execution. He now had an opportunity to restore wounded pride by joining the fight against Huerta, and he took it.

In March 1913, Villa sneaked across the border into Chihuahua with a handful of followers, certainly no more than a dozen. In a matter of weeks, he recruited five hundred troops. In six months, Villa led several thousand. He was a personable commander, mingling with his soldiers as though he were one of them and not the leader, making sure that daily rations of flour and beans were promptly allocated, encouraging troopers to bring along their families—wives, children, in some cases aging parents. To move this ever-growing horde, Villa bypassed traditional rebel travel modes of horseback, wagon, and foot in favor of railroads. Thanks to American investors, railroads extended in most general directions in the northern Mexican states where Villa initially operated. Villa loaded his followers into railroad cars—he eventually operated fifteen different trains—and placed his wounded in designated hospital cars, where they could receive treatment in relative comfort. Villa even paid his soldiers a regular wage of 25 pesos every fifteen days, in the form of his own specially printed scrip; Chihuahua shopkeepers and ranchers generally honored Villa's money, some in support of his efforts to unseat Huerta, others because they feared his wrath if they didn't.

In Sonora to the northwest, Carranza and Obregón had their own successes against the federals. In Nogales, Obregón drove the Huertistas to the U.S. side of the divided city. There the federal officers surrendered to American authorities, who reluctantly housed their new guests. The American consul based in Nogales wired Washington asking for instructions: Was America remaining neutral in Mexico's internal strife, and, if so, wasn't it taking sides by allowing the defeated Huertistas to loll comfortably just north of the border until they felt sufficiently rested to cross back and resume fighting the rebels? It was only one of the Mexico-related questions that vexed President Wilson and William Jennings Bryan, his secretary of state.

Wilson and Bryan disliked each other—Wilson thought Bryan made flowery speeches but had little common sense, and Bryan resented Wilson's rocketlike ascension from college to American president. But Bryan remained a Democratic Party force, obligating Wilson to offer him a prominent role in the new administration. Both held the opinion that America should exert foreign influence by peaceful means whenever possible. So Bryan was offered, and accepted, the job of secretary of state, considered the prime position in any presidential cabinet, and one in which Bryan, a devout Christian who believed every word in the Bible was literal truth, felt he could exercise his godly principles on behalf of the entire globe. In a major diplomatic step, Wilson allowed Bryan to negotiate new bilateral treaties requesting nations to bring disagreements before neutral investigative tribunals for at least a year's negotiations before resorting to war. With simmering tensions in Europe, it was a noble effort, though Germany refused to sign on. But Bryan also demonstrated his faith in even the smallest ways, including banning liquor at State Department events, which made him unpopular with foreign diplomats stationed in Washington.

For Wilson and Bryan, Mexico was an inconvenient distraction. Europe was their constant concern; they were determined to see war avoided there, or, if it did happen, to keep America out. Yet Mexico couldn't be ignored. America's most influential businessmen wanted Huerta firmly supported. On March 12, the *New York Times* reported that "in banking circles there has not been nearly as much shaking of heads over the fall of the Madero government as there was when Porfirio Díaz relinquished the power he had held so long." Americans living and working in Mexico were in just as much danger as Mexican nationals, sometimes more so since federal and rebel troops alike constantly demanded that U.S.-owned companies and ranches donate money, supplies, and livestock (cattle for beef, horses for transportation, mules for hauling loads), often confiscating what they needed if it wasn't reluctantly offered. President Wilson was unwilling to accept Huerta as Mexico's leader, and the rebels seemed unlikely to triumph in the foreseeable future. It was hard to get objective information about what was going on. Unlike Taft, President Wilson had grave doubts about the veracity of his ambassador to Mexico.

From the day they assumed office, Henry Lane Wilson bombarded the new American president and secretary of state with telegrams and private memos urging them to not only support, but to officially recognize the Huerta administration. He dismissed opinions expressed by various U.S. consuls that the rebels stood a good chance of eventually ousting Huerta. The ambassador argued that it was illogical for Wilson and Bryan to think that superior American morals could ever thrive in such a backward nation: "With 80 percent of the population unable to read or write, permanent democratic government cannot be established in Mexico." If the Huerta government did fall, the ambassador predicted, "absolute chaos will come and [American] intervention will be inevitable."

But by mid-March, Ambassador Wilson's continuing reports that the Mexican rebels were "decisively defeated" were contradicted by stories in American newspapers about revolutionaries' victories at Nogales, Ascensión, and in several other battles. On March 30, the ambassador requested that Bryan speak out against articles in U.S. newspapers that reflected negatively on Huerta and his federal troops: "I think it would be most useful if the Department would place the seal of condemnation on the sensational and wicked stories which are being sent out by certain portions of the press, and whose correspondents care nothing about the truth so they can get material for vivid headlines." Bryan declined.

In late spring 1913 President Wilson, despairing of constructive advice from his ambassador, asked journalist William Bayard Hale to go to Mexico City on his behalf and report confidentially about his impressions of the Huerta government. Hale's report expressed exactly what Wilson had anticipated: Huerta had to either voluntarily give up office or be forcibly deposed if Mexico was ever to have a truly democratic government. Huerta had recently announced he would stand for election in October. Now he received a private communication from President Wilson saying that the election should be held as scheduled, but Huerta must not be a candidate. Huerta was especially offended by the American president's assurance that he "counsel[ed] Mexico for her own good." He declined withdrawing from the race.

President Wilson suspected other nations might be engaging in secret negotiations with Huerta, and used a recently created U.S. government department as an active spy service. The Bureau of Investigation was established in 1908 by President Theodore Roosevelt and worked solely through the Department of Justice, freeing it from affiliation with any other government service. The bureau was originally intended to ferret out white-collar crime, but its purposes and number of agents rapidly expanded. Now many of its operations focused on Mexico, especially identifying border smugglers and foreigners working against American interests. Several agents were placed in jobs as border crossing officials. Others gained access to border post offices, opening, reading, and reporting suspicious mail. A major bureau effort was the hiring of "special employees" to infiltrate rebel supporters working out of the U.S. Any potentially useful information was welcomed, and from late spring through the end of 1913 there was plenty to report.

Most disappointing was the rush of foreign governments to grant diplomatic recognition to Huerta. Germany and Japan had been anticipated—both nations saw opportunities to increase their Mexican influence. But England's recognition of Huerta was a bitter disappointment. With prospects of war with Germany increasingly probable, the British chose access to Mexican oil over concern about the character of Mexico's president. In a meeting with an English official, President Wilson explained that "I am going to teach the South American republics to elect good men." The Englishman, realizing that Wilson really meant Mexico, replied that his government saw no difference among the leading contenders. But in the summer, word reached Washington of a new alliance that might very well dispatch Huerta from office. Carranza and Villa had met and agreed to join forces.

>-+-◆>--○--◆-+-◄

Though Carranza could never personally feel comfortable with someone as crude as Villa, the First Chief couldn't deny the man's fighting prowess. He sent emissaries to sound out Villa about an alliance. Villa realized that Carranza had the political skills that he lacked and, besides, it was never Villa's ambition to rule Mexico. He wanted great influence, but not ultimate responsibility. Above all, Villa hated Huerta, and joining with Carranza was the surest way to drive his enemy out of the presidential palace in Mexico City. He met with Carranza and agreed to fight for the First Chief, under one condition: Villa must operate independently in the field and appoint his own officers. Also, he wanted cannon. Carranza had several, and grandly allocated four to Villa. Now able to add bombardment to his signature cavalry charges and night attacks, Villa embarked on a fresh series of battles intended to bring the state of Chihuahua entirely into rebel hands. American newspaper and magazine correspondents, including John Reed and Ambrose Bierce, were welcomed to accompany Villistas, chronicling their gallant efforts for enthralled American readers. Villa's U.S. fans included Secretary of State Bryan, who was pleased to learn that Villa was a fellow teetotaler.

Despite Villa's success, and Zapata's persistent attacks in Morelos just south of Mexico City, Huerta remained determined to stay in office. He decreed that the October presidential election would be held as scheduled—he would abide by the decision of the people, leaving unsaid that most potential voters outside Mexico City would be too busy dodging bullets to utilize a ballot box. President Wilson was appalled; after an August speech to Congress when he demanded that Mexico must in some way depose Huerta, Wilson made clear in a public announcement that the U.S. would act if Huerta or the Mexican voters didn't: "The government of the United States does not feel at liberty any longer to stand inactively by while it becomes daily more and more evident that no real progress is being made towards the establishment of a government at [Mexico City] which the country will obey and respect. . . . We are seeking to counsel Mexico for her own good and in the interest of her own peace, and not for any other purpose whatever."

Secretary Bryan summoned Ambassador Wilson to Washington and informed him that the president would be pleased to accept his resignation. In another slap at Huerta, President Wilson did not appoint a new ambassador; after all, America still withheld diplomatic recognition of the Huerta government. Instead, the U.S. would be represented in Mexico City by Nelson O'Shaughnessy, the State Department's Mexican chargé d'affaires. Even with Ambassador Wilson gone, President Wilson still professed himself baffled by the actions of Mexican leadership. In a September letter to his wife, Ellen, who was seriously ill with Bright's disease, the president lamented, "I do not know what to make of Mexico. The apparent situation changes like quicksilver."

Huerta won the October 26 presidential election, but voter turnout was so sparse that even he could not pretend the results were valid. He announced another election would be held in July 1914. Woodrow Wilson had no intention of waiting that long. With Mexican conditions "quicksilver," he began considering an alternative plan that would remove Huerta from office and, hopefully, place someone in his stead who would be grateful to the U.S. and eager to bring complete American-influenced democracy to his troubled nation. To Wilson, Carranza seemed the logical choice. The First Chief was clearly no warrior, but Wilson had a plan to compensate for Huerta's inevitable decision to fight to the death. America would declare war on Mexico, allowing the U.S. to blockade Mexico's ports and cut off Huerta's access to arms purchased from foreign governments. Then American troops would set up battle lines just above Mexico's southern border and below the Mexican northern states controlled by Carranza's forces. These lines would be established with Carranza's permission. The American troops would fight only if it became necessary to protect

U.S. lives and American-owned property, while the Mexican rebels, led by canny generals like Villa and Obregón, would finish off Huerta. The federals would be hampered by lack of arms and ammunition while the U.S. ensured the Constitutionalists had all they needed. After Huerta was defeated, Mexico could hold an aboveboard presidential election. If Carranza didn't win it, any honest candidate who relied on American guidance would do.

In mid-November, the time seemed right to approach Carranza. Villa had just taken Juárez; after that victory, momentum was clearly with the rebels. Carranza was asked to meet with U.S. envoys in Nogales. There the First Chief was apprised of Wilson's plan. All that was needed was his agreement for American forces to temporarily enter Mexico. Carranza refused. Mexico would handle its own problems. American assistance was not needed or wanted, beyond the right to buy arms from the U.S. Would America sell him guns and ammunition? The stunned envoys tried to change his mind, but Carranza was unmoved: any form of American military involvement was unacceptable. That ended the meeting.

President Wilson did not, then or later, comprehend the extent of Carranza's nationalism, or his lifelong resentment of America's acquisition of half his beloved country. Perhaps granting Carranza's request for purchase of U.S. munitions would soften his puzzling attitude; the president lifted the arms sales embargo to Mexican rebels previously imposed by President Taft. Because rebel forces held Juárez directly across the border from El Paso, they now had convenient access to American munitions. Carranza remained adamant against any other form of U.S. assistance. Wilson was determined that America must do more to force out Huerta.

In November 1913, the State Department sent a telegram to several U.S. chiefs of mission in Central and South America. It warned, "While the President feels that he cannot yet announce in detail his policy with regard to Mexico, nevertheless he believes that he ought, in advance thereof, to make known to the Government to which you are accredited his clear judgment is that it is his immediate duty to require Huerta's retirement from the Mexican government, and that the Government of the United States must now proceed to employ such means as may be necessary to secure this result."

CHAPTER FIVE

Film Crews and the Refugees Nobody Wanted

The alliance between Carranza and Villa was shaky from the start. Neither man entirely trusted the other. The first sign of their inevitable break came in the days immediately following Villa's victory at Juárez—he was offended when Carranza offered only perfunctory congratulations. It was as though the First Chief considered taking the most important Mexican city on the border to be no more significant than winning some minor skirmish. Villa interpreted this as evidence that Carranza might be leading the revolution against Huerta to serve his own ends rather than the people of Mexico. But his suspicions about Carranza didn't prevent Villa from immediately attacking Chihuahua City, the state capital that he'd tried and failed to capture before. This time the garrison resisted briefly, then in early December retreated east toward the federally held town of Ojinaga 120 miles away on the Mexico-Texas border. Villa now controlled the entire state of Chihuahua.

Convinced he could follow and defeat the federals at will, Villa paused in Chihuahua City to act as self-appointed state governor. He issued a decree that all *hacendados* in the state would have their lands confiscated; profits from their operation would now engorge the public treasury, providing Villa with a steady source of money to pay his *soldados*. After Huerta was defeated, the land would be divided up among all the people of Chihuahua. Meanwhile, *hacendados'* cattle were butchered and the beef made available to Chihuahua's poor at drastically reduced prices. As historian Friedrich Katz observes in his definitive biography of Villa, this was the first time in memory that Chihuahua's state government had done anything specifically for its peasants.

During the first week of January 1914, Villa was ready to fight again; his forces, now known as the División del Norte, had swelled to at least thirty thousand. Many new soldiers were deserters from the federal army, freshly attracted to Villa's service either because of his generosity to the peasants or else terror at his willingness to execute captured foes. The División del Norte left for Ojinaga and what Villa anticipated would be the near-effortless destruction of federal troops making a stand there. The federals were commanded by Pascual Orozco; Villa looked forward to facing his despised antagonist. And when the Villistas moved east, they didn't travel alone. Besides soldiers and arms, their railroad cars were crammed with portable generators, motion picture cameras, and film technicians. Pancho Villa was going to be a movie star.

Money and reputation were equally crucial to Villa's cause. With so many soldiers to pay and arm, and so many of their families to feed and trains to keep fueled and repaired, there were never enough funds to pay for everything. On January 7, 1914, it was announced in the *New York Times* that Villa had agreed to "a moving picture venture" with Mutual Film Corporation of Hollywood. According to the *Times*, in return for granting Mutual exclusive rights to film the División del Norte in battle, Villa would receive 20 percent of all theater revenues, presumably a significant sum since in 1914 Americans bought a weekly average of 49 million movie tickets. (Other sources indicate Villa sold these rights to Mutual for a flat fee of $25,000.) The money was welcome, but so was the opportunity for Americans to see as well as read about Villa. Starstruck U.S. supporters could prove a valuable source of donations. So sweaty, equipment-laden film crews crammed into Villa's trains to Ojinaga alongside media correspondents. Villa had no doubt that his prowess would soon be on full, thrilling display in American movie theaters.

Ojinaga stood directly across the border from the small Texas town of Presidio. There were other tiny communities scattered on both sides, where Mexicans and Americans alike had rudimentary lives. Here the Rio Grande flowed shallow and slow, and there was no scenery beyond scrub brush, cactus, and a few low hills. It was an odd place for pitched battle, but Orozco and his federals had no other place left to run in north Mexico. Villistas were between them and retreat to Mexico City, and also blocked reinforcements from the south. There was nothing to do but dig in and try outlasting the rebel assault. The federals had to not only fight for their own lives but defend a mob of refugees who'd fled to Ojinaga from Chihuahua City along with them. Not all Mexicans idolized Villa.

The fighting began during the second week in January, and at first the federals held on. Villa let subordinates lead the initial attacks, but eventually took over himself. División del Norte's officer ranks had recently been bolstered by Felipe Ángeles, a former soldier under Porfirio Díaz whose belief in social reform eventually drove him to the rebels. Ángeles was an artillery expert, and his addition proved crucial at Ojinaga. Villa admired both Ángeles's skills at bombardment and as a strategist—his care in planning helped balance Villa's impulsiveness. With Ángeles's cannons blasting effectively, after several days of fighting the federals and refugees abruptly abandoned Ojinaga, splashing across the Rio Grande to sanctuary on the American side—3,352 men, 1,607 women and children, and 1,762 horses and mules, plus an ornate carriage bearing former Chihuahua governor Luis Terrazas and his family. Prior to the Villista victories in the state and subsequent confiscation of *hacendado* land, Terrazas's holdings totaled more than seven million acres. Orozco, who privately conceded defeat while demanding that his men fight on, disappeared deep into Texas.

There was consternation on both sides of the river. In Ojinaga, Villa was irked by news that the movie crew was unable to film usable battle footage. The combatants moved too much, and there was considerable dust. The movie deal hung in the balance. A compromise was reached. Villa switched from his ordinary clothes into a braid-bedecked general's uniform and dashed up and down Ojinaga's streets on his great war horse for the cameras, but this footage too proved unusable since Villa ignored repeated requests to ride slower. The film crew had better luck with members of the División del Norte, who obligingly faked some battle scenes. Afterward Mutual Films decided to switch from revolutionary documentary to melodrama, with a raffish professional actor hired to play the hero. *The Life of General Villa* debuted in May. It was not a box office smash, but afterward camera crews often came to Mexico, filmed reenactments, and sold them for inclusion in the newsreels that usually preceded feature presentations. American theater audiences were allowed to believe that the action in the newsreels was authentic.

The frustration felt on the south bank of the Rio Grande by Mutual Films and its would-be rebel movie star paled beside the alarm among Americans on the north bank. The Ojinaga refugees, nearly five thousand plus their animals, pushed to the breaking point a growing concern on the U.S. side of the border about desperate Mexicans and their need of American charity. The problem dated back to the French occupation of the 1860s, when Mexicans of all ages and backgrounds sought safety across the river in the United States. It was not lost on hardscrabble residents of the U.S. border towns they arrived in that many refugees were in states of near starvation or acute stages of illness. Food and medical care had to be provided; otherwise there would be dead bodies in the streets. The crisis was not temporary. As soon as one group of refugees was fed, another hungry, sick bunch appeared—plus, many of the neediest had nowhere else to go and stayed on, further draining the resources of residents who were hard-pressed just to feed and care for themselves.

Even more worrisome were male refugees who crossed the border in perfect health. Often they'd been soldiers in the federal army, and though they were required to turn over their weapons to U.S. authorities, many did not. In the small Texas coastal town of Refugio, there were reports of 1,000 to 1,500 refugees, most of them men who were armed and constantly drunk—only a dozen Anglos remained in town. The rest fled, in effect becoming refugees from the refugees.

All along the border, Anglo resentment flared. Some communities asked the military to intercede—wasn't it the Army's job to protect Americans from dangerous or pestilent foreigners? But the military lacked the manpower to guard the 1,900-mile border—the entire U.S. Army comprised just 4,800 officers and 77,500 enlisted men. One-quarter of its personnel were stationed overseas, mostly in America's new far-flung outposts—Hawaii, the Philippines, Puerto Rico, the Panama Canal project. And on the U.S. side of the border, Army presence often engendered hostility among transplanted Mexicans living and working there. When mine operators in the town of Terlingua requested troops to protect them from four hundred rough-looking refugees who gave no indication of moving on, they asked that the Army pretend it sent the soldiers without being asked. The Terlingua mines depended on Mexican labor, and if the workers knew their bosses called out the Army on their refugee countrymen, they likely would retaliate by striking or otherwise disrupting production.

With the exception of Zapata, fighting from the state of Morelos near Mexico City, revolutionaries battled Huerta's troops in northern Mexico. Refugees from the states of Chihuahua and Sonora and Coahuila could not flee even a few miles south—that's where the fighting was. The only available sanctuary was the American side of the border. Many refugees thought of the country immediately beyond the border as something of a promised land because they had relatives or friends who had emigrated there and found employment. America's southwest border states needed cheap labor on farms and ranches; Mexico was the best source. But inherent prejudices as well as charitable limits determined which Mexicans were acceptable. Mexican laborers who knew their place were tolerated—it helped that they usually kept to themselves in small communities away from where their white employers and fellow workers lived.

But so many able-bodied Mexican men now crossed the border that, for the first time, white American workers felt threatened. It was well known that Mexicans gladly worked for half or even a third of what Anglo laborers expected. If they kept coming, eventually these "greasers" would end up taking all the jobs. Then there were the innumerable elderly refugees too weak to work, or women with hungry children, or sick arrivals who would die without immediate care— these contributed nothing and drained limited community resources.

America had some immigration policies in place to restrict entry by specific undesirables: "Chinese immigrants, lunatics, people likely to become public charges . . . anarchists and others deemed undesirable," according to historian Rachel St. John. Customs officers at official border crossing points were responsible for deciding who the undesirables were, and did turn away many Mexican refugees. But most avoided the designated crossing places, because they realized they might be refused entry there or, more often, because they were running for their lives and desperate to get into America at the nearest possible point. A U.S. government report noted that so many "row boats, carriage roads and mountain trails" offered access that "however vigilant the border inspectors may be, [they] can accomplish next to nothing."

Because so many crossed undetected, it's impossible to know how many refugees and other Mexican immigrants entered the U.S. during the decade that Mexico's revolution lasted. Educated best guesses offer staggering estimates. In *The Injustice Never Leaves You: Anti-Mexican Violence in Texas*, Monica Muñoz Martinez suggests at least one million arrived in Texas alone. Arnoldo de León believes the number of refugees crossing all border points escalated annually, from perhaps 125,000 in 1910 to 252,000 in 1920. Arthur R. Gómez writes in *A Most Singular Country: A History of Occupation in the Big Bend* that by the end of the revolution in 1920, 10 percent of Mexico's roughly 15.6 million population had crossed into the American southwest. All that white border residents knew was that there were too many. In January 1914, when more than 4,600 refugees flooded into Presidio after Villistas stormed Ojinaga just across the Rio Grande, a breaking point was reached. Presidio was home to perhaps one thousand people, and a few smaller area towns totaled approximately five hundred more. Even temporarily, area residents could not assume the feeding and emergency medical care required for more than three times their number. Urgent messages were sent to the U.S. Army base at Fort Bliss in El Paso, two hundred miles to the northwest: *Do something.*

U.S. troops had already been sent to Presidio to protect residents there if the Ojinaga fighting spilled over the Rio Grande. Now, after some discussion, they led the refugees about twenty miles north to the village of Shafter and herded them into a cemetery. It was early afternoon, and the town school was let out early so students could stare at the refugees, most of whom were too exhausted to stare back. Then, from several directions, people arrived with food, portions of the same simple fare that would appear within hours on local dinner tables. When it grew dark, the refugees slept beside the graves and headstones, and the next morning, January 16, they were given breakfast. By then Major Michael McNamee, commander of the American soldiers temporarily stationed in Presidio, had received orders from Fort Bliss: Bring the refugees here.

Rail cars to convey them to El Paso would be waiting at the station in Marfa, but Marfa was forty stark, sandy miles away from Shafter, hard traveling even for healthy men on well-fed mounts. The horses and mules brought across by the refugees were almost uniformly starved and staggering. It was obvious many of the animals wouldn't survive the trek to Marfa, and the same was possible for some of the refugees. There were toddlers who would have to walk every mile because their mothers carried infants. Old people had difficulty even standing up from where they'd slept on the cemetery's ground. Several dozen refugees were too ill to walk a step. But all had to get from Shafter to Marfa, with the exception of badly wounded federal soldiers, who were left behind to be cared for by remaining Army personnel. There was nothing for it but for McNamee to order his troops to collect supplies of water and available food—there wasn't much of the latter, since most residents had already given the refugees what they had to spare. McNamee had a few wagons and an ambulance truck. The sickest among his charges were loaded on them. Those who had horses or mules mounted and everyone else walked, with the exception of Luis Terrazas and his family, who rode comfortably in their fancy carriage.

The road from Presidio and Shafter to Marfa was little more than lumpy ruts carved into hard-packed sand and rock. Though blazing summer heat was still months away, even in mid-January the sun burned down and the few thready clouds offered scant protection. During frequent rest stops—the children and old people grew weaker with every step—there were seldom trees providing shade. Water had to be carefully rationed. Everyone was thirsty. A pregnant woman gave birth to a stillborn child; the infant was buried by the road and the slow-moving procession crept on. About sixty animals died and were left for the buzzards. McNamee's report, submitted three weeks later, praised the refugees for making "every effort" despite "great hardships and suffering." For the first two days, the procession stopped for the night when the majority could no longer go on. During the marches, some dropped in their tracks. They were placed in the wagons, which soon overflowed with exhausted human cargo. On January 19, the third day, they arrived in Marfa, and the following morning the refugees were placed aboard three trains, which chugged to El Paso and Fort Bliss. A mixed reception awaited them there.

Six months earlier, El Paso had received and housed another massive glut of refugees, but these were white. Several thousand American Mormons, desperate to escape persecution in the U.S., had established colonies in northern Mexico. When Huerta murdered his way into the Mexican presidency and insurgency followed, the Mormon communities were in particular danger from *soldados* on both sides who confiscated their cattle for food and horses for fresh mounts, and were not above demanding money. An estimated 2,300 Mormons fled to El Paso, were housed there in a lumberyard's tin-roofed, dirt-floored sheds, and provided with food by various charitable organizations in the city. But their stay, and demands on local largesse, was brief. Most had relatives in the U.S., and departed El Paso within a few months to join them. About sixty-five or seventy decided to return to Mexico. El Paso offered the Mormons help in their moments of initial need, and then the Mormons helped themselves and El Paso was freed of responsibility for them. This was ideal.

When the Mexican refugees from Presidio arrived on January 20, there were no lumberyard sheds awaiting them. With the exception of Terrazas and his family, who took rooms at one of El Paso's finest hotels, these newcomers were interned inside a chain link fence topped with barbed wire on a flat, isolated area of Fort Bliss. They slept in canvas tents, and were given metal garbage cans to use for cooking food. Besides being fed, they received medical treatment from Army physicians, and El Paso churches and other community groups donated clothing. The internment camp was clean, and federal officers among the prisoners were tasked with maintaining order. There was some negotiation between the U.S. Army and Huerta's ministers—surely Mexico would pay at least some of costs for these refugees' care. The Mexican government agreed, but the payments were never made.

America was eager to return the refugees, but most did not want to go back. Former enlisted men had no desire to fight again in a war they expected would ultimately be lost, and the officers feared immediate execution—Huerta didn't tolerate losers of battles. Many civilian refugees believed they had no homes in Mexico to return to; their modest huts were surely destroyed during raging combat. The Fort Bliss camp remained occupied, and as months passed El Paso's citizens grew tired of their uninvited guests, who always needed something and showed no inclination to either go away or fend for themselves. Local leaders complained to Fort Bliss officials, who were equally tired of their Mexican wards.

In May 1914, refugees in the Fort Bliss camp were marched back to the El Paso train station and placed in boxcars that shuttled them farther west. They were taken to Fort Wingate in New Mexico, a military base that was shut down a few years earlier but now reopened to hold the refugees. Once again, they were surrounded by barbed wire, and now there were guard towers manned by U.S. soldiers with orders to shoot anyone attempting to escape. One refugee tried, and they did. The prisoners—they had no illusions about their status—were given Army rations to eat, and also additional vegetables. Some of the Mexicans brewed potent potato liquor. To amuse themselves in captivity, they formed musical groups and gave performances. A few of the refugees had been part of a circus troupe in Mexico, and their acrobatics were especially popular. The American guards were so impressed that they bought uniforms for the performers, who responded by concluding their shows with the singing of "The Star-Spangled Banner."

U.S. Army officials continued negotiating with Mexico—they could not, would not, take care of these refugees indefinitely, especially since Mexico had never sent any of the money promised to defray the costs. Years later Edith Lloyd, the wife of an Army physician assigned to the camp and who spent time there with her husband, described how the matter was finally resolved:

It did not seem as if they could keep the prisoners under canvas [tents]
as winter came on. . . . Then in early September an agreement was
reached. The Mexican Government would take back all their enlisted
personnel and their women. They could put them back in their army.
But the senior officers and the Generals were afraid to go back as
they were pretty sure to be shot.

Those being returned were taken to Eagle Pass on the Texas border
and handed over to Mexican authorities. Then, according to Lloyd,
"those who could not go back were left in El Paso. It was very hard for
a lot of them for they had no money or means of support. One cold
snowy day I saw . . . a poor little [refugee] general selling newspapers
on the streets of El Paso. I was so sorry for him [that] I gave him all the
money I had in my purse." Refugees kept coming—and Villa kept winning. Carranza felt the north was secure enough to move his own base
to Juárez. Villa then began attacking federal strongholds farther south.
By spring, counting Zapata's solid hold on Morelos, revolutionaries
controlled three-fourths of Mexico. Yet Huerta remained president.
His soldiers commanded Mexico City, and his supporters dominated
the Mexican congress. Huerta was very aware of the tension between
Carranza and Villa—if he held out long enough, perhaps they would
begin fighting each other instead. His government retained diplomatic
recognition from most foreign powers. Japan and Germany were especially friendly. Japan sold arms to Huerta—a clear violation of the
Monroe Doctrine—and the Germans seemed prepared to do the same.
War was imminent in Europe, and Germany approved of ongoing strife
in Mexico; it kept America distracted. Germans feared that when war
broke out, America, though claiming neutrality, might still support the
British with arms sales—better that the U.S. sell its surplus munitions
to the Mexican rebels. In March 1914 Germany secretly established
the War Intelligence Agency in New York City, placing agents there
to develop sources in U.S. government and military to pass along

critical information. German naval intelligence officer Felix Sommer-feld, posing as a journalist, became a helpful liaison between Mexico's Constitutionalists and the American press, giving Germany access to Huerta's rebel foes as well. Sommerfeld first embedded with Carranza, then moved over to Villa when it seemed that he presented the greatest danger to Huerta. Peace in Mexico was the last thing Germany wanted.

>--+-+>--0--<>-+-<

For years, whenever U.S. leaders in Washington believed that inter-necine Mexican conflict placed the lives and property of Americans in danger, they threatened not invasion but *intervention*, a word care-fully chosen to indicate limited action rather than any intention of permanent military presence. Mexicans were expected to understand the difference. Even as the Germans courted Huerta, a new American voice cautioned the U.S. government not to attempt any intervention to remove him from office. After assuming command at Fort Bliss in April 1914, General John J. Pershing studied the Mexican situation and notified the War Department that, in his opinion, if American intervention resulted in "a 'show-down' between this country and Mexico," Huerta and the rebels opposing him would stop fighting each other "and operate together" against U.S. forces. If President Wilson was informed of Pershing's prediction, he discounted it. The president was preparing to intervene.

CHAPTER SIX

Veracruz

On Thursday morning, April 9, 1914, Navy ensign Charles Copp and eight sailors on board the USS *Dolphin* anchored in Tampico's harbor received a routine order. After winning control of the north, the Villistas were attacking farther south in Mexico, including assaults in the state of Tamaulipas on the Gulf coast. Tampico was a port whose value lay in its proximity to the Tamaulipas oil fields; the town was full of refineries and holding tanks, and petrochemical stench was thick and constant. U.S. companies operated many of Tamaulipas's drilling sites and Tampico's refineries. More American citizens, two to three thousand, lived in Tampico than any other Mexican city besides the national capital. As fighting approached the oil fields and port, the U.S. Navy sent several vessels, including battleships under the command of Admiral Henry T. Mayo, to safeguard American lives and property. Huerta's federal forces still held the area, and imposed military zones in and around the port to thwart rebel provocateurs. Not all the locations were disclosed to the Americans anchored offshore.

Copp and his work party were assigned the innocuous task of taking a rowboat and fetching some supplies from a warehouse near the dock. Their small boat flew two American flags, and there was no chance of the sailors being mistaken for Mexican rebels. But as they loaded the supplies into the rowboat, they were surrounded by federal soldiers who held them at gunpoint and indicated that they were under arrest. Their crime was unauthorized presence in a military zone, though the Americans didn't know they were in a restricted area. Their captors spoke Spanish, which the sailors didn't understand. As a curious crowd looked on, the *federales* began marching the Americans off to jail. Colonel Ramón Hinojosa, their commander, arrived and was appalled at what his men had done. He sent word to General Morelos Zaragoza, commander of all federal forces in Tampico, who ordered the prisoners released at once and escorted back to their rowboat. Zaragoza then sent an informal message of apology to Admiral Mayo—a mistake had been made; Colonel Hinojosa, commander of the errant federal squad, would be charged with negligence. The general assured the admiral that nothing similar would happen again. Zaragoza thought that concluded the matter; Mayo didn't.

Without consulting his superiors in Washington, Mayo replied to Zaragoza that taking sailors from a boat flying American flags was "a hostile act, not to be excused." Zaragoza must immediately offer an official apology to Mayo—in person. Colonel Hinojosa must be severely punished. Finally, Zaragoza must "publicly hoist [an] American flag in a prominent position on shore and salute it with twenty-one guns." Mayo demanded Zaragoza's reply within twenty-four hours. After Zaragoza met these requirements, Mayo promised, an American ship would "duly return" the ceremonial salute. After sending this stern message, Mayo reported his action to Rear Admiral Frank F. Fletcher, commander of another American fleet some two hundred miles down the coast off Veracruz. Fletcher notified the Navy Department, which passed the news along to the State Department on Friday. Secretary Bryan and Navy Secretary Josephus Daniels weren't pleased with Mayo, but since the demand had been made, they felt it must be enforced; otherwise the U.S. might lose face. Woodrow Wilson wasn't at the White House; it was Good Friday, and he'd taken his seriously ill wife for an Easter weekend in the country. Bryan sent Wilson a message through White House staff explaining that Mayo had no other option. The deadline for Zaragoza's response was extended to Thursday, April 16, a week after the incident. The Mexican general could not make the decision; that fell to Huerta, Wilson's perennial antagonist. And, for the first few hours, Huerta made no response at all.

With the departure of Ambassador Henry Lane Wilson, American chargé d'affaires Nelson O'Shaughnessy represented the U.S. government in Mexico City. He spent Friday afternoon fruitlessly hunting for Huerta in the Mexican president's usual haunts—racetracks and bars. Finally, he found Huerta "taking a siesta," probably at the presidential palace, and asked that he be awakened for an urgent meeting. Huerta seemed puzzled by O'Shaughnessy's concern. He told the chargé d'affaires that he'd offer his own apology for the Tampico incident—was there anything else? O'Shaughnessy said, "That won't be enough"; President Wilson demanded "the salutes." O'Shaughnessy reported afterward that Huerta "immediately stiffened up," and said a formal response would be forthcoming. Two days later, it did: Mexico's public position was that the American military entered a restricted Mexican war zone without permission. President Wilson's decision allowing arms sales to Mexican revolutionaries bolstered the rebels. The U.S. government could not take exception to how the legitimate Mexican government defended itself. Huerta passed a private message to O'Shaughnessy—Mexico would give the American flag a public twenty-one-gun salute in Tampico if the U.S. Navy would simultaneously do the same thing honoring the Mexican flag, instead of waiting until after the Mexican cannons fired as Mayo had insisted. It would be a gesture of mutual respect, and a reasonable resolution to what should have been a minor disagreement. Huerta said that he could, and would, do no more. The proud Mexican people would never accept him completely capitulating to such a ridiculous demand.

Wilson had no interest in expressions of mutual respect. He felt Huerta was not acknowledging a reprehensible act against America.

When April 16 passed without Mexico's complete acquiescence, Wilson took his case to Congress and the Senate, asking in a joint session for permission to enforce America's demands by whatever means necessary. Congressmen and senators were feisty. America was a world power; Mexico must acknowledge it as such, and its own lesser status, or suffer the consequences. On April 22, a resolution approving use of force to make Huerta concur to U.S. demands passed by overwhelming majorities in both houses. But by the time the resolution was approved, Wilson already had acted.

>-+‹›-0-‹›-+-‹

On Saturday, April 18, the Americans learned that a German-registered ship, the *Ypiranga*, was steaming to Veracruz with a cargo of machine guns and ammunition for Huerta and the federals. The Monroe Doctrine was clear—the U.S. would not tolerate outside interference in America's sphere of influence. True, President Wilson had recently lifted his arms embargo on Mexico in February 1914, but that was for sales of American arms. Wilson could, and did, interpret Germany's imminent delivery of weapons to Huerta as foreign interference in America's dominion. Here was an opportunity to remind Germany, the rest of the world, and most of all Huerta who was master of the Americas. A dramatic gesture must be made. And according to prior planning, Veracruz was the best location in Mexico to initiate U.S. military action.

President Taft's plan to invade Mexico by capturing and occupying Veracruz, and attack the Mexican interior from a secure base there, remained in place. Now Wilson partially authorized their first step. American sailors and marines would take control of Veracruz's harbor and customs house and either turn back the *Ypiranga* with its munitions cargo intact or else confiscate the machine guns and ammunition. When Huerta was cowed enough to make the Tampico flag salute exactly as required, the U.S. forces would depart. In the interim, life in the rest of Veracruz would go on as normal. Wilson expected that the people living there would welcome an American act against Huerta—they surely despised such an unfit leader. The American fleet along the Mexican Gulf coast was ordered to Veracruz; as warships began bobbing menacingly outside the harbor, the townspeople stared in combined wonder and concern.

The *Ypiranga* was scheduled to arrive in Veracruz at 10 a.m. on April 21. About 5 a.m., Wilson wired orders, in capital letters, to Admiral Fletcher: "SEIZE THE CUSTOMS HOUSE. DO NOT PERMIT WAR SUPPLIES TO BE DELIVERED TO HUERTA GOVERNMENT OR TO ANY OTHER PARTY." Navy Secretary Daniels wired additional instructions: "If offered resistance, use all force necessary to seize and hold city and vicinity." More American ships were on the way; for now, Fletcher had about 1,200 men for a landing party. He estimated that 600 Mexican federal troops were presently in Veracruz. That numerical advantage would certainly make up for the fact that many of the Americans were sailors with no training to fight on land. Just before 10 a.m. and the *Ypiranga*'s scheduled arrival—the ship was running late—shifting breezes hinted at approaching bad weather, and Fletcher sent the landing party in.

William Cannon, a member of the U.S. consulate in Veracruz, telephoned General Gustavo Maass, commander of the federal troops in the city. Reading from prepared notes, Cannon declared that Americans intended only to take control of the customs house, the telegraph office, and the railway yards, where freight trains were standing by to deliver the arriving German arms to Mexican federal forces. U.S. troops would not fire unless fired upon; America requested that General Maass "remain on hand and lend all the assistance in his power to keep order in the city." Cannon was surprised when Maass abruptly hung up. The U.S. forces swarming into the Pier Four area of Veracruz's port encountered no resistance. By 11:30 they controlled their objectives. Apparently all that remained was dealing with the *Ypiranga* whenever it arrived. Crewmen on one of the American ships had spotted it on the horizon, still a considerable distance away.

But General Maass was active after slamming down the phone. He summoned his troops and instructed them to prepare for battle. A hundred were sent toward Pier Four, where it was anticipated they would lead an assault. To bolster his limited forces, Maass released inmates from the town prison, armed them, and also issued rifles to several hundred indignant civilians who offered to help fight the invaders. As this motley collection of defenders marched toward the pier, Maass finally wired his superiors in Mexico City, apprising them of the American landing. He was immediately ordered to withdraw all his forces outside Veracruz and await further instructions based on what the U.S. forces did next. But Maass couldn't recall the initial hundred troops he'd sent ahead, or some of the more enraged, rifle-wielding civilians. By this time, a squadron of American marines had pushed farther into the city. Inevitably, they collided with the aroused defenders.

As the first shots rang out, one of the U.S. officers signaled Fletcher on his ship that "a thousand" foes were attacking. Some of the American warships responded with salvos, beginning an extensive battering that turned much of Veracruz's charming seafront to rubble. The fight raged, and as bloody hours passed both sides were reinforced, the Americans by newly arrived sailors and marines, the Mexicans with more civilians and the teenaged cadets of the city's naval academy. The better-armed U.S. forces took control of Veracruz street by street. By the time the fighting stopped some thirty-six hours later, there were seventeen dead Americans and sixty-three wounded. The Mexican casualty list was less specific, with initial estimates of two hundred dead and three hundred wounded, though afterward the Veracruz city historian, undoubtedly exaggerating, recorded ten thousand fatalities.

Outside the harbor away from the fighting, the *Ypiranga* was stopped by an American warship and boarded by a U.S. officer, who informed the German captain that his cargo of guns and ammunition would not be delivered in Veracruz. An unexpected complication emerged. Based on sales receipts and bills of lading offered by the captain, the munitions were originally purchased in New York by Germans. Technically, they were American arms being legally delivered to Mexican federal forces. When this unwelcome news was reported to Washington, Secretary Bryan visited the German embassy to personally apologize. It was one thing to risk offending Mexico; Germany was a world power. Fletcher's action was the result of a misunderstanding, Bryan insisted. The admiral would also apologize.

But in light of its decision to take the Veracruz customs house and deny the weapons aboard the *Ypiranga* to Huerta, and especially after the fighting and American blood spilled in the Veracruz streets, the U.S. could not allow the cargo to be unloaded in the port and sent on to Huerta. Instead, the *Ypiranga* must sail away with its cargo still intact. To Bryan's relief, Germany chose not to press the issue. Its government made a public announcement that the arms were being returned to Germany. In fact, the *Ypiranga* with its load of weapons did sail away from Veracruz, but only for about a hundred miles along the Mexican Gulf coast, where it docked at another port with no U.S. troops present; Huerta's forces took grateful possession of the machine guns and ammunition. All America had to show for its Veracruz landing was possession of a port in a country whose fury was provoked by the U.S. presence.

Wilson and his advisors did not understand the humiliating significance of Veracruz in Mexican history. In 1519, Cortés brought his invaders ashore there, launching three centuries of enslavement by Spain. Veracruz was where America landed many of its troops during a war that took half of Mexico's territory. The French occupied Veracruz in 1864 as the first step in its Mexican conquest. The American arrival in 1914 was assumed to signal another full-fledged invasion. American military commanders in the field certainly thought so, and were surprised to receive orders to remain in Veracruz instead of next striking 230 miles west at Mexico City. Wilson had no such intention; the American president did not want all-out war with Mexico when conditions in Europe remained so ominous. On April 23, when it was clear that the Veracruz landing was a fiasco, Wilson reimposed a full American arms embargo on Mexico, including Huerta's government.

Mexican newspapers reflected the rage felt by its people. The *Independiente*, one of Mexico City's leading publications, predicted that Veracruz would bring Huerta and the revolutionary factions together against a common foe: "The Federal bullets will no longer spill brothers' blood, but will perforate blond heads and white breasts swollen with vanity and cowardice." Though Huerta and Carranza both criticized the American landing and demanded the immediate withdrawal of all U.S. forces in Veracruz, they still despised each other too much to put aside differences. For a change, it was Villa who took a nuanced view, telling an American official that so far as he was concerned, the U.S. could "keep Veracruz and hold it so tight that not even water would get in." Long-term American occupation of the port, Villa predicted, would ultimately work against Huerta. The Mexican people expected the government in power to expel the invaders, and when Huerta couldn't, his remaining public support would collapse. Villa did warn that America shouldn't attempt any other interventions in Mexico. That mistake would unite everyone against the gringos.

Huerta privately admitted to Chargé d'Affaires O'Shaughnessy that he would have eventually capitulated and given the twenty-one-gun salute, though that wouldn't have been enough for Wilson. Tampico, Huerta said, "was only a pretext." Wilson soon would have made some other outrageous demand. But Huerta remained president, and he could not ignore the insulting U.S. presence in Veracruz. He told O'Shaughnessy that "you have seized our port. You have the right to take it if you can, and we have the right to try to prevent you." About ten miles out of Veracruz, Mexican general Cándido Aguilar gathered federal forces and prepared a counterattack.

Wilson had no idea what to do next; he was thrilled when the governments of Argentina, Brazil, and Chile, all of which previously honored American requests to deny diplomatic recognition to Huerta, jointly volunteered on April 25 to mediate between Mexico and the U.S. The American president admitted to a friend that "I am hoping (I must admit a little against hope) for the best results of the mediation. We have been in a blind alley so long that I am longing for an exit." Huerta agreed to send representatives only when England pressured him to do so; Britain did not want a U.S.-Mexico war to cut off its access to Mexican oil. Carranza was asked to participate and refused, declaring he would never enter into even a temporary truce with Huerta. Villa, still considered subordinate to the First Chief, was not invited either, and didn't care. His complaint was that the U.S. should not have included his División del Norte in the new arms embargo— hadn't he been the only Mexican leader not to criticize America?

While mediation was being arranged (its location was Niagara Falls, New York), the U.S. still prepared to defend Veracruz if necessary, and installed an interim government to run the port for as long as American occupation forces remained. On April 27, the new U.S. military governor of Veracruz arrived. Forty-nine-year-old Frederick Funston's deserved reputation as a fighter overshadowed his modest height of five feet, five inches (the average U.S. soldier of the era stood a towering five feet, seven and a half inches). Funston had won a Medal of Honor during America's Filipino conflict and was personally promoted to brigadier general by President Theodore Roosevelt. But Funston spent the ensuing years chafing at an Army seniority system that essentially froze officers in rank during peacetime. Funston had greater aspirations for himself, major general at least, and believed his posting in Veracruz would finally provide a platform for promotion.

Almost immediately after his arrival, he received a threatening message from Mexican general Aguilar: "I am sorry to say I am no longer able to restrain my troops and I therefore take the liberty of suggesting your immediate withdrawal." Funston sent a prompt reply: "My dear General, if you can't hold your own troops, allow me to help you, because I can." Much to Funston's disappointment, Aguilar did not attack. When there was no further correspondence from Aguilar, Funston sent numerous messages to Washington, describing the certainty of imminent enemy attacks and promising he and the U.S. forces in Veracruz could reach and take Mexico City in a matter of days, if only President Wilson gave the order.

When the order wasn't forthcoming, Funston turned his energy and personal drive into a program that greatly benefited Veracruz and all who lived there. Though undeniably picturesque when viewed from its harbor, interior Veracruz was squalid. Gutters were clogged with effluvia ranging from dead animals to human waste. Open-air markets attracted as many flies as customers. Vultures perched everywhere, less to try to spot some decaying morsel than to choose among the infinite selection. Funston decreed that every street in Veracruz would be rendered spotlessly clean by American marines and sailors, and afterward kept immaculate by city residents on pain of fines or even jail. The civilian death rate from disease plummeted 25 percent. The U.S. military governor also ordered that all American personnel would behave appropriately, always demonstrating respect to the people of Veracruz. Most of the occupation forces were bored. They'd come to fight, not pick up litter. Even Funston's fearsome reputation as a disciplinarian couldn't keep the American troops from frequenting the brothels, so their commander took pragmatic action. Prostitutes were regularly checked for disease, which reduced but did not completely prevent syphilis among the occupiers.

What became known as the "ABC" (for Argentina, Brazil, and Chile) mediation conference in Niagara Falls got under way on May 20. Even Carranza reluctantly sent representatives. But it quickly became apparent that an agreement between Mexico and America would not be easily reached. The three organizing Latin nations wanted to broker a simple solution that would remove the U.S. from Veracruz and ease tensions. They suggested that "all parties involved in the Mexican civil war" put aside their differences and form a provisional government that the U.S. would agree to recognize. But Carranza wanted no part of this proposal. America had violated Mexico's borders. U.S. troops must abandon Veracruz immediately; only after that would he consider any additional steps, which would *not* include allowing Americans to organize or even supervise Mexican elections. By the end of June, the mediation process was at a standstill, with no resolution even remotely in sight. It seemed to American leaders that the situation in Mexico could not possibly become more complicated and dangerous. And then it did.

⊱┈◈┈○┈◈┈⊰

CHAPTER SEVEN

Carranza and Villa Collide

While the ABC mediation stalled and the U.S. reluctantly remained in Veracruz, the Mexican revolution raged on. Carranza, from his headquarters in Juárez, worked in close coordination with rebel general Álvaro Obregón in launching a series of successful attacks that left the First Chief convinced Huerta could not hold on much longer. Carranza began planning his ascension to the presidency; it must begin with Obregón expelling federal forces from Mexico City, followed by Carranza's triumphant entry. His rapturous greeting by adoring throngs would prove he assumed the presidency amid public acclaim. Afterward, Carranza would preside with a firm hand, leading Mexico to new heights while making clear to the rest of the world that outside guidance—outside *interference*—was not wanted or needed.

The greatest remaining obstacle to Carranza wasn't Huerta, or even the ceaseless meddling of Woodrow Wilson. The closer his own plotting and Obregón's battlefield success brought Carranza to the power he was certain that he deserved, the more Villa, his alleged ally, loomed as a threat. It began with Villa's battlefield victories, achieved separately from Carranza's direct command. Obregón, a general who reported to Carranza, won battles in methodical fashion. Villa's more dramatic conquering of federal troops was often accomplished with thundering cavalry charges. Once, when the federals brought up their own railroad train to block Villa's, the rebel leader loaded one of his boxcars with explosives and rolled it down the rails, blowing the fed-eral train to bits. These colorful acts won the fancy of the common people, who sang songs about the División del Norte, but not Carranza and the Constitutionalists. The most popular was "La Cucaracha," the reworking of a traditional Mexican folk song that jokingly compared Villa's bumptious band with cockroaches desperate for marijuana.

Villa's growing popularity threatened Carranza's ambition—Villa said he had no desire to be president, but if he changed his mind, there was no question whom most of the Mexican people would support. This especially frustrated Carranza because he knew how unsuited Villa was to lead Mexico. In February 1914, one of Villa's bloody, en-tirely unnecessary acts had required all of Carranza's guile to avoid an international incident. Like Carranza's Constitutionalists, the Villistas frequently fed themselves by confiscating cattle, often from ranches owned and operated by foreigners who sometimes asked their govern-ments to demand restitution. Most of the American ranchers were resigned to losing some stock; Secretary Bryan chided those who con-tacted him for assistance, asking why, with their vast herds, they were so concerned that "one of your steers will be killed and eaten by Mexi-cans." But William Benton, an Englishman whose property was one of the largest in Mexico, had been a friend and supporter of Porfirio Díaz and had little regard for Villa, whom he considered a bandit. When some of his cattle were filched by hungry Villistas, Benton rushed to Juárez to personally confront Villa, who was there to receive some goods sent from El Paso. Villa was in a bad mood, and later claimed Benton drew a gun during their quarrel. Afterward, Benton was dead—there were several versions of how he died, from a firing squad to being personally shot by Villa, who couldn't understand the fuss. So far as he was concerned, Benton deserved to die.

The British government wanted to punish Villa, but the Monroe Doctrine prohibited that. Americans, particularly Texans, took up the cause—a white man was murdered by a Mexican. Huerta took full advantage, citing the incident as proof foreign governments should fully support him against the rebels. Villa's blustering only exacerbated the situation, and Carranza stepped in. He released a formal statement that all inquiries about Benton's death must be directed to him "as First Chief of the Revolution." Then he simply refused to answer the questions, since even foreign demands for an investigation violated Mexico's sacred sovereignty. Villa essentially got away with murder, leaving Carranza more convinced than ever that Villa was unfit for leadership. His fighting skills and, more important, his devoted troops remained necessary to oust Huerta. But when the incumbent president was about to topple, Carranza was determined that it must not be Villa who delivered the deciding blow and received ultimate public acclaim.

>-+-+>-0-<+-+-<

By June, it was obvious to everyone but Huerta that the end of his presidency was near. Obregón grinded down from the north, and the Villistas now swung south in a parallel, pincerlike movement. Carranza tried to slow Villa's momentum by announcing thousands of Villistas would be transferred to another command. But Villa said he'd quit, his officers informed Carranza that they would obey only Villa, and the First Chief backed down. Villa, gratified and still acting on his own rather than consulting Carranza and Obregón, now decided to attack Zacatecas, a mining city and railroad hub that, if it fell into rebel hands, would serve as the perfect jumping-off point for an attack on Mexico City, 375 miles away. Huerta understood the necessity of holding the town. He bolstered its garrison to about twelve thousand troops, all he could muster since federal desertions were rampant. The Villistas numbered twice that, but the high hills surrounding Zacatecas worked to the defenders' advantage—gun crews commanding those heights awaited the rebels. No cautious general would have accepted the inevitable mowing down of his troops, but Villa wasn't cautious. His battle plan was always the same. His forces would charge again and again, taking whatever losses were necessary to wear down the enemy, and finally the Villistas would sweep through any remaining resistance. Villa wasn't oblivious to the welfare of his *soldados*. The ambulance cars on Villista trains were unique; he provided post-battle care for his wounded, and pensions to the families of those who died under his command. But victory was more important than lost lives. Men joined him to fight, and as a result some would die.

Many Villistas did die in the daylong battle, at least three thousand, but they killed twice as many enemies before the federals ran in the late afternoon. Now Villa was poised to go on to Mexico City. All he needed was coal for his trains and ammunition for his men. He notified Carranza of the great victory and asked for the necessary supplies to be sent immediately. Carranza refused. Reduced to control of Mexico City, Huerta would have to resign at any moment in hopes of escaping with his life. When he did, Carranza was determined that Obregón, not Villa, would take the capital. Without coal to fuel his engines, Villa was either stranded in Zacatecas, or, since there was no federal resistance remaining in the north, he could march his troops back to Chihuahua. Furious, but without any better option—the *federales* had already used up most of the available food in and around Zacatecas—Villa led his followers home.

Woodrow Wilson suggested an armistice. Why not accommodate both sides in a provisional government to preside until democratic elections chose a Mexican president serving by will of the people rather than force of arms? During this interim, a Constitutionalist (obviously the First Chief) would share authority with a three-member board, at least one of whom would be a conservative who'd supported Huerta. Carranza refused—the federals must unconditionally surrender. Villa, trudging back north with his troops, apparently knew nothing of the proposal. Like Carranza, he waited for Huerta to give up. Representatives of the Villistas and Constitutionalists met and hashed out their own agreement. Villa would publicly *and* privately recognize Carranza as First Chief. In return, Carranza would acknowledge Villa as leader of the División del Norte and would allow deliveries of coal and munitions to Villa, but Villa would not attack Mexico City. That honor, as Carranza always intended, would fall to Obregón.

On July 15, Huerta resigned the presidency and fled to exile in Spain. The rebels let him go. Weeks later, Obregón occupied Mexico City, and Carranza arrived to assume control of the government. Francisco Carvajal, foreign minister under Huerta, served as interim president for a few weeks until Carranza took over. Now Woodrow Wilson communicated again: When would free elections be scheduled? Once those were held, and a democratically elected Mexican president was in power, America would make an orderly exit from Veracruz. Carranza's response was brusque. Elections would be scheduled according to his wishes, not Wilson's. The U.S. must get out of Veracruz immediately—if that didn't happen, it would prove the U.S. action was taken against Mexico, not Huerta. Also, Carranza intended to punish all Veracruz officials who'd cooperated with the American occupiers, for this was a betrayal of their homeland. For the moment, Wilson let matters rest. He had much more on his mind than Mexico.

Part was personal. On August 6, 1914, First Lady Ellen Wilson succumbed to Bright's disease, but Wilson could not indulge very long in mourning. Long-dreaded war had erupted in Europe, and the American president's full attention was required. Wilson longed for America to successfully arbitrate this overseas conflict, demonstrating to the world that negotiation and compromise were always preferable to combat. Two days before losing his wife, Wilson tore himself away from her bedside for an address to Congress, where he stressed the importance of the U.S. maintaining absolute neutrality in the European conflict. The next day, Wilson obeyed his own mandate. England successfully cut the Atlantic Ocean cables that allowed Germany's American embassy to directly communicate with Berlin. Sweden, another neutral nation, offered Germany the use of its cable services, and Wilson ordered German access to U.S. cable systems as well. This, he believed, offered proof to Germany that America did not, as the Germans suspected, favor their foes.

The gesture made no difference to Germany. Perhaps America was neutral at present, but it would eventually favor England and the British allies unless its attention—and munitions—were occupied elsewhere. The longer Mexico remained chaotic, the more likely the U.S. would feel compelled to intervene beyond occupying Veracruz. If U.S. leaders didn't understand the Mexican national pride that abhorred American interference, the Germans did, and took advantage. Quietly, they offered Carranza not instructions, but respectful assistance—for now, a few German military advisors to join Constitutionalist armies in the field. At the same time, Germany made overtures to Huerta in Spain. Was he perhaps contemplating an attempt to recapture Mexico's presidency? Germany would consider financing such an operation. Both Carranza and Huerta were receptive, neither realizing the Germans were also assisting the other. So far as Berlin was concerned, more raging internecine war in Mexico would keep the U.S. preoccupied with its own border on its own side of the Atlantic. This strategy became more imperative within a few months, when it became obvious that, rather than the quick victory Germany originally anticipated, the war in Europe was settling into an extended, bloody struggle.

><+>+O+<>+<

In late August, Obregón left Mexico City to visit Villa in Chihuahua. The two men initially got on well, especially when Villa learned that Obregón did not consider Carranza to be the automatic choice for president. They embarked on a train trip through the northern states to Nogales. When the Mexican leaders arrived in Juárez, General Pershing insisted they cross to El Paso, where they were feted by civilians as well as the military. Pershing passed a private message to

Villa: Secretary Bryan sent his personal thanks for "valuable services." Obregón and Villa took advantage of their time together to compose a memorandum, calling for Carranza to be formally recognized over Carvajal as Mexico's interim president, but prohibiting Carranza from becoming a candidate for the presidency in the formal election that would be held as soon as possible. Carranza immediately rejected the proposal. He'd anticipated Villa's eventual disloyalty, but Obregón's acquiescence was an unpleasant surprise.

Villa returned to Chihuahua. Messages from Zapata reached him. The rebel leader in Morelos, who had yet to recognize Carranza as First Chief, interim president, or his leader by any title, warned Villa not to be taken in by frauds pretending to share concern for Mexico's poor. It fell to himself and Villa, Zapata wrote, to identify and execute all "enemies of the people." In September, upon learning the First Chief intended to keep him isolated in the north, Villa repudiated Carranza and his interim government. Unfortunately for Obregón, who'd just come to Chihuahua at Villa's invitation to observe a military parade, his host was immediately on the lookout for more enemies of the people. Obregón fought for Carranza's Constitutionalists—that immediately made him Villa's enemy, too. In another act of spontaneous fury, Villa ordered his men to form a firing squad and execute Obregón. Cooler heads, probably Felipe Ángeles's among them, talked Villa out of it. Obregón was put on a train and sent back to Mexico City instead. He spent the entire trip expecting Villistas to intercept the train at any moment because their impulsive leader changed his mind again, but he reached the capital safely. Afterward, Obregón never trusted Villa.

It was apparent that Villa and Carranza would fight each other, with Zapata certain to attack the First Chief, too. Anxious for a solution that avoided additional war, revolutionary leaders from both sides called for a convention in the town of Aguascalientes; all opinions would be expressed and, hopefully, a government formed by delegate votes rather than bullets. The site was selected because Aguascalientes was located about halfway between Carranza in Mexico City and Villa in Chihuahua. Obregón was a delegate. Carranza and Villa, the two individuals with the most at stake, were not, though both sent several representatives. Carranza would not commit to recognizing the convention's authority. Villa surprised most participants when he swore to abide by the will of the delegates. Zapata initially chose not to have anything to do with the convention. But when delegates endorsed Zapatista demands for land and water rights reforms, he allowed some followers to participate. They predictably joined the anti-Carranza wing.

Deliberations began on October 10, and late in the month delegates decreed that both Carranza and Villa must step aside. Villa agreed, and Carranza tentatively did but then reneged. When he did not surrender authority in Mexico City by the November 10 deadline, the convention declared Carranza to be in rebellion, named Villa commander in chief of convention forces, and chose nonentity Eulalio Gutiérrez as provisional president. But Carranza's cause was far from lost; most of Mexico's seasoned military commanders preferred him to Villa, whose troops largely comprised peasant volunteers rather than professional soldiers. The *hacendados* also preferred Carranza over Villa and Zapata. Álvaro Obregón had a hard decision to make. For a time, it seemed as though the convention would deadlock, leaving Obregón as a compromise candidate for the presidency. But now he must choose between Villa and the First Chief. The deciding factor was that two months earlier, Villa had tried to execute him. Obregón announced for Carranza. He and some of the Carranza-leaning delegates raced back to Mexico City to rally the officers and soldiers there who remained loyal to the First Chief. On November 19, certain that Villa would soon arrive in force, Carranza and Obregón led the remaining Constitutionalist forces east out of Mexico City. Their destination was Veracruz.

After months of refusal, Carranza was ready to discuss terms with America. So far as President Wilson was concerned, Huerta was gone and a democratic convention had chosen an interim Mexican president, with a formal presidential election promised soon. America could depart Veracruz with its announced objectives achieved and honor intact. The only question was who would occupy Veracruz after them. The Villistas would certainly want it, but U.S. officials were well aware that Carranza's Constitutionalists currently controlled nearby Tampico and its oil fields. These must remain open, especially since many were at least partially owned and operated by American business interests. Carranza swore they would be protected. With Villa dominant along the U.S.-Mexican border, Carranza desperately needed a seaport to receive supplies. If America left the city to him, he promised to pardon all Veracruz officials who had cooperated with the U.S. occupiers. That satisfied Wilson. On November 23, 1914, American forces boarded ships and sailed away from Veracruz. As soon as they were gone, Carranza and the Constitutionalists marched in. In a matter of weeks Veracruz's streets once again were full of reeking trash. Disease reached its previous fatal frequency. Vultures flapped back to perch on roofs. It was as though the Americans had never been there.

On November 28, church bells pealed and welcoming crowds filled every open space in the national capital as Villa and Zapata, riding fine horses at the head of an impressive procession, entered Mexico City. It was the first time the two men had met; when Zapata insisted on a celebratory toast of cognac, teetotaler Villa gamely took a swallow and promptly gagged. After the leaders posed for ceremonial photos in the presidential palace—Villa jokingly sat in the president's personal chair—they retired to plot strategy for obliterating the Constitutionalists. Interim president Eulalio Gutiérrez was not included; both Zapata and Villa considered him an unimportant figurehead and certainly not their commander. Villa hoped for a coalition of fighting forces. Zapata wouldn't consider it. He intended as always to stay and fight in the south. Villa must return to the north and fight there. Villa was disappointed, but felt forced to accept. If he refused, Zapata would probably declare war on him as well as Carranza.

Villa stayed on in Mexico City for another few days, strategizing with Felipe Ángeles, who had become his closest confidant. Ángeles wanted Villa to take the División del Norte and strike Carranza hard at Veracruz; a decisive victory there would settle matters by finishing off the main body of Constitutionalists for good. But Villa hesitated. Constitutionalists were lurking up north, unsurprising since Obregón, Carranza's chief general, was from Sonora. Villa was prideful and couldn't abide active enemies in his home region. Also, his most devoted, long-term followers were also from the north, proud peons who wouldn't understand Villa leading them to Veracruz when their villages in Sonora and Chihuahua and Coahuila were in jeopardy. Villa prepared his troops to go north.

Before he left Mexico City, Villa learned that Interim President Gutiérrez hoped to form his own army, comprised of former Díaz supporters, Constitutionalists desiring a leader other than Carranza, and anyone else who despised Villa. Then, with Villa and Zapata away from the capital, he would either take control of Mexico City or else resign the interim presidency, retreat with his followers to some safe place, and wait out events. Perhaps Villa, Zapata, and Carranza would destroy each other, leaving Gutiérrez to take control of Mexico. Villa's contempt for Gutiérrez was such that he didn't slaughter the interim president on the spot. He ignored him instead—what harm could the fool really do?

Villa didn't ignore a suggested foreign alliance. A Japanese warship unexpectedly sailed into a Mexican port; its commander came to Mexico City and requested an audience with Villa. Treating Villa like the true head of the Mexican state, the Japanese officer presented a query from his government. If, at some future point, Japan should declare war on the U.S., how would Señor Villa react? Might he consider an alliance with the Japanese? Villa replied that his services, and those of the entire División del Norte, would be at America's disposal in any foreign war.

In January 1915, Villa once again demonstrated his loyalty to America. Since December, Villistas and Constitutionalists were engaged in a lengthy, bloody stalemate at Naco near the Arizona-Mexico border. Americans on the U.S. side were in constant danger from stray shots. General Hugh Scott, soon to be elevated to Army chief of staff, went to Naco to broker a cease-fire. The Constitutionalist commander was willing; the Villista commander refused. Scott asked that Villa himself come to negotiate. Scott had served in the Philippines; he was comfortable dealing with rough-mannered rebel leaders, and took an immediate liking to Villa. They quickly made a deal. Both sides would leave Naco. In return, the Villistas would have border entry rights at Nogales and the Constitutionalists at Agua Prieta—each a critical means of obtaining supplies. Afterward, Scott and Villa enjoyed pleasant conversation. Villa told the American general about Japan's recent query, and promised Scott his cooperation in any future disputes. Scott was so impressed with Villa that he considered offering him a chance to attend the U.S. Army's officer training school at Fort Leavenworth, Kansas, "where he might learn the rudiments of morals." Scott also sent a message to President Wilson, urging him not to support Carranza since Villa was America's friend and Carranza, obviously, was not.

Outspoken regard for the U.S. would have earned any other leader the condemnation of the Mexican people, but Villa's equally public devotion to the welfare of the poor, so notably absent in Carranza, was a mitigating factor. It helped, too, that the colorful Villa was so *entertaining*. Amid lives of endless hardship, many Mexicans found Villa's bombast and contempt for elitists to be refreshing. The humorless Zapata stayed anchored in his southern home state. Carranza seldom mingled; it was impossible to imagine him hugging villagers or treating hungry peasants to freshly butchered beef, as Villa often did. So far as most of Mexico's common people were concerned, if Villa didn't hate America, it was perhaps unfortunate but forgivable when weighed against his attributes.

Even as Villa enjoyed overwhelming popular support, his battlefield momentum abruptly lagged. Part of his allure was based on widespread belief that Villa could not be defeated. He might occasionally lose a battle, but afterward he would regroup and triumph again. But that was when his opponents were mostly conscripted soldiers reluctantly fighting for Díaz or Huerta. Now circumstances changed—and so did Villa's luck.

Problems began soon after the División del Norte left Mexico City for the north. Interim President Gutiérrez gathered forces loyal to him, cleaned out the national treasury, and abandoned the capital. His hope of gaining permanent power for himself came to nothing. Whatever support he initially attracted eventually melted away, but for the present he siphoned off some of Villa's potential recruits, perhaps ten thousand in all, and his treasury looting left Villa without funds to buy the guns and ammunition and other supplies he required to fight the Constitutionalists. Previously, Villa raised money by selling off cattle taken from confiscated estates in the north, but now those once bounteous herds were so reduced that they weren't a source of any significant income. Villa was no longer in position to pay his troops, or to grant pensions to the widows of those who fell in his service. His trains needed coal, his wounded needed medicine, and Villa couldn't afford enough of either. Meanwhile, Carranza was relatively well funded. The Constitutionalists controlled most of Mexico's oil and coffee fields; they also controlled agave and sisal harvests, enjoying profits from the sale of these prized fibers required to make everything from liquor to paper, hats, and carpets. In a very competitive global market where warring European nations bid up prices for available munitions, Carranza could afford to purchase most of what his forces required.

Villa fought anyway, and initially won battles in Monterrey and

Guadalajara on his way back north. But Obregón, patient where Villa was impulsive, bided his time, waiting to choose just the right places and times to fight, and was counseled by German military advisors who suggested a new battle strategy against the Villistas. Villa wore down opponents by sending wave after wave of attackers; that tactic should be countered by the Constitutionalist forces digging in and firing from trenches, spreading out barbed wire barriers, and letting the valiant soldiers of the División del Norte essentially batter themselves into defeat with minimal damage to the defenders. Unlike Carranza, Obregón did not believe that accepting useful advice from foreigners was a sign of weakness. He proved an apt pupil.

When Villa had moved far enough north, Obregón and the bulk of Constitutionalist forces attacked Zapata in the south, driving him and his troops back into Morelos. Obregón then took Mexico City— for now, control of the capital was mostly symbolic. Then in early April Obregón led his army 135 miles north to Celaya, still far from Villa's home state of Chihuahua, but close enough so that Villa's pride would require him to come and fight. As his German friends advised, Obregón dug in at Celaya and let Villa attack. There were two great battles, the first a sound defeat for the División del Norte when Villa backed off to regroup, and the second a panicked rout after the Villistas decimated themselves with fruitless charges against their entrenched foes, just as the Germans predicted. Villa and his remaining troops ran, leaving behind all their artillery, thousands of rifles, many of their horses, six thousand captured soldiers, and three thousand dead ones. Villa's remaining troops still trusted their commander; the problem, most believed, was their ammunition. The bullets they'd purchased at minimal cost from questionable dealers must have contained sawdust mixed with gunpowder. It may have been true.

Villa's invincible image was shattered; he was obsessed with regaining it. Obregón must be faced again, and routed in his turn. For much of May the Villistas tended their wounds, scrambled for funds to replenish their badly depleted arms—for the first time, Villa was compelled to demand money from rich American landholders in the north, his friendship for the U.S. notwithstanding—and Villa himself sought the perfect battleground for his rematch. His choice was León, eighty miles north of Celaya. Villa and Ángeles realized how Obregón's entrenchment strategy had won in Celaya. Now they'd use the tactic against him.

The Villistas dug in outside León, and the Constitutionalists did the same opposite their position. Both sides attacked, but more as probes than all-out assaults. Like the trench warfare bogging down war across the Atlantic in Europe, León became a seemingly endless stalemate. After almost six weeks, Obregón's officers began arguing that he must force the issue. Though the German advisors counseled continued restraint, the Constitutionalist soldiers demanded to either finish the fight or simply leave, which Villa would claim was the same thing as retreat. Obregón agreed that if conditions remained the same by June 5, he would assault Villa and accept the consequences. But Villa's patience ran out first and on June 2 the División del Norte charged instead. It was a brutal fight. At one point cannon fire blew off Obregón's right arm. He screamed for aides to kill him; they dragged him to safety instead and the German advisors took command. Under their direction, the Constitutionalists held out until the attackers were exhausted. Then they counterattacked, and once again the Villistas had no option other than flight, leaving another three thousand of their comrades dead on the battlefield.

Villa led his remaining forces, perhaps twelve thousand men, back into Chihuahua to hide in the mountains and hope the Constitutionalists wouldn't immediately pursue. With their commander badly injured, Obregón's forces stayed where they were. Villa seemed eliminated as a real threat. He could be finished off later. Carranza proclaimed himself president and began pressing for U.S. diplomatic recognition of his government. He claimed that, following Villa's humiliating retreat, Constitutionalists controlled seven-eighths of Mexico, were endorsed by twenty of twenty-seven Mexican state governors, and so had the support of at least thirteen million of Mexico's fifteen million people. At some point, when events and his own best judgment allowed, Carranza would preside over the drafting and implementation of a new Mexican constitution that would place Mexico at the forefront of progressive governments. Meanwhile, America must acknowledge the obvious fact that he controlled Mexico. There was no immediate response from Washington. President Wilson had more urgent matters claiming his attention—one involving German aggression in the Atlantic, and the other threatening to further complicate the situation in Mexico.

>-+>-O-<+-<

At the outset of the First World War, England identified the North Sea as a war zone—any ships passing there risked being identified as German war vessels and sunk. Germany announced the same for all seas off the coasts of the United Kingdom. By 1915, German submarines known as U-boats (*Unterseeboot,* or undersea boat) had become the scourge of the Atlantic. U-boat aggression became so pronounced that in April Germany placed an advertisement in newspapers around the U.S., warning that "vessels flying the flag of Great Britain or any of her allies are liable for destruction . . . travelers sailing in the war zone on the ships of Great Britain or her allies do so at their own risk." In early May the *Lusitania,* a flagship British ocean liner, was sunk by a U-boat as it approached Liverpool after cruising from New York. One thousand one hundred ninety-eight passengers were lost, including 128 Americans. Germany responded to the ensuing uproar by referencing its warning in America newspapers. The *Lusitania* was in an identified war zone, and, besides passengers, its cargo also included some munitions. Therefore, the sinking was justified.

Woodrow Wilson's policy of strict neutrality had been embraced by most Americans, but now widespread public outrage convinced the president that he must take action. Wilson sent Germany several stiff notes, warning the Germans that America would not tolerate attacks on its citizens. The clear implication was that American forbearance must not be tested further unless Germany was prepared for the U.S. to join the war against them. The president's protest was sufficiently threatening that Germany announced it would give up its policy of unrestricted submarine warfare; U-boat commanders would be more selective in their targets.

Secretary of State Bryan believed that Wilson's notes violated American war neutrality, and resigned in protest. That was fine with the president; he had Bryan's replacement already in mind. Robert Lansing favored a reasoned but firm approach to Germany. He already served as a State Department consultant. Bryan was known for making speeches. Lansing preferred a much lower profile, and in taking preventive action rather than letting events dictate reaction. Among his immediate goals upon taking office was to bring about the end of conflict in Mexico. America had greater priorities. If the Mexicans wouldn't settle matters themselves, the U.S. would do it for them.

If Wilson and his new secretary of state needed additional incentive, Victoriano Huerta provided it. In April he left Spain for New York City, ostensibly to enjoy metropolitan life there but in reality to plot further with the German agents who used New York as their base. The U.S. government correctly believed Huerta was preparing a takeover attempt in Mexico; even as American intelligence agents monitored Huerta, German agents began hiring mercenaries—an estimated ten thousand soon arrived in or around Juárez, waiting for Huerta and the exiled general who resurfaced to lead his new army. Pascual Orozco was ready to avenge himself on Villa, Carranza, and anyone else standing in the way of his own return to power. The plot's German financiers had no real confidence that Huerta could actually regain the presidency. But he would fight for it, preventing Carranza and Obregón from finishing off Villa and placing the Constitutionalists in undisputed power. Meanwhile, Germany would also encourage Carranza and Obregón, and even find ways to help Villa resurrect his battered División del Norte. Especially with the furor following the *Lusitania* sinking, Germany needed the ongoing distraction of Mexicans fighting each other on America's border.

In June, Huerta left New York by train, supposedly to visit the grand Panama-Pacific Exposition in San Francisco. But he furtively switched to a southbound train in Kansas City, heading for New Mexico and a rendezvous with Orozco and a final dash into El Paso. Then Huerta and Orozco would cross into Juárez, link up with the mercenaries waiting there, and begin their march through Mexico. It didn't happen thanks to Zach Lamar Cobb, a U.S. customs collector in El Paso who doubled as a spy for the State Department. Cobb learned that Huerta and Orozco were en route, and led a contingent of soldiers from Fort Bliss; they arrested the duo at a train station in Newman, New Mexico. Both men were held in El Paso for violating U.S. neutrality laws and inciting an armed revolt against a friendly nation. Orozco eventually escaped, only to be killed in August by a posse of federal marshals, Texas Rangers, and troops of the U.S. 13th Cavalry. Huerta remained in custody in El Paso until his death, probably from alcoholism-related disease, in January 1916.

With the Huerta plot thwarted and Villa apparently eliminated as a threat, Venustiano Carranza believed he had no substantial opposition remaining. In July 1915 he left Veracruz, returned to Mexico City—if the cheering throngs he once anticipated did in fact turn out, there seems to be no record of them—assumed government leadership, and badgered Wilson and Lansing for diplomatic recognition. It was a gesture of respect that Carranza believed he deserved. Wilson wasn't convinced; instead of Carranza, there surely must be a potential Mexican president friendlier to the U.S. "who could be commended by our confidence to the trust of the rest" of Mexico. Lansing would have preferred someone else as well, but he wanted Carranza recognized so Wilson's attention could be fixed on Europe. Then bloody events on the Texas-Mexican border indicated that America's problems with Mexico were far from settled.

><+>·○·<+·<

CHAPTER EIGHT

The *Plan de San Diego*

D r. Andrés Villarreal was an outspoken Villista who lived on the
American side of the border in Texas's Rio Grande Valley. The
U.S. Bureau of Investigation was aware that Villarreal spent much of
his time recruiting Tejanos—Texas residents of Mexican descent—to
cross over into Mexico and fight for Villa. Agents monitored him but
did not interfere; Villarreal wasn't arming men with the intention of
personally leading a Mexican revolutionary faction. Proselytizing for
Villa was not in itself a violation of U.S. neutrality laws.

On the night of January 22, 1915, Villarreal contacted authorities
in McAllen, Texas, and informed them that he'd been approached by a
Mexican activist claiming to represent mysterious leaders who wanted
Villarreal's participation in a plot against the United States, something
called the *Plan de San Diego*. Villarreal agreed to lure this Mexican
into another meeting, and the following morning a federal marshal
arrested Basilio Ramos Jr. The short, scrawny prisoner with moles near
his mouth and nose looked harmless, but the papers Ramos carried
were not. Their carbon-copied *Plan de San Diego* contents described
an armed takeover of at least a half dozen American states and the
slaughter of all white males in them aged sixteen or older. Part of the
reconquered territory would become an independent Hispanic nation
that might eventually join Mexico; another section would be allocated
to American blacks as compensation for their enslavement by U.S.

Anglos, and a final portion returned to Indian tribes. Long-suffering Tejanos living on the north side of the Texas-Mexico border were expected to eagerly join the cause. Recruitment was under way, with 2 a.m. on February 20 designated as the starting time of a multifront assault.

Ramos was chatty after his arrest. He claimed that a year earlier in Mexico, Constitutionalists jailed him for supporting Victoriano Huerta. In late May, he was released on the condition that he leave Mexico at once. For a while, Ramos worked for a brewery in San Diego, a tiny town about 150 miles above Texas's southern tip. But in late December he returned to Mexico, where he was arrested and jailed in Monterrey. While Ramos was incarcerated, another prisoner showed him the *Plan de San Diego*, and Ramos, along with eight other inmates, signed the document as a gesture guaranteeing their participation. When he was released, Ramos immediately returned to Texas; his assignment was to recruit there on behalf of the plan. He approached Villarreal because the doctor was prominent in the local Tejano community. Ramos was disturbingly matter-of-fact. The plan was well under way. No one could stop it. Ramos was charged with conspiracy to commit treason and bound over in Brownsville, the major southernmost city on the Texas border, until he could be tried there in the May term of the federal court.

There was nothing original about would-be Mexican revolutionaries, jailed or roaming free, writing and distributing *plans* describing their intentions. Madero had done it; Carranza, too. Printed *plans* were a means of legitimizing revolutionary ambitions. As a recruiter, it was natural for Ramos to have a copy of the *Plan de San Diego* in his possession—potential enlistees would be reassured by it even if they couldn't read. *Plans* were traditionally named for the location where they were conceived. This one citing an insignificant town in Texas stood out from most others, which contained detailed proposed policies involving land redistribution, water rights, and other political and economic issues. The *Plan de San Diego*, historian Miguel Levario believes, was almost "too elementary. Raise up a force, kill who you want." In a less incendiary region of the U.S., it might have been dismissed as a hoax. Ramos was hardly an intimidating figure, most of America recognized "San Diego" as a city on California's Pacific Coast, and if Mexicans couldn't even whip each other south of the border, a pack of them could hardly take a substantial chunk of America by force, killing thousands in the process. But on the U.S.-Mexican border, particularly the Texas portion marked by the Rio Grande, it was less a question of whether such an uprising was possible than why one had been so long in coming.

Widespread Mexican resentment of the U.S. had its roots in Texas. In January 1915, American annexation of Texas was just seventy years in the past, and the humiliation of the U.S.-Mexican war, which began in Texas, was about the same. All along the north side of the Texas border, Mexicans were marginalized to the point of subservience, in the Rio Grande Valley most of all. After the arrival of the railroad in 1904, the small family *ranchos* owned there by generations of Mexicans-turned-Tejanos were targeted by wealthy Americans bent on acquiring vast acreages for commercial farming. Because of demand, property values skyrocketed. Many Tejanos faced the choice of selling the land they cherished or else being ejected for failure to pay new, astronomical taxes. Returning to Mexico meant exposing themselves to the very real dangers of war, which for men of all ages included potential conscription into either federal or revolutionary armies. Those staying on the American side of the border were able to find only menial work, and at lower pay than the poorest Anglos would accept. Their resentment was natural, especially since white Texans along the border and in the Rio Grande Valley did not differentiate between them and the bandits from the Mexican side who regularly rustled livestock and occasionally committed other forms of theft.

The advent of the Mexican Revolution only escalated the

prejudice, as rebels began crossing north to steal not only horses, but guns and ammunition. With large sections of the border virtually unsupervised, many towns formed militias to patrol and, without legal standing, capture, beat, and sometimes kill any Mexican deemed suspicious. One militiaman complained it was harder tracking rogue Mexicans than Comanches. All Comanches were clearly enemies, but "you meet a bunch of Mexicans, you don't know what you're up against, whether they are civilized or not." It was useless appealing to Anglo authorities, who often believed that the beatings or deaths of innocent Mexicans served as warnings to the guilty ones.

The suspicion was mutual. Historian Arnoldo de León explains, "Those *Tejanos* who tried to remain where they were in what was now America faced all kinds of racism, segregation, and even lynchings. These things confirmed the suspicions that they'd had. Mexican children, Tejano kids, were taught by their parents and grandparents not to trust white people because they were always out to harm us. It was a form of self-protection to always be distrustful."

With racial paranoia already rampant, law enforcement officials hoped to keep Ramos's arrest and the purported *Plan de San Diego* quiet—no sense stirring up panic while authorities tried to find out more. But the Associated Press broke the story on February 2, and two days later the *Brownsville Daily Herald* printed additional coverage. White Brownsville residents braced for battle; armed citizens in automobiles fanned out to protect their town. Tension mounted as days passed, until 2 a.m. on February 20 when nothing happened. In May when Ramos was brought to trial, the federal judge remarked that he should have been on trial for lunacy rather than conspiracy, then ordered him released on bond. Ramos vanished, and so did Texas border fixation about the *Plan de San Diego* attacks he had insisted were imminent.

Concern about overall border safety remained. On June 2, with the Mexican Revolution still unsettled, President Wilson announced that the U.S. was prepared to act: "We must presently do what [we] have not hitherto done or felt at liberty to do, lend active moral support to some man or group of men, if such may be found, who can rally the suffering people. . . . I feel it to be my duty to [say] that, if they cannot accommodate their differences and unite for this great purpose within a very short time, this government will be constrained to decide what means should be employed by the United States in order to help Mexico save herself and serve her people." Nine days later, Texas governor James E. Ferguson asked the president to provide him with $30,000 to hire additional Texas Rangers to guard the border or, failing that, to assign fifty U.S. soldiers to serve as border patrols under the command of the Rangers' adjutant general. Wilson passed along the request to the new commander of the Army's Southern Department in San Antonio—Frederick Funston, promoted to major general for his service in Veracruz and, upon the American departure from that port city, transferred to this prominent administrative post. Funston informed Wilson that Ferguson's border concerns were something for the state of Texas to handle on its own. The cause of border raids, Funston declared, was probably Mexican nationals living on the Texas side of the border rather than Villistas or Constitutionalists. America's posse comitatus regulation forbidding federal troops to enforce civilian law except in cases of extreme emergency applied. Governor Ferguson must learn the difference between marauding revolutionaries and common bandits. No money for additional Rangers or U.S. Army troops assigned to the Texas adjutant general was forthcoming.

About the same time Funston refused Ferguson's request, a band of suspicious-looking Mexicans was reported just north of Brownsville. The city's home guard raced after them, but their quarry eluded capture. For a few more weeks, it seemed that these uncatchable riders were just an annoyance. Then in July, much to their consternation, Texans along the border and in the Valley learned that the essential element of the *Plan de San Diego*—killing white men in retaliation for insults suffered by Mexicans and, especially, Tejanos—was not a hoax after all.

Reports abounded that bands of Mexican riders roamed the Valley border region roughly between Brownsville and Laredo—not one or two horsemen, but dozens of rough-looking characters. Posses searched for them, these often a mix of local lawmen, Texas Rangers, and civilians either deputized or self-appointed to grab their guns and come along. Though the rumored bandits were never encountered, let alone cornered, there was an ominous sense that something was about to happen. Cameron County sheriff W. T. Mann, calculating without actually seeing his quarry, estimated there were "20–30" Mexicans on the prowl and that they were "raiders from the other side" rather than Tejanos. Mann also claimed he'd received an anonymous letter that a hundred armed Mexicans were gathering in Matamoros across the river from Brownsville, preparing to attack the neighboring American city. The posses remained in the field, where the going was hard. Border terrain in South Texas was frequently thick with snarls of mesquite, cactus, and other prickly impediments. The Rio Grande meandered within short riding distance; bandits could easily splash across it and jeer at pursuers from the sanctuary of the south bank. At this point, no one linked the rumored threat with the debunked *Plan de San Diego*.

On July 9 there was finally a confrontation. A foreman at the sprawling King Ranch, hundreds of thousands of acres and growing steadily as its namesake family acquired additional Tejano family parcels, killed an assumed Mexican bandit and wounded another. A few days later, two lawmen were shot to death at a dance near Brownsville—their assailants escaped across the Rio Grande. Then a dozen raiders ransacked a general store. In itself this wasn't unusual, but it was accompanied by aberrant bandit behavior when phone lines were cut. The next night, assassins shot at but missed a white rancher. On July 18, an Anglo ranch hand was murdered. There were too many consecutive violent acts to be dismissed as coincidental; some coordinated strategy must be in place, and now whites on the South Texas border remembered the *Plan de San Diego*.

Despite renewed pleas for assistance, General Funston remained unmoved. He reiterated that local authorities had to handle their own problem—these were raids, not an invasion. Were he ordered to use Army troops to seal the border tight, Funston claimed, he would require at least fifty thousand soldiers, clearly an impossibility given the Army's depleted ranks. If the federal government must get involved, Funston belatedly endorsed providing funds to the Texas governor to hire more Rangers. Washington wouldn't do it—if the government granted financial assistance to Texas for additional border security, the governors of Arizona, New Mexico, and California would surely demand defense subsidies for their own states.

Carranza, encouraged by Villa's concurrent battlefield defeats at Celaya and León, promised he would eliminate this burgeoning Texas border threat if the U.S. granted the diplomatic recognition that his administration clearly deserved. To South Texans, Carranza seemed in position to do so—Constitutionalist troops under the command of General Emiliano Nafarrate controlled Matamoros and the southeast Mexican border across from where most of the attacks occurred. But Nafarrate's soldiers were not only failing to bar the raiders' crossing into Texas, witnesses to the attacks reported with growing frequency that Mexican federal troops participated.

There was further escalation in late July; raiders burned a railroad bridge outside Brownsville and tore up the tracks. This was taken as certain proof that all or at least most of the attacks during the month were coordinated rather than random. Bandits usually stole stock or supplies and fled. This was no longer the case in South Texas.

August was worse. A party of surveyors was attacked but escaped. An estimated twenty-five to fifty raiders engaged in a running firefight with a posse that included some American soldiers. The raiders killed a private and wounded three other pursuers before eluding capture.

More phone lines were cut and a railroad trestle outside Brownsville was burned to the ground. The small town of Sebastian was ravaged, its store looted, and A. L. Austin, president of its home guard, shot—local Tejanos were supposedly complicit. Then came the most frightening incident of all. A large band of raiders, estimated at anywhere from fifty to seventy-five, attacked South Texas's virtual holy of holies—the King Ranch, a property so sprawling that it was divided into five divisions. The extended King family wielded such economic and political clout that most Texas governors gained and retained office only with their support. No one crossed the Kings until the evening of August 8, 1915, when Mexican raiders swarmed their legendary property.

The attackers chose the buildings making up a subdivision headquarters near the small town of Norias, seventy miles north of Brownsville. It wasn't entirely a surprise attack; Caesar Kleberg, subdivision foreman related to the Kings by marriage, was warned earlier that suspicious riders had been spotted in the vicinity. He sent word to the governor and the Army that help was to be sent immediately; it was an order rather than a request, and promptly obeyed. During the morning and afternoon of the eighth, reinforcements arrived on horseback and by train.

Just before dusk, the Rangers rode out to reconnoiter; ranch boundaries extended into the distance and they were soon within sight and earshot of the Norias headquarters. Sixteen men—soldiers, ranch hands, a deputy sheriff, and three customs inspectors—stayed behind, and about half an hour after the Rangers rode out, someone saw riders approaching. It was assumed the Rangers were returning. But as they rode closer, their sombreros gave them away. The defenders snatched up rifles and the Mexicans charged. The fight lasted for several hours, ending only when one of the defenders put through a call to Caesar Kleberg reporting the attack and begging for reinforcements—the raiders had neglected to cut the phone lines. Several defenders were wounded; five raider bodies were found afterward. In terms of numbers, the attackers lost. But their temerity in attacking hallowed King Ranch property signaled that no Anglos in South Texas were safe.

Posses scoured the region, looking for raiders or at least clues that might offer information about who organized and led them. They were helped in August by the plotters themselves, who published a series of flyers claiming stunning but fictional triumphs. One of the publications was a freshly edited version of the *Plan de San Diego*, supposedly issued in celebration of the raiders occupying San Antonio and establishing a "general headquarters" there. Its signatories were "First Chief of Operations" Luis de la Rosa, a former deputy sheriff in Cameron County, and "Chief of the General Staff" Aniceto Pizana, who owned a small South Texas ranch and was known to neighbors as an aspiring poet. Here was proof that Tejanos were among the *Plan de San Diego* leaders. Both de la Rosa and Pizana were known to be former followers of Ricardo Flores Magón. That solved the mystery of why the *Plan* promised to share some conquered American territory with blacks and Indians; Flores Magón had always included these races in his polemics demanding reparations for the oppressed.

Having finally identified local plotters, the posses and Rangers and civilian home guards launched energetic assaults on any Tejanos even suspected of connections with de la Rosa and Pizana. Arrests were common, executions scarcely less so. The September 11 *San Antonio Express* reported that the "finding of dead bodies of Mexicans, suspected for various reasons of being connected with the troubles, has reached a point where it creates little or no interest. It is only when a raid is reported, or an American is killed, that the ire of the people is aroused." In the century since, historians have argued over the number of Tejano deaths, with estimates ranging from a few hundred to several thousand. Few records were kept, so there is no way to know for certain. But it's inarguable that, beginning in late summer and early fall of 1915, South Texas Tejanos began choosing the risks of war in Mexico over the immediate dangers north of the Rio Grande. Immigration officers in Brownsville estimated that four or five families a day left the U.S. at that crossing point alone.

General Funston acknowledged the emergency was greater than he'd previously believed. Army troops were dispatched to South Texas, where they were ordered to form scattered groups of sentries on the north bank of the Rio Grande. There was soon an unanticipated problem— Mexicans on the south bank began taking potshots across the river at the American soldiers. Some snipers wore the uniforms of Carranza's troops. This suggested that the *Plan de San Diego* was Carranza's brain-child. If not, he would surely order General Nafarrate, his area commander, to get his troops under control. But the shots across the river kept coming, and U.S. soldiers were forbidden to retaliate.

In his memoir, General Pershing took issue with that restriction: "We should have informed the de facto government that . . . any Mexican bandits or others invading American territory or attacking American citizens would be regarded as international outlaws and that we would hunt them down wherever they might take refuge." As the commander at Fort Bliss, and the officer in charge of border troops from West Texas through New Mexico and into Arizona, Pershing informed Washington that "if any depredations [are] committed on that section of the border under my command, the bandits [will] be pursued immediately into Mexican territory if necessary." His superiors responded that if Pershing disobeyed orders and sent unauthorized pursuit across the border, he'd be court-martialed. Pershing replied that they could expect "the opportunity to haul me before a court if anything of that sort occur[s] in my front." But Pershing knew there was no real risk of that—*Plan de San Diego* raids were focused on South Texas, many hundreds of miles away.

On September 13, raiders crossed the river and attacked a small U.S. cavalry outpost, killing three soldiers. Four days later, there was fighting on the outskirts of Brownsville. Five local lawmen responded by standing on the north bank of the river and firing at random targets in Mexico. On September 23, the worst atrocity occurred. Three U.S. soldiers guarded the tiny village of Progreso on the river's north bank about twenty miles west of Brownsville. Raiders attacked. Two of the American soldiers escaped, but Private Richard Johnson was taken prisoner. His captors hauled him across the river into Mexico and shot him to death. Then they decapitated him and mockingly stuck his head on a pole, placed in clear view from the American side. Johnson's headless body was dumped in the Rio Grande. U.S. troops pleaded for the chance to retaliate, at least with attacks on Mexican army camps across the river. Washington was steadfast—nothing must be done that Carranza could construe as invasion. That would surely result in even more widespread bloodshed, and possibly full-scale war.

Funston informed the War Department that only an immediate show of force by the U.S. could prevent catastrophe: "If I do not have an adequate force ready for instant use, a single act of indiscretion by a subordinate commander on either side may start a conflagration that will extend along the entire border, and result in an international crisis." Anticipating the usual response that there was no available budget to increase his available forces, Funston declared that this excuse would no longer do: "The time for economy has passed, more troops should be supplied regardless of cost." But no reinforcements arrived, and the attacks continued.

CHAPTER NINE

The Texas Rangers and Their Bandit War

While the Army was restricted in its response to *Plan de San Diego* raids in Texas, another entity meted out retributive punishment at will. In a letter written to his mother in June 1915, Ranger Roy Aldrich bragged, "The soldiers are mighty careful about what they do but the Rangers butt in and do as they please." For anyone remotely familiar with the history of the Rangers, their brutal conduct in 1915 and the next few years was unsurprising. Since their first iteration in 1823, Rangers were called on as a last, lethal resort when Texas intended the eradication of an enemy: first Indians, then rustlers, Union troops in the Civil War, and now murderous Mexicans. In every instance, no matter how barbaric the offenses of their foes, Rangers' counterattacks were worse. Their reputation was such that intimidation was as much a factor in their effectiveness as violence.

There were never many full-time Rangers, often no more than a few dozen, in part because their salaries were comparable to those paid to ranch hands while the Rangers' lives were so often at risk. Though they were expected to exhibit total loyalty to the governors who hired them, that loyalty was seldom reciprocated. When things in Texas appeared relatively calm, Ranger rosters were thinned in deference to the state budget. When a crisis occurred, their depleted ranks were expected to recklessly charge in and restore order even as state officials dithered over hiring reinforcements, seldom more than a few dozen. The numbers involved were consistently appalling; in mid-July 1915 when the *Plan de San Diego* erupted, twenty-six Rangers were available to help defend some 1,500 miles of territory on and around the Texas border. They received reinforcements over the next few months, but by August they still totaled only about fifty.

But many were former prison guards or civilian lawmen, men who were tough and accustomed to violence. They gloried in acting without concern about consequence. It was Ranger tradition to provide the sketchiest possible reports about activities in the field. In 1875, after cornering a pesky band of Mexican rustlers, Ranger captain Leander McNelly sent a message to his adjutant general in Austin: "Had a fight with raiders, killed twelve and captured two hundred and sixty beeves [cattle]. Wish you were here." Forty years later, describing the capture of alleged *Plan de San Diego* killers, Ranger Aldrich—then an enlisted man, but soon promoted to captain—laconically wrote, "The two men responsible for this crime were afterwards apprehended, and met the fate they so well deserved. They were taken to the scene of the murder and summarily executed." Because of federal rules, Rangers could not cross the Rio Grande with impunity, but within their state they often made rather than obeyed the law.

Over the decades, Mexicans and Tejanos served as the Rangers' most consistent targets. Any "greasers" were considered suspect, because to the Rangers they all looked alike; any of them could be Mexican raiders skulking north of the Rio Grande for the opportunity to filch cattle, rob a store, or kill a white person. All Tejanos potentially harbored these villains, abetting their crimes. Particularly in the Rio Grande Valley, the Rangers routinely stormed Tejano gatherings such as *bailes* (dances), firing shots in the air, making their presence known. As a result, one Ranger recalled, "We were feared as men were never feared before on that border," and he made this boast decades before the *Plan de San Diego*. White Texans celebrated the Rangers as the only lawmen in the state who were proactive rather than reactive. Historian Carlysle Graham Raht, who won his own accolades as a U.S. Army scout, recalled that Rangers were considered "as courageous as a Numidian lion and tougher than a Mexican burro . . . his language, perhaps, could not pass in a London drawing room, but he could successfully ride a bronco and kill a Mexican horse thief at 500 yards."

The challenge, always, was that there were so very few Rangers to patrol such vast territory. Texas law permitted any state citizen to apply for Ranger assistance by submitting a request to the adjutant general's office in Austin. Only a few could be honored, usually those where civil authorities attached statements of support. Requests by rich, politically powerful families with extensive ranch or farming operations, often in the Valley, always took precedence. Otherwise, the Rangers typically operated in small bands based at great intervals around their sprawling state, patrolling as best they could, riding hundreds of miles each week to maintain visibility, reminding everyone that the Texas Rangers were *there*.

For men who craved action, such routine was boring, especially in the months immediately following the promised February 20, 1915, launch of the *Plan de San Diego*. The Rangers anticipated lots of fighting, and, when there wasn't any, they were left to their dull patrol assignments. In April, back at his base in Rio Grande City directly on the border, Roy Aldrich lamented in a letter to his mother that "there is mighty little to do here. No use whatsoever for Rangers." Aldrich enjoyed being a fighting man, even serving with the British in South Africa during the Boer War. Afterward in Texas he made his living selling real estate until early 1915, when, with trouble apparently brewing from the *Plan de San Diego*, Aldrich enlisted in the Rangers and looked forward to combat. When February 20 passed and he didn't use his gun, Aldrich grumbled. There were rumors of bad Mexicans being spotted near Brownsville, and he wrote home that a fight "will come off soon I think probably tomorrow & I would like to be there but there is no chance."

Then, beginning on June 2, Aldrich and the rest of the Rangers got their chance. Bands of Mexican gunmen were suddenly reported all around South Texas, and mixed posses that included local sheriffs, Rangers, and civilian militias went after them. It was still frustrating, because their quarry was never sighted. Aldrich blamed the rough Valley terrain: "The thousands of square miles of brush make it almost impossible to find them." But the marauders had no difficulty finding victims; on July 12 near Brownsville, a deputy sheriff and deputy constable were murdered at a dance. Six days later, raiders killed a young white ranch hand. The federal government continued insisting that the raids were a state and regional matter. Texas governor Ferguson, denied the federal assistance he requested, reluctantly dug into his own state treasury and hired a new Ranger captain, one destined to extend the Rangers' reputation for brutal law enforcement.

Henry Lee Ransom was a veteran of the Spanish-American War and the U.S.-Filipino conflict. As a civilian, he managed a Texas prison farm and then cracked heads as a special enforcer for the mayor of Houston. Ransom had two previous, abbreviated Ranger stints prior to 1915, leaving both for better-paying jobs as a deputy sheriff. But the burgeoning uprising in the Valley promised the nonstop excitement that he craved, and as a Ranger captain he would no longer be subject to the kind of legal restrictions forbidding civilian peace officers from exercising harsher law enforcement. Governor Ferguson placed Ransom in charge of newly recruited Ranger Company D, seven men consisting of former prison guards and other "shooters," and ordered him to eliminate Valley troublemakers. Ferguson later said he specifically commanded Ransom "to kill every damned man connected with it" if necessary.

Ransom had his squad in place by mid-July; almost immediately after Company D arrived, raiders burned a railroad bridge outside

Brownsville. King Ranch manager Caesar Kleberg, anticipating trouble, wired the adjutant general demanding that Rangers immediately be assigned to guard his property. The Kings were one of the most influential families in Texas; if they were pleased with the Rangers' service, Governor Ferguson would be in the Rangers' debt. When a more senior captain prepared to lead a squad on this critical mission with almost guaranteed fighting, he was informed by his Ranger superiors that Ransom and Company D had the assignment. They failed to prevent the attack at Norias, but for the next several months Ransom and his hard-bitten men exacted fearsome vengeance. The Rangers had names of suspected raiders and their alleged local abettors, all to be hunted down and killed as examples to other "greasers" contemplating insurrection. Local authorities claimed *Plan de San Diego* plotters were the source of all the Valley's troubles. The Rangers called it the Bandit War because, to them, Mexicans lacked the mental acuity to be anything more than bandits.

Ransom's simple motto was "a bad disease calls for bitter medicine," and Company D acted on that philosophy, with each individual act against supposed *sediciosos* intended to also serve as a deterrent. In September, Company D encountered Jesús Bazán and Antonio Longoria riding horses along a road in Hidalgo County just north of the border. The Rangers' kill list included "Longoria," a relatively common surname among Tejanos. Antonio Longoria had committed no criminal act, but his last name was on the list. The Rangers shot him dead, and Bazán as well. Then they left the two bodies to rot in the road. The victims' families, Stephen Harrigan writes, "fled their homes, convinced that they would be killed as well if they tried to retrieve their loved ones. *Tejanos* driving their wagons down the road skirted around the bodies, fearful that a show of human sympathy would mean, to the Rangers, proof of conspiracy."

The Longoria-Bazán murders weren't isolated cases. A few weeks earlier, the Rangers attacked a ranch where they suspected "alleged bandits" were hiding, suspects in a double murder of whites in Sebastian, Texas. There was no notion of arrests and subsequent trials. Instead, the Rangers went in shooting and killed three suspects, a father and his two sons, one of the latter shot while hiding under a bed. Two of the three victims were unarmed. In another incident, the corpses of fourteen Mexicans were found near the Longoria-Bazán death site, these bodies neatly left in a line, bullet holes in their skulls indicating they were formally executed rather than gunned down in battle. Five of the corpses had empty beer bottles shoved in their mouths. No one recognized the dead, and their killers left no identifying signs—but they were assumed to be Rangers, and the Rangers did not deny it.

The Texas Rangers, historian Doug J. Swanson believes, became "nothing less than death squads." Those who weren't yet in on Mexican kills hoped for the opportunity. Roy Aldrich, stuck with other Rangers guarding the King Ranch, wrote on August 13, "We can't leave the ranch so can't get in on the scouting & am afraid won't see any fighting. The other companies and the Sheriff's posses are getting a lot of undesirable Mexicans. No news of this gets in the papers. . . . This is the King Ranch which explains why they can have a whole [Ranger] company as guard."

Scattered complaints from ordinary citizens about Ranger rather than raider depredations began reaching Austin. Valley resident R. B. Creager argued that "in my judgment 90 percent of those [Mexicans] killed were as innocent as you or I of complicity in those bandit outrages." But the majority of white Texans in the Valley supported the Rangers' actions and encouraged them to do more. The *Kingsville Record* rhapsodized, "It's no wonder Mexican bandits tremble in terror at the word [*Rangers*]. Strong, determined men they are, with courage and daring written on their faces, dead shots, tireless on the trail . . . a mighty army within themselves, the State's best gift to her people."

It was the Rangers' intent to batter Valley Tejanos into submission, and to a great extent they succeeded. But their brutality had another, less desired, consequence. Though they might have initially opposed the *Plan de San Diego* and its promised slaughter of Anglos, the attitudes of many border Tejanos radically changed as the summer of 1915 passed and more innocent Mexican blood was shed. Their term for the Rangers became *los rinches*, "*rinche*" being an adjective translating as "full to the brim." Besides being a play on the sound of "Rangers," *rinche* identified the Rangers as full of themselves, an overflowing, messy force.

Many Tejanos began sympathizing with the Mexican raiders; some joined in their attacks. As many as one to three thousand Tejanos eventually participated in, abetted, or at least knew about in advance but did not report *Plan de San Diego*/Bandit War raids. Almost as bad were the changed attitudes of many previously pro-American Tejanos in the Valley. David Montejano writes that "Mexicans who had always been tractable and friendly became sullen." U.S. soldiers assigned to border duty noticed, and informed their superiors. Soon local Texas lawmen and the Rangers' adjutant general in Austin were instructed by the federal government to cease all summary executions of Mexican suspects. It had little effect on the white civilian militias and none on the Rangers.

To assist regional lawmen and the Rangers in pinpointing actual *sediciosos* rather than harassing every Tejano in the Valley, the federal government stepped up interception of area mail by agents of the Bureau of Investigation. Letters by the thousands were opened and inspected, but little information was gleaned. Most of the agents could not read, let alone speak, Spanish. The same deficiency prevented the bureau from placing effective spies in Texas border towns.

Despite the Rangers' efforts, by fall of 1915 the situation in the Valley was worse than ever, and their means of combating it remained extreme. Aldrich, still pulling guard duty at the King Ranch, wrote in September that "the 'bandidos' broke out again yesterday and are killing Gringos and burning ranches and bridges. They sure are crazy people. They will all be killed in the long run." Meanwhile, the Rangers, along with dozens of civilian militias and members of the U.S. Army (General Funston finally assigned about 2,500 soldiers to help guard the Texas border) killed as many as they could. Although the death toll among Mexicans and Tejanos mounted, the raids continued.

>·+·>·0·<+·<

American authorities became increasingly frustrated by their failure to identify the masterminds responsible for the raids. The possibility of the *Plan de San Diego* being an organic movement among resentful Mexicans along the Texas border was almost universally dismissed—those people weren't considered capable of such strategy. A few of the attacks might have been the work of ordinary bandits, but many were carried out over days or even weeks by packs of raiders committing murderous acts that did not involve robbery. At some level Carranza was surely involved—Mexican federal troops were known to have participated in some raids north of the Rio Grande, and they frequently provided covering fire for raiders splashing across the river to evade American pursuit. But Carranza denied it—why would he direct such inflammatory actions when he so badly desired diplomatic recognition by the American government? A few papers recovered from the bodies of felled raiders indicated that Germany might in some way be supporting the raids, but World War I was in progress across the Atlantic and authorities hoped that Germany had all it could do on its own battlefronts. President Wilson's intent was that both sides in the European conflict would eventually invite him to act as arbitrator in peace negotiations. If the U.S. either publicly or privately accused the Germans of colluding with Mexican raiders in Texas, Germany's indignation might be such that it would never accept Wilson as a peacemaker.

To Secretary of State Robert Lansing, one thing was clear. The chaos in Mexico had to end. President Wilson's full attention was required on the war in Europe. Sending the Army into Mexico again was a nonstarter—if America was drawn into the war across the Atlantic, it couldn't have a significant portion of its military tied up fighting south of the Rio Grande. Staying neutral while one Mexican government after another fell to revolutionaries clearly didn't work. That endless cycle distracted the president and endangered Americans in Mexico and on the U.S. side of the border as well.

Lansing blamed Germany. He wrote in his diary that "Germany desires to keep up the turmoil in Mexico until the United States is forced to intervene; therefore, we must not intervene. Germany does not wish to have one faction dominant in Mexico; therefore, we must recognize one faction as dominant in Mexico. . . . It comes down to this: Our possible relations with Germany must be our first consideration, and all our intercourse with Mexico must be regulated accordingly."

The immediate step the U.S. must take, Lansing urged Wilson, was conveying diplomatic recognition to one man in Mexico, making it clear that in return for this favor he would be expected to shut down the Texas border raids, protect Americans and American interests in Mexico, and get his country under control. And once recognition was granted, the U.S. would unequivocally support its recipient, meaning that Woodrow Wilson must accept a Mexican head of state who did not completely match up to the American president's rigorous democratic standards. Then peace in Mexico might be achieved, and Germany's meddling thwarted.

In October, Wilson reluctantly agreed.

CHAPTER TEN

Wilson Chooses Carranza

With the decision made to grant diplomatic recognition to a Mexican leader, America had to select from a limited pool. Villa was hiding in the Sierra Madre, his reputation for invincibility shattered at Celaya and León. Zapata was no factor outside his home state of Morelos—General Pershing described him as "little more than a brigand." That left Carranza, whose disdain for the U.S. was reciprocated by American leadership. But Carranza's forces controlled most of Mexico; recognizing his administration would be accepting what increasingly appeared to be inevitable.

Villa sensed what was coming. He sent word to Wilson and Lansing that he was prepared to leave Mexico if Carranza would agree to step down, too. Some compromise candidate could head a new, American-approved Mexican government. The U.S. enthusiastically endorsed the proposal, but Carranza predictably refused to consider it.

Villa tried proving he was a true friend to America. Although he'd reeled back to Chihuahua, Villa still had about twelve thousand troops, enough to hold out for some time if Carranza sent his forces north to finish off his hated rival. Feeding his men, let alone paying them as he always had, was almost beyond Villa's power. For years he'd funded his operations with his own privately printed scrip, which many ranchers and merchants accepted in the belief that the Villistas would eventually prevail and govern Mexico. From 1912 through early

1915, each "Villa peso" was worth about 30 U.S. cents. Now its value cratered to a cent and a half, if anyone would take Villa pesos at all. This left Villa no option other than to confiscate edible crops and live-stock from farms and ranches, and to extort money from manufactur-ing operations (otherwise the Villistas would destroy their equipment) around Juárez and Chihuahua City, areas he still controlled. Most of these entities were American-owned, and they complained to their government.

In early August, General Hugh Scott was dispatched to meet with Villa, whom he'd previously persuaded to abandon fighting at Naco when the lengthy battle endangered U.S. civilians. The two men re-spected each other, but Scott was still surprised when Villa agreed not only to stop extorting Americans, but to return about $6 million in cash, livestock, and other supplies that he'd taken from them. Scott wrote in his memoir that Villa "gave all this up only because I asked him to." The American general, in turn, urged his government not to choose Carranza, "who [has] rewarded us with kicks on every occa-sion," over Villa, who, Scott insisted, remained a loyal ally.

Wilson and Lansing weren't persuaded. A meeting was arranged between U.S. officials and representatives of Argentina, Brazil, and Chile, the same ABC coalition of South American governments that unsuccessfully attempted to negotiate an immediate American with-drawal from Veracruz. On October 9, there was consensus. America would be first to recognize Carranza; immediately afterward, the three South American nations would do the same. A new American arms embargo would prohibit sales to any Mexican faction other than the now-recognized Carranza government. That would surely convince Villa and Zapata that further opposition was hopeless. Secretary Lan-sing set in motion the somewhat ponderous process of formal recog-nition, a week or ten days for formal papers to be drawn up, and an announcement made. But Villa had his own plan, and his schedule conflicted with the U.S. State Department's.

Pancho Villa was no great battle strategist, but he realized that, at least for the present, he could no longer directly challenge Carranza's main forces under Obregón. Yet with his remaining force of twelve thousand, it was still possible to assault smaller Carrancista garrisons in parts of the north where the Villistas still enjoyed numerical advantage. Villa retained control of Juárez; if he could strike out west and take one or two other critical border towns, then he, not Carranza, would have the best access to weapons and munitions peddled by area smugglers. One target in particular seemed ripe—Agua Prieta, directly across from the Arizona border town of Douglas. There was no Mexican railroad providing direct access to Agua Prieta. When Villa attacked, Carranza could not rush in reinforcements. Once Agua Prieta was taken, Villa would rest his troops and begin attracting the same flocks of volunteers that had joined his previous campaigns. Once he raised a sufficient force, he would march south, first taking Hermosillo, the capital of Sonora, and then fighting his way south toward Mexico City, beating Obregón and avenging Celaya and León in the process. Zapata could move up from Morelos, join Villa, and Carranza would be crushed between them.

It was a fine plan with only two troubling elements. It assumed Zapata would finally fight somewhere other than his home state, and ignored the three hundred rugged miles of mountain and desert between Villa in Chihuahua and Agua Prieta in Sonora. Just as Carrancistas had no convenient railway access to the Arizona border town, neither did the Villistas. Their fearsome journey would have to be made on horseback, so long as the horses could survive, and probably at least part of the way on foot, dragging cannon along behind them. Villa discounted these concerns. He believed his own iron will would inspire his troops through any hardship, and now he lacked a strong subordinate to argue otherwise. Felipe Ángeles had provided a calming voice of reason for Villa, but after Celaya and León he fell out of favor with his leader. Villa wouldn't accept responsibility for his own poor battlefield decisions; Ángeles became his scapegoat. With Villa's permission, Ángeles left Mexico for a small ranch on the Texas side of the border. That left Villa to make arbitrary decisions. He sensed U.S. recognition of Carranza might be imminent, while his own fate hung in the balance. Taking Agua Prieta might, *should*, cause America to reconsider. Getting his forces from Chihuahua to Agua Prieta would take weeks; already in late September there was ice up in the mountains, and the parched deserts had only widely scattered sources of water. Time was of the essence; Villa left two thousand men behind to defend Juárez and Chihuahua City. He and his ten thousand remaining troops set out west.

When they passed villages along the way, the Villistas confiscated whatever food was available. Instead of payment they offered promises. Assist the noble Villa now, and he won't forget the favor. But pleasantries were punctuated with coercion. Villa asked and then demanded that the able-bodied men in each village volunteer to join his forces. When few did, Villa conscripted them, making clear that refusal meant death. Reluctant additions swelled the Villista ranks, but also increased the amount of food and water required. There was little forage in the mountains, and horses and pack animals dropped; so did men, many exhausted not just from the steep ascents, but the effort at hauling up cannon by hand. Most commanders would have turned back. Villa, coaxing and threatening for more than three weeks, led his troops through. By the last few days of October, his plan was no longer secret. Federal scouts spotted the Villistas a few days' march from Agua Prieta. Villa's own spies reported good news—there apparently were just three thousand or so *federales* holding the town, and no way for Carranza to send forces in time to reinforce them before the Villistas attacked.

A few daring American reporters who rode down to meet and interview Villa brought him bad news. On October 19, while the Villistas were still struggling through the mountains, Woodrow Wilson and Robert Lansing announced that America recognized Venustiano Carranza's administration as the legitimate government of Mexico, de facto (in place) until such time as democratic elections either confirmed Carranza with votes or replaced him. Villa seemed calm as he heard the news. He told the reporters that the diplomatic recognition of his enemy made no difference, and on November 1 he attacked Agua Prieta, certain that his forces outnumbered defenders by at least three to one. They didn't.

Instead of thanking America for its diplomatic recognition, Carranza made an immediate demand. Pancho Villa and a large body of troops were marching on Agua Prieta. If the U.S. was truly Carranza's ally, it must prove it by aiding him now. There were Mexican federal troops available to reinforce Agua Prieta, but the only way to rush them there in time was for America to permit them to proceed by train on American rails through U.S. territory, to Douglas, Arizona, where they would disembark and cross directly into Agua Prieta. This was hardly the way Wilson and Lansing hoped to begin their reluctant partnership, but they couldn't refuse. Some five thousand Mexican federals crossed U.S. territory by rail to reinforce their three thousand comrades in Agua Prieta, and Villa had no idea that they were there. These were battle-tested *federales*, many of them veterans who'd fought at León and Celaya. Villistas held no terrors for them. They strung barbed wire boundaries, set up machine gun nests, and dug in. When Villa attacked, they were ready.

The early flow of battle baffled Villa. There must be more than three thousand defenders to repulse his first charge so briskly—but that was impossible. He tried again, with similar results. The Villistas' supply of ammunition was limited; they had not anticipated an extended fight. Villa resorted to his favorite tactic—a night assault. But thanks again to the U.S., the defenders were prepared. Prior to the battle, General Funston personally came to Douglas to observe. Great floodlights were moved to the perimeter of the anticipated battlefield—there's no certainty whether they were furnished by the Mexican or the American government. But at Funston's direction,

American generators in Douglas provided the necessary power, and when Villa's cavalry and troops charged under what they believed would be cover of darkness, they were lit up into easy targets and slaughtered as they came.

The next morning, an American news correspondent walked along the American side of the border fence near the battlefield. On the other side were heaps of Villista dead; the wounded begged for water. Villa, uninjured but dazed all the same, was there—the journalist later described "a startled, haunted look" in his eyes. Villa asked what had happened, and the writer explained that the U.S. allowed federal reinforcements to cross American territory by train. According to the journalist, "Villa said nothing. His jaw dropped weakly and he hung his head in utter despair."

Naco was only twenty miles away. Some of Villa's surviving troops had already fled or else surrendered. He led the remainder, perhaps two-thirds of those who made the original attack, toward Naco, taking advantage of the federals' reluctance to pursue. The Villistas brought along as many of their wounded as they could. The U.S. manager of the Consolidated Copper Mine outside Naco took pity on the battered procession and sent two of his company's American doctors out to do what they could for the injured. Villa's temper flared. He told the physicians that "I will devote my life to the killing of every Gringo I can get my hands on, and the destruction of all Gringo property." Then he ordered the doctors to be executed, before relenting at the last minute and letting them go.

Villa considered, then abandoned, an attack directly on Douglas and the Americans there who had betrayed him. He didn't have enough men left to attempt it. Anticipating an eventual federal advance against him, Villa had to get his badly shaken troops moving. Before he did, he posted a manifesto expressing his outrage. In it, Villa charged that the U.S. granted Carranza diplomatic recognition in return for ownership of all Mexican oil, and made other concessions that robbed the Mexican people. Villa sarcastically thanked Woodrow Wilson, "since he has freed me of the obligation to give guarantees to foreigners." Then the Villistas retreated—but not far.

It seemed to Villa that perhaps all was not lost. The Villistas had failed to take Agua Prieta as he planned, but there might be a different opportunity. It had been Villa's intention to attack the Sonora capital of Hermosillo next, 175 miles to the southwest. Perhaps in their rush to reinforce Agua Prieta, the federals had left Hermosillo relatively unguarded. Although his troops were in poor condition, Villa led them toward Hermosillo. Capturing and holding the city for even a short time would prove he remained unconquered. But the *federales* holding Hermosillo also blunted Villa's attacks with entrenched defense, and he was beaten again.

With Carranza's forces to the east between them and their iso-lated mountain lairs in Chihuahua, the Villistas turned north. When they came to Nogales, battle ensued when one of Villa's men fired on American soldiers guarding the U.S. side of the border. American troops unleashed cascades of return fire, and Carranza's federal troops posted on the Mexican side began shooting, too, claiming afterward that they accidentally directed some fire at the Americans after mis-taking them for Villistas. Villa lost another fifty men in the brief, confusing fray and retreated again, this time in an almost blind rush, desperate to get someplace where enemies weren't. A few days later the Villistas straggled into the tiny Sonoran village of La Colorada. Here, at least, they were still an intimidating force, and Villa permit-ted morale-restoring looting. The Villistas, formerly renowned as champions of the poor and downtrodden, stole whatever they wanted and, at Villa's command, summarily executed sixteen Chinese, a peo-ple loathed by their leader.

A few days later in the hamlet of San Pedro de la Cueva, it was worse. Townspeople there, mistaking approaching Villistas for at-tacking bandits, fired on them, wounding several before Villa's men identified themselves. It was an unfortunate misunderstanding, but Villa had no patience for explanations. He ordered the execution of every village male aged fourteen and over. When the San Pedro de la Cueva priest begged Villa to spare them, he was shot too. In all, seventy-four villagers were murdered. The slaughter made no sense, morally or strategically. Villa didn't care. His fury boiled over and someone had to pay.

By early December, Villa and his remaining troops were back in Chihuahua. Villa still controlled most of the territory there, but obviously not for long. Federal troops massed to the west and south, and not enough Villistas remained to hold them off for long. In the state capital of Chihuahua City, Villa ordered everyone to come hear him speak from the balcony of the municipal palace. He declared that Carranza sold out to the U.S., including among his many traitorous guarantees that all American property in Mexico would be protected. Well, Villa would show the *yanquis* otherwise. He and his followers would no longer waste even a single bullet on their fellow countrymen. Instead, they would fight the gringos, who were intent on claiming Mexico for themselves. From now on, no American property—or American—would be safe from Pancho Villa.

The small Villista garrison in Juárez surrendered to the federals on December 23; the next day, Villa abandoned Chihuahua City, taking about four hundred hard-core followers back into the Sierra Madre with him. The U.S. provost marshal in El Paso reported to Washington that Villista defectors arrived at Juárez "in droves" to surrender, and to offer their services to the federals: "Those that have not already joined [Carranza] are only waiting for a chance to come in." General Pershing and El Paso mayor Tom Lea jointly announced that no Villistas would be granted sanctuary in El Paso; any already in town were given six hours to leave, or face arrest.

>-+-◆>-◦-<◆-+-<

As Villa lurched from one defeat to the next, Carranza embarked on a tour along the border. America's assistance at Agua Prieta was reciprocated; though Carranza did not acknowledge any direct connection to the *Plan de San Diego*, the *Plan*-related border raids immediately ceased after he received diplomatic recognition from the U.S. and railroad privileges for his soldiers. On November 23, Carranza met with Texas governor Ferguson in Nuevo Laredo, and after their conversation a clearly delighted Ferguson announced that border conditions were back to normal. Six days later in Matamoros, across the Rio Grande from Brownsville, Carranza urged residents "to keep the peace" with Americans. News of Villa's ignominious loss at Nogales had just reached Matamoros, and Carranza assured his audience that this would surely be the last time Villa caused trouble between Mexico and America.

Carranza envisioned a rosy future for himself and his beloved country. Zapata still opposed him in Morelos, but with Villa eliminated as a threat and the U.S. embargoing arms sales to any Mexican leader other than Carranza, General Obregón should make short work of this lone remaining revolutionary. The Mexican economy was still in shambles, but with American diplomatic recognition now secured, U.S. banks would undoubtedly offer loans at reasonable terms. The state of Chihuahua on the border was problematic—many former Villistas were returning there, and until the Mexican economy recovered, jobs would be scarce. But the American economy was robust—the unemployed Villistas could find plenty of work just above the border. Best of all, America had recognized Carranza on *his* terms, with no real concessions beyond his promise to protect U.S. businesses in Mexico. Carranza wanted these to thrive anyway, because taxing them provided desperately needed income. America realized Mexico no longer had a pliable president yielding to every *yanqui* whim. So far as Carranza was concerned, he'd won.

Six weeks later, he learned otherwise.

CHAPTER ELEVEN

>-<+>-O-<+>-<

Santa Ysabel and the El Paso Riots

On Thursday evening, December 30, 1915, El Paso's civic and business leaders gathered at a banquet held in one of the city's finest hotels. Its honoree was General Álvaro Obregón, hero of Celaya and León, conqueror of Pancho Villa, and now personal emissary of Mexican president Venustiano Carranza. Obregón was in El Paso to open an office for the Carranza regime, intended as a headquarters where American businessmen seeking investment opportunities in Mexico could get any information and assistance they required. Loquacious and constantly smiling, apparently at ease in virtually any setting, the one-armed Obregón was a far more efficient spokesman for a new era of Mexican-U.S. relations than Carranza, who abhorred social mingling of any sort unless it was among like-minded upper-class Mexican nationalists who disliked Americans as much as their leader did. Obregón gave every impression of pleasure at his warm reception, reminding his hosts how much he'd enjoyed his previous visit sixteen months earlier, when, accompanied by Pancho Villa, he'd met with city dignitaries and promised that, very soon, peace would come to Mexico and with it a time of mutual respect and prosperity.

So many things had happened since, but now Obregón was back to usher in that era with his El Paso friends. Foremost among them was the U.S. Army officer who'd hosted Obregón and Villa on their August 1914 visit. Fifty-five-year-old Brigadier General John J. Pershing, commander of Fort Bliss, had an almost royal presence in El Paso. Firm yet friendly, a career Army officer who still demonstrated a tactful understanding of civilian concerns, Pershing was considered an integral part of city leadership since his arrival in April 1914. That he was proving an outstanding commander of the local Army base came as no surprise to anyone familiar with his career. Pershing always excelled.

The son of a middle-class merchant in Missouri, Pershing was solid though not outstanding in West Point classrooms. But his personal comportment and natural air of pragmatic authority were such that Pershing was named First Captain, the highest rank among cadets. At five feet, nine inches, Pershing was only slightly above average height, but because he always stood and even sat ramrod-straight he gave the impression of being much taller. As a young officer fighting the Apache and Sioux, Pershing was cited for gallantry; his marksmanship ranked him among the Army's top five sharpshooters. Then and later, Pershing was respected but not liked by the troops serving under him. In the field he shared their hardships, forgoing the fancier tents and special meals enjoyed by many officers in favor of the same flimsy pup tents and near-inedible rations provided to the noncoms and privates. But Pershing also enforced strict discipline under every circumstance—there was never any sense that the general, at heart, was one of the guys. Even after transferring from combat to classroom, teaching at an officers' school in Nebraska, Pershing stood out. Studying at night while serving by day as an instructor of military tactics, Pershing earned a law degree, then returned to the field commanding the legendary all-black 10th Cavalry Buffalo Soldiers before being appointed to the faculty at West Point. The cadets resented his demanding teaching style, and nicknamed him "Nigger Jack" for his time with the Buffalo Soldiers. Pershing disdained the epithet but not the association, and the reworked nickname "Black Jack" stuck.

Pershing served with distinction in the Spanish-American War, and then in the Philippines. Because of Army rules tying promotion to

seniority, he was mired at mid-officer rank. President Theodore Roosevelt, an avid admirer of Pershing, stepped in and arbitrarily promoted
him to brigadier general over eight hundred more senior officers. That
made Pershing the object of jealousy among many Army peers, and
their resentment intensified when he married Helen Warren, the
daughter of Francis E. Warren, U.S. senator from Montana and chair-
man of powerful Senate committees. A prestigious assignment for
Pershing followed—he was placed in command of a brigade in San
Francisco that was soon relocated to Fort Bliss at the center of border
tensions. It was in this capacity that he met with Obregón and Villa
in August 1914, and it was with Pershing's encouragement that the
pair worked out a tentative plan for Carranza to temporarily take the
reins of Mexican government, then step down in favor of a candidate
chosen in a democratic election. Carranza refused, he and Villa soon
split, and Obregón, nearly murdered during one of Villa's paranoiac
fits, took Carranza's side.

During the ensuing border chaos, Pershing's area of responsibility—
roughly three hundred miles from El Paso to Nogales—remained
relatively calm, due at least in part because *Plan de San Diego* raids
focused mostly around Brownsville, more than eight hundred miles
away on the southernmost Texas-Mexican border. But El Paso leaders
felt certain the raids never came their way because Pershing was on
guard. Their admiration for his dedication to public service intensified
four months before the Obregón banquet. When Pershing was transferred from California to Fort Bliss, he left his wife and four children
behind in San Francisco, planning to bring them to El Paso after he
felt sufficiently settled in to his new command. But in August 1915,
Helen Pershing and their three daughters burned to death in a fire at
their San Francisco home. Only Pershing's six-year-old son survived.
Emotionally shattered—despite persistent Army gossip that he'd married a senator's daughter to further his military ambitions, Pershing
was devoted to his wife—the grieving general brought the boy back to

El Paso and immediately resumed his duties. On the night of December 30, these included making Obregón welcome, and encouraging El Paso's civic leadership to do the same.

Obregón helped his own cause with a rousing speech following dinner. Peace had finally come to Mexico, Obregón promised. A sensible leader now occupied the presidential palace in Mexico City, a man who realized Mexico's future depended in great part on friendly relations with the United States. Recent years had put an understandable strain on that friendship. Of course, the fine Americans who invested in Mexican properties and operated factories and mines there previously had cause for concern. But now was a time of reconciliation and fresh opportunity for mutual gain. Obregón identified Villa as the chief cause of the trouble. It was Villa who'd refused to make peace with Carranza, and Villa who'd recently so terrorized American businessmen and workers in northern Mexico that many simply abandoned their mines and factories, fleeing north of the border while their equipment stood dusty and unused.

Yes, Obregón conceded, they'd been right to run. Villa had promised to kill them if they didn't go, and Obregón knew how menacing Pancho Villa could be. But now Villa was done for, reduced to hiding in the Chihuahua hills with an insignificant band of rabble, afraid to show his face for fear President Carranza's mighty forces would finish him off, an eventual, inevitable result. Federal troops commanded Chihuahua, and the northern Mexican states of Sonora and Coahuila, too. No Americans there need fear Villa any longer. President Carranza and General Obregón personally guaranteed it. Pershing's smiling presence at the banquet provided additional reassurance to El Paso leadership. If the Fort Bliss commander trusted the new Mexican government, so could they.

Obregón became specific. He knew that this evening's attendees included officials from U.S. mining concerns in Chihuahua, responsible businessmen who waited in El Paso until they believed northern

Mexico was safe again. That wait was over. Come back now and enjoy the protection of the Carranza government. Obregón's persuasive powers were such that officials of an American-owned silver mine outside Cusihuiriachi, a small village in central Chihuahua, decided to return there and resume production.

Because they believed Obregón, they died.

>-+∙>-∙0-∙<∙+-<

Pancho Villa did not understand that Woodrow Wilson and Robert Lansing meant no personal insult to him when they granted diplomatic recognition to Carranza. The Americans chose to support the Carrancista faction because of its increasing dominance, and to stymie Germany's hope of America kept occupied with fighting on its Mexican border. If Villa held the upper hand against Carranza, the U.S. likely would have recognized him, though Villa insisted all along that he had no desire to become Mexico's president. He'd said it and meant it, but Villa was determined that Carranza shouldn't be president either. Some historians believe the reason was simple: to Villa, Carranza was not concerned enough about the welfare of the poor. But it was more than that. During the brief period when they were at least theoretically aligned, Villa felt Carranza did not show him sufficient respect, using him to hammer Huerta's troops while reserving certain glories, like a triumphant entrance into Mexico City, for himself and Álvaro Obregón, once Villa's presumed friend but since revealed as Carranza's lickspittle crony. Then Carranza sold out to the U.S. and became its lackey; when Villa accused Carranza of giving away Mexico's oil and its most productive lands and their grazing and mineral rights to the *yanquis*, he did so in the firm, convenient belief that these claims were close enough to the truth, whatever it was.

For the present, Villa had lost not only his mighty División del Norte but also the reputation for invincibility that once raised him up from relative obscurity. He retained his matchless understanding of Mexico's common people and their ingrained mistrust of America. This would be the tool Villa used to regain his previous stature and, in the process, exact vengeance on Carranza and Wilson. What must happen was for the gringos to send their soldiers back into Mexico, especially since the insult of the Veracruz occupation was still fresh in the people's memories. Any U.S. incursion would do, no matter how minor—Villa could claim that even a dozen U.S. troops crossing the border heralded a full-scale American invasion, and, unless Carranza risked his new alliance by demanding their immediate withdrawal, Villa could label him a co-conspirator with the *yanquis*. Either way Villa, now an outspoken foe of the Americans, would begin regaining his former place as the defender and hero of Mexico's commoners.

Even as he retreated through Chihuahua in late November and early December, Villa set his simple plan in motion by pausing at U.S.-owned ranches and factories, ordering all Americans there to leave Mexico or die. Cognizant of Villa's proclivity for murder, many fled back to the U.S., shutting down operations and, of course, complaining to their government about Villa's threats. Villa hoped for immediate armed *yanqui* response, but none came. Instead, Carranza declared that Villa was now at bay in the mountains, far away from Chihuahua's mines and factories. Federal troops had the state and the rest of the north under control. Then, at the El Paso banquet in his honor on December 30, Obregón urged American managers and workers to return, guaranteeing their safety. The *El Paso Herald* printed its editorial doubts on the front page of the next day's paper, predicting that Villa probably planned raids on the U.S. side of the border. But General Funston, commanding the Army's Southern Department, responded in an interview that he didn't believe Villa was capable of any further aggression—he was too badly beaten. In Washington, Secretary of War Lindley Garrison asked Secretary of State Lansing if it might not be possible to withdraw most U.S. troops from the border thanks to "improved conditions" there. For the moment, Lansing declined.

Villa plotted further provocation. On January 8, 1916, he dictated a long message to Emiliano Zapata, addressing it to "Your Camp Wherever You May Be," though he knew that Zapata, as always, was in Morelos, fighting federal troops southwest of Mexico City. In the message, Villa described to his "fine friend" how American perfidy caused his recent defeats: "Could there be a more offensive act [against] the Mexican people and its national sovereignty?" Villa proclaimed himself far from beaten. He planned to "prepare and organize and then attack the Americans in their own territory to let them know that Mexico is a free nation." Such an attack could only be made from the northern Mexican states; Villa asked Zapata to "come over here with all your troops, and please specify the date so I can greet you personally and together we can reconstruct and engrandize Mexico, defying and punishing our eternal enemy."

Zapata didn't respond. Even if he'd wanted to march north and join with Villa, federal troops were massed between them. But to Villa, it was worth a try. The letter mentioned his ultimate plan, a risky act to force Wilson's hand and bring U.S. troops into Mexico. Villa wrote that he was preparing to attack "Americans in their own territory." But that would be a last resort. Even as he sent his letter off to Zapata by a trusted messenger, Villa planned to kill Americans in Mexico. He still had spies in El Paso, and learned that a number of American managers and engineers had been persuaded by Obregón to return and reopen a silver mine in Cusihuiriachi, just south of Santa Ysabel and only a few hundred miles from where Villa and his remaining followers made their main camp. It was easy for Villa to learn the time when the train bearing them would pass through Santa Ysabel and begin the final miles to the mine on a route that passed through isolated country.

>·⊹·○·⊹·⬩

On Saturday, January 8, Charles Watson, general manager of the "Cusi" silver mine, boarded a train in El Paso along with more than a dozen other American miners and engineers who worked for him. Watson had already made preliminary visits to Cusi; he found no Villistas in the vicinity. Passes approved by the state's governor were required to cross Chihuahua—Watson arranged them for his employees. He also offered to pay for some Mexican federal troops to guard the train, but was informed that this wouldn't be necessary because Villa posed no threat to Americans in Cusi.

It was about 250 miles from El Paso to Chihuahua City, and there the Americans spent the remainder of the weekend. On Monday morning they took another train, this one with two passenger cars. Americans rode in one, Mexicans in the other. Some of the Mexicans also worked at the mine, but they did not sit with their Anglo co-workers in the American car, by custom rather than rule. This second train reached Santa Ysabel in the early afternoon, stopping briefly at the station there to refuel. It was later reported that as the train paused on the tracks, two armed men rode alongside its passenger cars, looking to see who was inside. But they made no threats, and soon the train left for Cusi. A half dozen miles outside Santa Ysabel the train slammed to a stop—El Paso newspapers later reported it was "derailed," either by rails torn out of place or else a railroad car lying on its side across the tracks.

Tom Evans, one of the Cusi crew, jumped out to see what was the matter. So did Thomas Holmes, a young American who did not work at the silver mine. To their horror, they saw Mexican riflemen standing on an embankment shooting down at the train; windows shattered and passengers screamed. Charles Watson jumped out and began running, but he was cut down. Some of the attackers boarded the Mexican car. They robbed the passengers they found there, taking not only money and jewelry but food packed for the trip. Then the leader of the brigands, subsequently identified as Pablo López, one of Villa's most trusted lieutenants, suggested that the terrified Mexican passengers ought to enjoy watching the gringos die.

The Americans were herded out of their passenger car at gunpoint, then ordered to line up alongside the train and strip. A few, like Watson, who tried to run were gunned down. Thomas Holmes managed to roll beneath some bushes; the Villistas didn't notice, and he survived to tell the tale. No other Americans did. Eighteen in all were executed, including Manuel Romero, a native of Las Vegas, New Mexico, who defiantly told the Villistas that he, too, was an American, and died because of it. Those who hadn't tried to run were shot where they stood, and extra bullets tore into their fallen bodies to ensure they were dead. The naked corpses were left to the sun and the buzzards. López and his murderous companions, estimated by Holmes and the Mexican passengers to number about fifty, rode off wearing some of the clothing taken from their victims. The train backed up to Santa Ysabel; when word of the slaughter reached American authorities, it included descriptions of how the Villistas desecrated the dead, puncturing their naked bodies with bayonets and gouging out their blank, unseeing eyes.

The corpses were placed in coffins at Chihuahua City, and then on Thursday, January 13, returned by train to Juárez and moved on a side rail across the Rio Grande into El Paso, where outraged citizens waited. Their fury had built since Monday, when the *El Paso Morning Times's* front-page headline read "SLAY FIFTEEN: A Confirmed Report Reaches El Paso of Bloody Massacre at Cusi, Chih., of Mining Men." Details in this first story were sketchy; the death toll was unconfirmed, the perpetrators remained unidentified, and the paper sought more information from the Carranza government. But the *Morning Times* headline on Tuesday, January 11, was graphic: "MINING MEN STRIPPED NAKED AND RUTHLESSLY SHOT BY BAND OF VILLA SAVAGES." The death count was confirmed at eighteen. According to the newspaper, the atrocity—described by the *Morning Times* in horrific detail—was directed "by General Francisco Villa in person." It wasn't—ever since, some historians have written that Pablo López must have acted on his own, with Villa learning of the murders only afterward. But Villa's lieutenants always followed their commander's orders—any freelancing might elicit his wrath and place their own lives in jeopardy. It was Villa's plan, although the immediate assumption that he must have been present was incorrect.

The coffins were unloaded in El Paso and taken to various funeral parlors prior to local burial. A crowd gathered in front of U.S. consul T. D. Edwards's office, shouting that not enough had been done to protect the men returning to Cusi. That much was true, but the accusations that Edwards, who'd befriended Villa during the Mexican's earlier exile in El Paso, must have helped plan the Santa Ysabel attack were not. The commotion sparked discussion among crowd leaders about forming a vigilante committee, a thousand civilian volunteers to storm into Mexico with Carranza's blessing to track down and kill Villa—surely the Cusi mine owners would fund the operation. Some El Paso civic leaders offered encouragement; it was better for them if the demonstrators blamed Villa entirely, forgetting that it was the local businessmen who six weeks earlier hosted the banquet where Obregón extended his fatal invitation.

By midafternoon, after discussions moved from the streets to El Paso saloons, talk segued into violence. El Paso contained its own Mexican-Tejano neighborhood, known locally as "Chihuahita," the local equivalent of a Chinatown in New York or San Francisco. Previously, it was considered an exotic playground offering authentic Mexican atmosphere to Anglo El Paso residents without the inconvenience of actually crossing over the International Bridge into Juárez on foot or by trolley. Now, with the sight of the Santa Ysabel victims' coffins so fresh in memory, the angry crowd evolved into a violent mob—perhaps two or three dozen at first, then hundreds, finally an estimated 1,500, charging into Chihuahita and brutalizing residents there. Mexicans of any age or gender were assaulted: Hortencia Villegas, who lived in Chihuahita, later recalled that "everyone receiv[ed] blows, the elderly and young people, everyone."

It took El Paso police three hours to arrive in Chihuahita. In that interim, Mexicans in Juárez learned what was happening and rushed across the bridge with sticks and lengths of pipe, wading in to fend off the attackers. Even federal soldiers on duty in Juárez felt compelled to cross the bridge and enter the fray. By the time El Paso cops finally reached Chihuahita, fighting was so widespread in the narrow streets and small open neighborhood squares that the melee was beyond their control.

The El Paso mob included a few off-duty soldiers from Fort Bliss. Now a flood of on-duty soldiers lined up four abreast and charged into Chihuahita, shoving combatants aside, posting armed guards at intersections and on entrances to neighborhood squares. General Pershing, despairing of civilian authorities' ability to quell the riot, had ordered in the 16th Infantry. Bloodied Anglos drifted back to their own neighborhoods, prodded along by soldiers but otherwise unmolested. Mexicans from Juárez were herded back home over the river, Carranza's federal troops among them. This was a crucial moment: if Pershing sent squads of his American soldiers across the bridge for even a few hours to ensure that the Mexicans stayed on their side of the Rio Grande, Villa would have the American incursion that he needed.

But the American troops stayed on their side of the bridge. Some were ordered back into Chihuahita, where shaken residents nursed their wounds and wondered why, if the *yanquis* were so furious with Villa, they'd been attacked instead. The indignity stung almost as much as their wounds, and the insult was compounded when, instead of leaving the stunned residents to recover, the American soldiers and city police began a joint building-by-building search for armed Villista sympathizers. It was after midnight before they concluded that if any had been in Chihuahita, none remained.

There was more. Pershing announced the implementation of martial law, but only in Chihuahita and not the rest of El Paso. Further trouble, he explained, would inevitably come "on the streets separating the Mexican from the American part of the city." Until further notice, Mexicans living in Chihuahita were restricted to their neighborhood, and Anglos could not enter it. Pershing also shut the International Bridge. These restrictions remained in place for almost a year.

Another incident further alienated El Paso Hispanics from city Anglos. Rumors reached El Paso of a typhus epidemic across the river. Fearing contamination and subsequent spreading of the disease, and certain the illness was carried by lice, officials decreed that all Mexicans in the city's jail or hospitals must take delousing baths "in a mixture of kerosene, gasoline and vinegar." Anglo patients and prisoners were exempt. On March 6, twenty-seven prisoners in the El Paso jail burned to death in a fire caused by a match lit too close to one of the delousing baths. Nineteen of the dead were Mexican.

><+>-o-<+><

Two days after the El Paso riot, Villa ordered his officers to begin a new round of active recruitment in the small villages around the Sierra Madre. They would probably have to forcibly conscript the men—it both dismayed and frustrated Villa that most peasants no longer volunteered to serve under his command. How could they forget how Villa fought for them and their families? But willing or not, he needed more fighters immediately. The blatant atrocity at Santa Ysabel had failed to lure vengeance-seeking American soldiers into Mexico. Instead, President Wilson demanded that Carranza capture and punish the perpetrators. That was more problematic for Carranza than the American president realized. It was winter, and many federal troops in Mexico's northern states were suffering from the unfamiliar cold. Like their hardy leader, most Villistas hailed from Chihuahua, where, particularly in mountain regions, temperatures during winter and early spring routinely fell near or below freezing. In early December 1915, when Carranza's forces had reoccupied Juárez, the U.S. provost marshal noted in a dispatch to Washington that "a great many [are] sick from exposure. . . . They [are] all from the southern part of Mexico and unable to stand the cold of this [northern] climate." Even if Carranza had been able to set healthy soldiers on his trail, Villa had nothing to gain by fighting Mexican federal troops; two months earlier, he'd sworn to use bullets only on *yanquis*. So Villa prepared to prod the gringos again, this time killing them on their own side of the border. Wilson would surely send troops after Villa then.

Villa's lieutenants returned with a few dozen men they'd managed to round up by promising to kill their families if they didn't come along. Villa gathered old and fresh forces, perhaps 250 in all, and revealed that they would shortly set out toward Ojinaga, where they'd bypass the Mexican federal garrison and assault Presidio and other Texas towns in the vicinity. In terms of potential spoils, there was nothing in it—these were poor communities. But they were on the U.S. side of the border, so when the Villistas retreated back into Mexico, American soldiers would have to come after them.

Around the end of January, Villa and his troops set out. The way was hard; they had no access to rail and weren't a strong enough force to travel openly. The 150-mile trek was anticipated to take about a week, but beginning on the first night there was a spate of desertions. Most of the recruits and more than a few of the veteran Villistas feared American soldiers too much—plus, Presidio was in Texas, and that meant the terrifying Texas Rangers, *los rinches*, might get involved. After forty men deserted, Villa feared he wouldn't have a sufficient force to overrun Presidio and reluctantly turned back.

Only weeks later, he sent out his officers to recruit or conscript again, particularly in the well-populated town of Namiquipa. Men there were told they must either come or be shot, and their families would die with them. The threat was effective. By late February Villa had about five hundred troops, enough to attack a reasonably substantial American border town. On February 23, Villa again marched his men out, this time northwest, heading for a ripe target just across the

Mexico–New Mexico border. Most of his men, especially the con-scripts, were not told this time that they would be attacking in the U.S. Many assumed they'd be raiding ranches in northern Chihuahua. During the early days of the march Villa didn't disabuse them of that belief, and after that the men were too exhausted to care much about anything beyond getting to whatever their destination might be. And so, on March 9 the Villistas found themselves just outside Columbus, New Mexico, and about 4 a.m. Villa ordered them to attack.

CHAPTER TWELVE

>-·+>-·O-·<+-·<

Columbus

In the years since Porfirio Díaz embraced widespread trade with the U.S., "bifurcated cities" sprang up on opposite sides of the border, usually in convenient crossing places—El Paso and Juárez, Brownsville and Matamoros, Douglas and Agua Prieta, Calexico and Mexicali, the two Nogaleses, several dozen in all. Most experienced mutual growth. Shoppers from both countries enjoyed access to products that were either unavailable or exorbitantly priced on their own side of the border. Customs officials from both countries collected taxes; U.S. border patrols supervised immigrants and day laborers. Some twin border communities, like Ojinaga and Presidio, were less cities or even small towns than outposts. But few were more isolated in desolate terrain than Columbus and Palomas along the Mexico–New Mexico border, in a sprawling valley sloping toward the south, dotted with spiny scrub brush and infested with rattlesnakes. In the winter, cold wind howled in unhindered from the north; in the summer, the sun baked every shadeless inch, and always, given lack of rain, dust swirled in thick, stifling clouds. Columbus and Palomas, separated by a few miles of craggy dirt road, existed because they had to. Some sizable American-owned ranches spread out past Palomas—the 2.5-million-acre Palomas Land and Cattle Company was the flagship—so there were cattle herds to drive north, and *yanqui* cowboys and Mexican *vaqueros* and their families who needed supplies, and taxes to be collected daily on both sides of the official border crossing point.

Columbus wasn't entirely without amenities. It had two hotels, the Commercial and the Hoover, which provided housing to drummers hawking their wares to town merchants; a couple of saloons, a munitions dealer, cafés selling basic American and Mexican food, and even a small venue, the Crystal Palace, where events like boxing exhibitions were occasionally held. But there still wasn't much to the place. People there eked out a living. The lucky ones enjoyed socializing in midsized Deming, thirty miles to the north, or, on special occasions, whooping it up in El Paso, eighty miles east. Trains stopped daily at the small station in town, dropping off a few passengers, collecting a few more.

Life in Columbus was hard, especially for members of the U.S. Army's 13th Cavalry stationed there. It was their responsibility to guard sixty-eight miles of border, most of it rough and ideal for rustlers, smugglers, and other miscreants who wanted to avoid official border crossing points. In March 1916, the ranks at Camp Furlong in Columbus consisted of 21 officers and 532 enlisted men—ten times that number could not have effectively blocked border access in their assigned region, flat for a few miles and then ringed with mountains, cut across with rugged draws and difficult to traverse on horseback or foot. The smugglers and rustlers knew the area and could pick their way through. The soldiers of the 13th, even those who were veterans of fighting in the Philippines, were usually no match for their elusive quarry. With poor pay and few if any prospects for advancing in rank, many men served in America's military because they had no other viable options. Substance abuse was rampant. During 1916, 9.7 percent of the entire Army was convicted at least once of alcohol abuse. It was even worse in the Army's Southern Department commanded by General Funston and headquartered out of San Antonio. That year, 12.4 percent of soldiers in the district, including those stationed at or near the border, were found guilty of alcohol-related offenses. No record is available regarding drug abuse, but morphine was legal, and other substances were readily available, especially marijuana. A modern-day Army study in the Fort Bliss archives notes, "It's clear that at least some of the 13th [Cavalry in Columbus] would have been under the influence of alcohol and drugs at any given time." Sunstroke, infected cuts from cactus and other sharp-edged vegetation, food poisoning, and venereal disease also kept the Camp Furlong sick bay crowded. No one assigned to the camp wanted to be there. This was especially true of the camp's commanding officer.

Colonel Herbert J. Slocum served honorably during the Indian Wars, in the Spanish-American War, and in the Philippines before taking command in Columbus in September 1914. Slocum was some-thing of a dandy and a man of considerable self-regard. He proudly claimed direct descendance from Myles Standish, and Slocum, like Pershing, married well, to the daughter of a New York state senator. Though Slocum was a West Point dropout, he still managed to get an Army commission and painstakingly worked his way to colonel's rank with some hope of an eventual general's star. Unlike Pershing, no U.S. president ordered him promoted over the hundreds of more senior officers; Slocum found himself instead stuck in Columbus, charged with the impossible task of guarding a particularly difficult stretch of border. His first wife had died; the second, considerably younger Mrs. Slocum lived with her husband in what passed in Columbus for a decent house. Married officers lived with their families outside Camp Furlong, which had only bare barracks amenities for men and none for women and children. The town was roughly divided into quadrants, bisected by the Deming–Palomas road running north and south and the railroad running east and west. Camp Furlong and the railroad station occupied the southeast quadrant. The limited town business district and some "nice" houses, including Slocum's, were in the northeast. The northwest contained most of Columbus's residents, and in the southwest quadrant was a customs house, a few businesses, and tiny Cootes Hill, the only vantage point in the valley. Enlisted men were mostly limited to the meager recreations Columbus had on offer. Off-duty officers escaped to parties in Deming and polo matches in El Paso, traveling to Deming by car—at least two hours, more likely three, to drive the thirty miles along the bumpy road—or taking the train to El Paso.

Occasionally, Columbus's civilian population practiced evacuations in case of Mexican attack, but with no real sense of imminent threat. Border raids on Americans were almost universally confined to South Texas during the *Plan de San Diego* attacks. U.S. border residents in California, Arizona, and New Mexico considered themselves relatively safe. Columbus had the 13th Cavalry if defense ever proved necessary, and Anglos felt no particular discomfort on the frequent occasions when Mexican strangers crossed the border into town. They shopped for American goods in Columbus stores or visited with Tejano friends and relatives. Approximately half of Columbus's civilian residents were Hispanic.

Every day, squads of horsemen departed Camp Furlong on patrol. They occasionally encountered a few smugglers or rustlers, but never engaged in any full-scale fighting. Slocum, as did all Army commanders on the border, had strict orders not to send American troops across into Mexico, either in direct pursuit of raiders or even to scout for them. Slocum initially depended on information from friendly Mexicans around Palomas, who sometimes warned that dangerous men were rumored to be riding in his direction. Nothing ever came of these tips, and after a while Slocum habitually ignored them. He was indefinitely stuck in stifling backwater duty, a dismal fate for a direct descendant of Myles Standish and an officer who had served his country honorably and well.

⊱•❀•⊰

Prior to 1903, when ranchers first began building barbed wire barriers, the U.S.-Mexico border was marked by widely spaced columns that were often dozens of miles apart.

Victoriano Huerta rose to military prominence through battlefield prowess, and ascended to Mexico's presidency by first deposing, then ordering the assassination of, Francisco Madero in 1913.

2

3

Venustiano Carranza led the rebellion against Huerta, but his lack of military skills made him dependent on subordinates who were better fighters. Carranza deeply resented American condescension toward Mexico.

4

Francisco "Pancho" Villa's colorful exploits endeared him to Mexico's peasant class, and he fancied himself a man of the people. He opposed the Carranza government, bringing him into conflict with the U.S.

On April 21, 1914, U.S. forces occupied the Mexican port of Veracruz, destroying much of it in a bungled attempt to stop a shipment of arms from reaching Mexico's federal army. At least two hundred Mexicans were killed and another three hundred wounded.

6

In August 1914, rebel generals Álvaro Obregón and Pancho Villa enjoyed a cordial border meeting with U.S. general John J. Pershing. Their friendly relations proved short-lived.

7

Emiliano Zapata and Pancho Villa drove Carranza's forces from Mexico City in November 1914. They triumphantly posed for photographs in the presidential palace.

Desperate for money to buy arms and supplies, Villa sold film rights of his battles to an American movie company. Here, a cameraman stands between two Yaqui Indian riflemen.

During the Mexican Revolution, both sides were quick to condemn captured or even suspected enemies to firing squads.

Desperate to escape the carnage enveloping their villages, thousands of Mexican refugees fled to the American border, where many U.S. communities lacked the resources to feed and shelter them or care for their sick and wounded.

U.S. citizens sought vantage points to gawk at fighting across the border, placing themselves in danger from stray bullets.

German advisors attached to the Mexican federal army instructed troops on the tactics of trench warfare.

Several raiders were captured during Villa's March 9, 1916, attack on Columbus, New Mexico. The bodies of those who'd been killed were stacked and burned.

The Punitive Expedition dispatched to Mexico in pursuit of Villistas found it hard going in the rugged region. Cavalry troops had to pick their way along primitive trails.

Mexican cavalry lurked about the Punitive Expedition everywhere. Its presence was a constant reminder that the American troops were considered invaders rather than partners in capturing Villa.

Texas Rangers proudly pose with corpses of Mexican raiders during the *Plan de San Diego* terrorism spree along the South Texas border.

The Mexican government labeled Villa an outlaw, and offered a reward for information leading to his capture. But it was politically essential to Carranza that federal forces rather than Americans catch or kill Villa.

President Wilson ordered General Funston to meet with Álvaro Obregón and persuade the Mexican government to cooperate better with the Punitive Expedition in efforts to capture Villa. But Obregón conveyed Carranza's message that the American troops must leave Mexico at once.

On February 5, 1917, General John J. Pershing reviews the men of the Punitive Expedition from a temporary stand as they cross the border from Mexico back to Columbus. Although Pershing lauded his men, Villa remained at large.

About 2 p.m. on Friday, March 3, Zach Lamar Cobb, director of customs for El Paso and also a government agent who had the best network of spies and sources among American officials on the border, cabled Secretary of State Lansing in Washington: he had solid information that Villa, "with three hundred men," was marching toward Columbus, New Mexico. Referring to a widespread rumor that Villa at some point intended to surrender to U.S. authorities and claim he had no knowledge of the murders at Santa Ysabel, Cobb added that "there is reason to believe that he intends to cross to the United States and hopes to proceed to Washington. Please consider this possibility and the necessity of instructions to us on the border." There was no immediate response from Lansing. That same day, the Mexican commander in Juárez contacted Pershing at Fort Bliss, warning him to disregard the possibility of Villa coming to America to proclaim his innocence regarding Santa Ysabel. Instead, he intended "some act of violence" that would force the U.S. to send troops into Mexico. Pershing reportedly commented that he took such warnings "with a grain of salt."

If either civilian officials or Pershing passed along these warnings to Slocum in Columbus, the colonel was not alarmed. For his weekly report to Southern Department command, Slocum needed only one sentence: "Border conditions in this patrol district for week ending March 4, 1916 have remained normal." But the next day, Funston notified Slocum from the Southern Department command in San Antonio that "reliable" sources indicated Villa might surrender to American border authorities. Funston added that less reliable informants suggested Villa planned to raid some U.S. border town.

On March 6, Cobb cabled Lansing again: his earlier report about Villa was confirmed. He believed Villa would reach Columbus that night or the next day. Cobb added that he'd sent a deputy to Columbus to investigate and report further. On March 7, Cobb wired additional information. A Mexican consul claimed that "Villa with 500 men" had raided the Palomas Land and Cattle Company, but the same source believed that Villa was now fifty miles away from Palomas and heading south. Perhaps he had no designs on Columbus after all.

Slocum sent his regular patrols out along stretches of the border. None reported sighting Villa or observing any unusual activity. These latest rumors appeared unfounded, just like all the earlier ones. To Slocum, jumpy civilians like Cobb suspected Villa somehow lurked behind every clump of cactus. But on the afternoon of March 7, two visitors arrived at Slocum's office, and in separate conversations each insisted that this time the threat was real. Both Juan Favela and Antonio Muñoz worked for the Palomas Land and Cattle Company; they often came to Columbus, where they were known and well regarded. Each told Slocum that he'd spotted Villa and a large force—other ranch hands had been taken prisoner and at least one was murdered. The Villistas were close by, though for the moment still across the border in Mexico. The colonel had to do something right away. But Slocum's options were limited, and the most obvious—sending a squad of cavalry across the border to reconnoiter—was forbidden by his superiors. Instead, Slocum offered Muñoz $20 to ride back into Mexico the next day, look around, and then return and report. The *vaquero* agreed. The colonel was less direct with Favela, who later recalled that Slocum told him, "If Villa comes . . . a reception will be waiting for him. Do not be concerned."

That night, Slocum and Major Frank Tompkins rode down to the border crossing at Palomas and were assured by the Mexican commander there that, so far as he knew, Villa was not in the area. Tompkins was suspicious. He wrote later that the Mexican soldiers on guard at the Palomas crossing had their rifles handy and all faced toward the American rather than Mexican side of the border. Besides the *federales*—about forty—there was no impediment to raiders crossing into America beyond a barbed wire fence. Slocum didn't press the issue. Even if Villa had been in the vicinity, he'd probably turned back south.

But Slocum received additional warnings on Wednesday, March 8.

When Columbus merchant Louis Ravel delivered a wagonload of goods to Palomas, a Mexican customs official asked him to send three telegrams from the railway station in Columbus—Palomas had no such facility. The messages were intended for Mexican federal officers at three different border locations in the region, alerting them that Villa was nearby. Back in Columbus, Ravel took the messages instead to Slocum, who had them translated, shrugged, and told Ravel to "stop spreading rumors." Late in the afternoon, Antonio Muñoz returned from his paid scouting expedition. Muñoz testified afterward he told Slocum that Villa and at least five to seven hundred men were just across the border and "headed this way." Slocum, however, swore that Muñoz had assured him Villa and his forces were moving southeast, away from Columbus. Misunderstanding rather than prevarication on the part of either man is possible—Muñoz spoke very poor English and Slocum had no Spanish at all.

Slocum was convinced these latest Villa rumors had little if any substance. Perhaps the Mexican rebel and some followers had briefly been in the area, but they were surely gone by now. Even if Villa remained nearby, he would never attack Columbus with its military camp. Still, the colonel hedged his bet. As a forty-year Army veteran, he understood that in the unlikely event of a substantial cross-border raid by Villa in Slocum's designated region, probably on some ranch and with resulting public uproar, the scapegoat would be Camp Furlong's commander. Slocum accordingly issued orders intended to indicate that he'd taken appropriate preventive measures. Two officers and 65 cavalrymen were sent to guard the U.S. side of the Palomas border gate overnight; another 7 officers, 126 cavalrymen, and 25 additional troops were dispatched to Gibson's Line Ranch fourteen miles west of Columbus, considered by Slocum to be a likely spot for Villa to raid. That left a dozen officers and 341 men at Camp Furlong in Columbus, although 79 of the latter were noncombatant personnel such as cooks and veterinary specialists who cared for the 13th Cavalry's horses and mules.

Around twilight, Slocum received a phone call from George Carothers, a U.S. government official who served in various border capacities. Carothers told Slocum he should disregard any reports that Villa was moving away from Palomas and Columbus. Slocum's response, Carothers testified later, was to "ridicule" his message, insisting that according to his own reliable information, Villa was already sixty-five or seventy miles away.

Then Slocum left town. Some information suggests he and a few of the Camp Furlong officers not sent out on special guard assignments attended, along with their wives, a party at a ranch some dozen miles away; other sources indicate the Slocums drove to a social gathering in Deming. But in any event he was gone, leaving in place the same minimal camp security assigned on any other night—one soldier guarding the facility where machine guns and ammunition were locked away, another at the camp stables, a third at the headquarters building, and a fourth moving between the hospital and barracks. A sergeant and three enlisted men made periodic patrols through town. First Lieutenant James Castleman was officer of the day and therefore responsible for overall security. All the other officers were either at home with their families in other parts of Columbus, away from town at parties or on leave, or else assigned to the patrols at the Palomas border gate and Gibson's Line Ranch. No additional sentry was placed atop Cootes Hill, where a night approach up the valley slope would have been detected, at least by sound if not sight.

The train from El Paso chugged into the Columbus station around midnight. First Lieutenant John P. Lucas disembarked. Lucas, who commanded the 13th Cavalry's machine gunners, was returning to town after playing in an El Paso polo tournament. He and Castleman exchanged a few words about the Villa alert and then Lucas, worn out from polo, made his way across the Palomas Road to the small adobe house a few dozen yards from Cootes Hill that he shared with Lieutenant Clarence Benson—both officers were unmarried, and rooming together allowed them to make the best of Columbus's very limited rental facilities. Benson wasn't there—he was part of the group Slocum assigned to spend the night on guard at the border. Acting on what he later termed a hunch, Lucas checked and loaded his service revolver, went to bed, and soon slept. It was very quiet in Columbus.

CHAPTER THIRTEEN

The Raid

When the Villistas attacked Columbus just after 4 a.m., they split into two dismounted columns of about two hundred men each, just as their leader ordered. One column jogged north across the railroad track and then swerved east, targeting the town's business district with its shops, bank, post office, and hotels. The other moved south and east back across the Palomas Road, tearing into Camp Furlong with its stables and supplies of arms and ammunition. Neither column encountered any immediate opposition—total surprise was achieved. This heartened the Villista conscripts, most of whom had never even fired a gun. Now they did, not only shooting but shouting as they charged forward, caught up in the excitement.

As the column attacking the business district swept in, panicked civilians began stumbling out into the streets, some from their houses, others from the Commercial Hotel. Some Villistas chose victims in the same random way many of their fellow attackers snatched items from store shelves. It was a simple matter of selecting whoever appealed—the pickings could not have been easier. One man trying to escape in his car was shot as he fumbled at the steering wheel. Raiders herded guests together inside the Commercial Hotel, stripped them of their valuables, dragged several of the men outside, and gunned them down. Town veterinarian Harry Hart was the object of especially cruel sport. He was ordered to run down the street, and the Villistas blasted away at their moving target until their bullets blew him to bits. A newlywed husband was ripped from his wife's arms and murdered. The Villistas savaging the business district did observe one limit, obeying orders to kill all the men, but to spare the women, whose shrieks added to the cacophony of one-sided gunfire. After perhaps a half hour of unabated rampage, some of the raiders began lighting torches to burn buildings; the Commercial Hotel erupted in flames. None of the business district attackers had been even slightly wounded until they were surprised by a barrage of machine gun fire from the south. Things had not gone as smoothly for the raiders attacking Camp Furlong.

Lieutenant John Lucas had slept for only a few hours when he was awakened by the sound of a rider outside his tiny house. Looking out the window, Lucas saw several horsemen whom he immediately identified as Villistas because of their wide-brimmed sombreros—it was Villa and his small guard, remaining behind to observe the raid from near the base of Cootes Hill, while the column ordered to attack Camp Furlong charged in. Lucas grabbed his pistol and waited for the Mexicans to storm into his house, "determined to get a few of them before they got me." But instead, a Camp Furlong guard also spotted the raiders and fired at them. The Villistas returned fire, mortally wounding the American soldier, and then ran past him toward the camp barracks and mess hall three hundred yards away. Lucas fumbled in the dark for his boots, couldn't find them, and ran barefoot toward the camp, hoping to gather his machine gun squad and mount a defense.

Not all camp personnel were asleep. In the mess hall, a squadron of cooks commanded by a mess sergeant busily prepared breakfast for the remainder of the troops. The initial target of the attackers was the Camp Furlong stables just east of the mess hall. The unarmed cooks were an unexpected but not daunting obstacle between the Villistas and the Army horses and mules just steps away. But instead of cowering behind their ovens, the noncoms stood their ground, flinging pots of boiling water in the raiders' faces and bashing at them with an axe normally used on firewood and some baseball bats stored nearby with other equipment for the camp team. An axe stroke made one of the raiders the Villistas' first fatality. This ferocious, completely unexpected defense momentarily slowed the attackers, and that gave Lieutenant James Castleman, officer of the day and, in fact, the only officer on duty, the opportunity to rally the first soldiers emerging from the barracks. Castleman and Sergeant Michael Foudy ordered their men to shoot, but finding targets was difficult. The night was still pitch-black; all around them Villistas howled and fired. The largest concentration seemed to be across the railroad tracks in the business district, but it was mostly dark there, too.

Meanwhile, Lieutenant Lucas, limping on bare feet badly torn by sand burrs, made his way to the barracks housing his squad, leading them toward the guard tent above the barracks where the camp machine guns were locked away. Thanks to the heroism of the mess hall cooks, Lucas and a few of his men beat the Villistas to the tent. He unlocked the machine guns, picked one out, and dragged it outside, aiming across the tracks toward the business district. Almost immediately, the machine gun jammed.

Castleman led a squad of about twenty-five soldiers a few dozen yards east of Lucas and his machine gun team. The Castleman squad fought its way toward the railroad tracks, killing a few Villistas and suffering their own casualties. It remained difficult for both sides to see. Dawn was still almost an hour away, and neither Columbus nor Camp Furlong had streetlamps. The only illumination came from gunfire. But then the Commercial Hotel went up in flames, and the fire backlit the Villistas in the street. Now they offered clear targets to the soldiers across the railroad tracks. Castleman's squad began laying down effective fire, and Lucas's men got three machine guns in place that functioned properly, cumulatively blasting five thousand shots over the next forty-five minutes. The initial confidence of Villa's untrained conscripts melted away. Battle wasn't as exhilarating when the gringos fought back.

>–◦–◦–◦–◦–◦–‹

Nineteen-year-old Susan Parks spent the early part of the raid cowering in the Columbus business district. Parks's husband was out of town, and her initial concern was to protect their infant daughter. At one point Parks believed that she saw Pancho Villa in front of the Hoover Hotel, directing his raiders: "I [had] seen so many pictures of the man that there could be no mistake." It was a mistake; during the attack, Villa never left his post at Cootes Hill. But Parks was a courageous woman who worked as the town's telephone operator. After hiding her daughter under a bed, Parks used the Hoover switchboard to notify Fort Bliss, eighty miles away in El Paso, that Pancho Villa and his men were at that very moment murdering and looting in Columbus. With that accomplished, Parks afterward told the *Columbus Courier* she then made calls "to surrounding towns," certainly including Deming, warning as widely as she could that Villistas were raiding in force. Somewhere, Colonel Herbert J. Slocum learned that the camp he commanded was under attack.

The fight raged for another hour. U.S. troops now held an advantage in firepower, but they were still outnumbered by almost two to one. They had some hopes of reinforcements—perhaps the sounds of fighting had reached the Camp Furlong troops guarding the border gate three miles to the south—but none appeared. There was nothing to do but dig in and keep fighting. Raiders in the Army camp were able to steal some horses and mules, but never gained access to weapons and ammunition. In the business district, the Commercial Hotel burned down to smoldering cinders. As dawn neared, probably not much after 6 a.m., the Villistas began a reasonably controlled retreat south, pausing five hundred yards past Cootes Hill and leaving behind about seventy dead and wounded; reports of that number would vary. American corpses lay in the Columbus streets, though not nearly as many—eight soldiers and ten civilians. Just as the sun rose, Slocum arrived at Cootes Hill, where the bulk of the American defenders now gathered. Slocum claimed that he, like most of his other officers, had been cut off from the fighting by the riders between his Columbus home and Camp Furlong, but now he would assume command. The colonel was uncertain whether the force beyond the hill was comprised of attackers or some of the 13th Cavalry personnel he'd previously ordered to patrol near Gibson's Line Ranch. One of the other U.S. officers ordered his men to snap off a few shots in their direction; heavy return fire confirmed that these were Mexicans.

Major Frank Tompkins approached Slocum and told the colonel that "the Mexicans were whipped." When Tompkins requested permission to "mount up a troop and take the offensive," Slocum granted it. After twenty minutes Tompkins had gathered thirty-two cavalrymen, and when they charged, the Villistas, still numbering about four hundred, fell back toward the place where they'd previously cut through the border fence. The U.S. troops raced after them, halting when covering fire erupted from the rearguard Villa had left in place to cover any retreat. Tompkins led his men at an angle along the fence, ordered them to cut their own opening, and led another charge. His men "socked in the spurs" and "swept forward." The remaining Villistas turned their mounts and fled. The American soldiers engaged in their own target practice, shooting some Mexicans off their horses before the raiders stopped out of range about 1,500 yards away.

Tompkins realized that, after cutting the fence and charging through, he and his cavalry were now in Mexico. He held the troops in place while he scribbled a note to Slocum, notifying the colonel of his position and requesting permission to continue after the Villistas. Forty-five minutes later he received Slocum's reply, which was for Tompkins to use his own judgment. Since Castleman had just arrived with another twenty-seven riders, Tompkins chose to move forward. For almost the entire morning, the Villistas kept running—Tompkins wondered why, since they greatly outnumbered their pursuers, the raiders didn't stand and fight. But he and his force took full advantage, firing and bringing down several dozen more, until finally the Villistas did turn, at which point Tompkins, now fifteen miles deep into Mexico, cut off pursuit and led his men back to Camp Furlong on the U.S. side of the border. Tompkins later estimated that his chase after the Villistas lasted about seven and a half hours, with "between 75 and 100 Mexican bandits killed on Mexican soil." Tompkins and one of his soldiers had minor bullet wounds. Slocum unsuccessfully nominated Tompkins for the Medal of Honor, but the major was eventually awarded the Army's Distinguished Service Cross.

Tompkins and his cavalrymen arrived back in Columbus just before 1 p.m. They found soldiers and civilians dragging dead Villistas into a pile just outside town. The sixty-seven collected corpses were soaked in kerosene, then burned. Before this crude cremation, the contents of the dead raiders' pockets, packs, and saddlebags were examined. One of the saddlebags contained a leather diary with entries describing the Santa Ysabel massacre, as well as Villista payroll and expense records and a copy of Villa's January 8 letter to Zapata imploring his fellow rebel to join him in killing Americans "in their own territory." Seven captured Villistas were held to be handed over to federal authorities; within a few months six were hanged, and the seventh sentenced to life in prison. Ranchwoman Maud Wright and black cowboy Bunk Spenser, hostages released by Villa just before his remaining forces retreated south, provided eyewitness testimony that Villa had personally led the raiders to Columbus, then directed the raid.

Slocum was ordered by General Funston to immediately submit a report about the raid and his actions prior to it. He was not allowed even a day to organize his thoughts—Secretary Lansing was hounding Funston for information. While the Villista corpses still smoldered,

Slocum retreated to his office to craft a statement that might salvage his reputation and military career. But before he set pen to paper, the colonel summoned *vaquero* Juan Favela, who had spent the previous night in Columbus and survived the raid. Years later, Favela said that Slocum "gave me a pass to go anyplace in the United States. 'Just get out,' he ordered me. 'I don't want you talking to the newspapermen who will be pouring into town.' He gave me some money."

Favela went to Deming for a few days, then returned to Columbus. Though he didn't want to anger Slocum, his pregnant wife was there and he wanted to be with her. But by the time he returned, there was so much chaotic activity in town that neither Slocum nor the dozens of reporters there noticed Juan Favela at all.

CHAPTER FOURTEEN

"The Most Serious Situation"

For several years, Cleveland mayor Newton D. Baker refused Woodrow Wilson's frequent requests to serve as his secretary of war. But after completing his mayoral term in late 1915, Baker finally agreed. A lawyer by trade and a political strategist who worked diligently to win Wilson the Democratic nomination in 1912, Baker had no experience in military matters. But, like the president, he adamantly opposed American involvement in the European conflict—some observers believed Baker was a pacifist. On March 8, 1916, President Wilson personally escorted Baker to the War Department and introduced him to staff there. Army chief of staff Hugh Scott immediately offered his resignation, telling Baker that, as new secretary, he had the right to promote the officer of his choosing to that post. Baker replied that he didn't know any other Army officers, so Scott should stay. Further, "I am going to do what you advise me."

By the time Baker began his first day in office on the morning of March 9, word had already reached Washington about Villa's attack on Columbus, and Wilson and Secretary of State Lansing were in agreement that this time America must not trust Mexico to bring the perpetrators to justice. Beyond the indignity of the assault itself, Wilson was aware that 1916 was a presidential election year. So far, the American public supported the president's determination to keep their country out of an overseas war, but voters would surely reject a White House incumbent who failed to avenge fellow citizens murdered by invaders of the United States. Less than two miles away at the Capitol, Senator Albert Fall of New Mexico was advocating recruitment of 500,000 soldiers to storm into Mexico, seize all critical ports and railroad lines, and then "assist" the Carranza government in eradicating every Mexican bandit. (During his tirade, Fall failed to mention to his fellow senators that he had extensive properties and business interests in Mexico.) In a hurriedly convened meeting, the rest of Wilson's cabinet concurred when the president instructed Secretary of War Baker to mount an expedition into Mexico for the purpose of capturing Pancho Villa and bringing him back to the U.S. to answer for his foul crime. Lansing immediately announced the decision to the press—within hours, newspapers across the nation declared that Villa would be the object of an immediate manhunt, and that the only acceptable result would be his capture and execution.

Baker went to his office at the War Department and summoned General Scott, who recalled being told, "I want you to start an expedition into Mexico to catch Villa." Scott thought that order was "strange"—clearly, the inexperienced Baker hadn't sufficiently thought the situation through. The general asked, "Mr. Secretary, do you want the United States to make war on one man? Suppose he should get on a train and go to Guatemala, Yucatan, or South America?" Wilson's instructions to Baker hadn't included those contingencies. Though he knew nothing about military operations, the legally trained secretary fully understood the ramifications of arbitrarily crossing multiple national borders with armed forces. Baker told Scott he wanted American forces sent only into Mexico. The general pressed his boss further: as an individual, Villa would be difficult to apprehend in his native country, where he but not his pursuers would be familiar with the rugged terrain. A U.S. expedition could operate in Mexico for only a limited time. "You want his band captured or destroyed," Scott suggested, noting in his memoir how he emphasized the word *band*. That would eliminate the Villistas as a threat and satisfy the American desire for retribution. Baker replied, "That is what I really want." He and Scott made their case to Wilson and Lansing, who consented. The expedition's mission would be completed with the eradication of the raider force that assaulted Columbus, whether Villa was captured or not.

Baker and Scott next sent a wire to General Funston in San Antonio, ordering him to organize "an adequate military force of troops from your department" that would "proceed promptly across the border in pursuit of the Mexican band which attacked the town of Columbus, New Mexico . . . the work of these troops will be regarded as finished as soon as Villa's band or bands are known to be broken up." There were limits to where this expedition could go, "the state[s] of Chihuahua and Sonora, or roughly, the field of possible operations by Villa." Funston was in full agreement with the instructions, except for one directive contained in the first sentence—the troops would be "under the command of Brigadier General John J. Pershing." As commander of the Army's Southern Department, Funston believed it was his right to lead this prestigious expedition; he'd been promoted to his current position in recognition of his service two years earlier in Veracruz. His performance as military governor there was exemplary, but Scott remembered how the hot-tempered Funston constantly pleaded with his superiors for permission to move on Mexico City. The expedition pursuing Villistas required a cooler head, and Scott convinced Baker that Pershing was a better choice than Funston to lead it. Funston couldn't refuse an order from Baker and Scott, but he could, and soon would, take out his resentment on Pershing.

Though it was only a matter of hours since Major Tompkins and his cavalry chased the Villistas back into Mexico, America had already planned its pursuit and selected the officer to lead it. Now, Wilson and Lansing believed, came the easy part—notifying Carranza, and obtaining his consent. The usually difficult Mexican president would surely cooperate this time; America was going to eliminate the Villistas for him. At 4 p.m. on March 9, Jesús Acuña, Mexico's secretary of foreign affairs, received his first official communication from Lansing: America considered the Columbus raid to be "the most serious situation." The U.S. expected that Carranza "will do everything in his power to pursue, capture and exterminate this lawless element." Wilson and Lansing expected Acuña to promptly reply that Mexico was suitably appalled by the raid, and Carranza was ready to cooperate in any way America wished. But no response was forthcoming until the next day, when Acuña merely observed that Villa's attack on Columbus was proof that the Mexican government was effectively dealing with him—Villa undoubtedly crossed the border while avoiding pursuit by *federales*. There was no apology or promise to partner with America toward Villa's apprehension.

Lansing immediately wired back asking what, specifically, Mexico was doing to capture Villa, and where, exactly, the Mexican government had believed him to be just prior to the raid. Acuña's reply this time noted that President Carranza was "pained" by the events in Columbus. The Mexican government now formally requested U.S. permission to pursue Villa north over the American border; in return, the U.S. would be permitted to do the same going south "if the raid effected at Columbus should unfortunately be repeated at any other point on the border." Wilson was aghast—Carranza apparently expected America to wait for *another* Villa attack in the U.S. before pursuing him into Mexico. But Carranza was unaware that the U.S. had decided to withdraw the expedition after eliminating the Villistas, even if Villa himself remained at large.

The Mexican leader was usually oblivious to his country's lower classes, but he well understood the risk to his administration. If he not only permitted a new American military presence in Mexico, but allowed these despised, invading gringos to catch and hang Pancho Villa, Mexico's working class and peasants would surely embrace Villa as the greatest martyr since Christ himself, while reviling Carranza as the equivalent of Judas. If Wilson's expedition didn't catch and kill Villa, Americans might vote their president out of office. But if the *yanquis* succeeded, it might well cost Carranza not only his presidency, but his life. Despite the Mexican leader's personal determination to eventually destroy Villa, Americans could not be permitted to kill his longtime enemy. Offering permission to enter Mexico if Villa raided the U.S. again seemed the perfect ploy, because in the aftermath of Columbus the Americans would surely line their side of the border with troops to prevent such a recurrence. Carranza believed the matter was settled.

He was almost correct. Later, in an off-the-record interview with journalist Ray Stannard Baker, who later served Wilson as a press spokesman, the U.S. president acknowledged that he was reluctant to offend Carranza in light of what Wilson believed was America's previous, shameful aggression against Mexico, especially during the U.S.-Mexican war. Additionally, Wilson told the journalist that he did not want a significant percentage of America's available troops engaged in Mexico "at the very moment that the [U.S.] might need all its forces to meet the German situation."

But Wilson couldn't delay. Members of his cabinet warned that the American public expected immediate action. Government agent Cobb wired from El Paso that Carranza was "rushing troops to Juarez . . . I think as a predicate to claim ours are unnecessary. Ours are necessary." If the U.S. Army didn't act, Cobb warned, American civilians on the border, particularly near Columbus, would. Already, Anglos in Columbus suspected at least some of the Mexicans living there, maybe most of them, must have been Villa informants. The Mexican residents were warned to clear out of town, and stay away for a while. There were rumors of Mexicans being randomly killed in the area, and their bodies left in the open to rot. Cobb insisted that the only way of preventing additional violence was for white people to believe that their government was aggressively responding.

Wilson and Lansing decided to move forward. Rather than demand that Carranza adjust his offer of mutual border crossing rights in the event of another Villa raid, they chose to deliberately misinterpret it. They responded to Carranza that "the Government of the United States understands that in view of [the] reciprocal agreement proposed by [the Mexican government], the arrangement is now complete and in force and the reciprocal privileges thereunder may accordingly be exercised by either government without further interchange of views." The American expedition was coming whether Carranza liked it or not. He demonstrated that he didn't like it by declaring that the expedition could not use Mexican railroads to move troops or matériel, a daunting limitation considering the number of soldiers and animals involved, plus the massive amount of supplies required to support and sustain them. Horse- or mule-drawn wagons would be slow; whenever possible, trucks must be used, and that meant adding engineers to the expedition, and the heavy equipment necessary either to improve Mexico's primitive roads or cut new ones through desert sand and mountain rock, plus the mechanics needed to maintain the machinery and countless gallons of gasoline to keep the vehicles running. Logistics would undoubtedly be a daily frustration, but that was Pershing's problem. The president and the War Department had an even more pressing issue: Should some American be held publicly responsible for the debacle in Columbus, where, despite numerous warnings, Villa took the town and Camp Furlong by surprise? Slocum was the obvious candidate, but the colonel had no intention of taking the blame.

On March 10, only a day after the raid, Funston released to the press a copy of Slocum's initial report. Slocum claimed Villa "made the attack with 1,500 men" and "intended capturing the town, looting the bank and killing all Americans." He speculated that spies informed Villa that the garrison at Camp Furlong was depleted after Slocum sent out troops to guard the border gate and the ranch west of Columbus. The colonel ignored how the soldiers remaining at Camp Furlong were still caught by surprise, emphasizing instead how "our troops turned out quickly. . . . Villa's attempt to capture town and camp was a complete failure." Funston was unimpressed; he wrote privately to General Scott, "Had I been in command [at Columbus] and had heard that Villa was anywhere near the border, I would have had the town and camp protected by heavy guards. . . . I have always had a fine opinion of [Slocum], and cannot for the life of me understand his apparently 'casual' way of doing things on this occasion."

Many civilians in Columbus also believed that the colonel was culpable. One wrote to Pershing that Slocum "should, in my opinion, be tried for murder, for he had notice that night . . . that they were coming and took no precautions to protect the town, nor the boys in his own regiment." General Tasker Bliss was assigned to lead a full investigation. But for the time being the president, Lansing, Baker, and Scott agreed that the public could not be allowed to think that Villa had caught an Army officer so disgracefully unprepared. Slocum was ordered to lead the portion of the 13th Cavalry assigned to Pershing's expedition.

While pursuing Villa in Mexico, Slocum provided a fuller written report, this time declaring that he was in Columbus at the beginning of the raid, but unable to reach the rest of his men in the embattled camp for almost two hours. The real problem, Slocum insisted, was the lack of light in town and the camp: "On a dark night, such as selected for this attack, a sentinel or member of patrol could not see twenty feet in front of him." The colonel pointedly noted that this lack of visibility wasn't his fault, "[my] requisition for oil and street lamps for this purpose having been previously disapproved." By June, Slocum was publicly exonerated.

▷·┤◇├·○·┤◇├·◁

Since Villa was presumed in full flight south, Pershing was instructed to quickly assemble what was labeled the "Punitive Expedition," which besides support personnel, two infantry troops, and two artillery batteries consisted of the 7th, 10th, 11th, and 13th Army cavalry regiments. The 7th was once famously led by Lieutenant Colonel George Armstrong Custer, and the 10th comprised the legendary Buffalo Soldiers, who earlier counted "Black Jack" Pershing as one of their officers. Though Pershing had been told that he could request all the troops and supplies he considered necessary, in formal orders his superiors reminded him of the mission's constraints: "The President desires that your attention be especially and earnestly called to his determination that the expedition into Mexico is limited to purposes originally stated, namely the pursuit and dispersion of the band or bands that attacked Columbus, N.M., and it is of the utmost importance that no color of any other possibility or intention be given . . . neither in size or otherwise should the expedition afford the slightest ground of suspicion of any other or larger object."

Pershing arrived in Columbus on March 13, with the intention of launching the expedition the next day. The tiny town was a maelstrom of activity. Trains unloaded troops, equipment, and horses by the thousands. Trucks rolled in, but not many—there were only about one hundred in the entire U.S. Army, though purchase orders were now issued for more. The expedition was to employ the latest military innovation, a fleet of eight fragile JN-2 "aeroplanes" for use in scouting and sending messages. These had to be disassembled, loaded on trains along with their pilots and repair crews, then reassembled in Columbus before they could be flown into Mexico days after the expedition set out.

Pershing picked most of his expedition staff from officers already serving under him at Fort Bliss. His subordinates clamored to be chosen—gallantry in the field remained the only means other than seniority to advance in rank. One of the most vocal, and surely the most disappointed not to be initially selected, was 2nd Lieutenant George S. Patton, whose border cavalry unit was not part of the overall expedition force. At age thirty, Patton's career was already unique. While in military service he competed in the 1912 Olympics, finishing just short of a bronze medal in the pentathlon. No one in the Army was a better equestrian or pistol shot, and Patton's fencing skills carried over into use of battlefield sabers—the young officer not only developed new saber-fighting techniques for the military, he invented a new "Patton saber" that became standard-issue.

His lust for advancement sometimes worked against him; few superior officers wanted such an openly ambitious subordinate outshining and second-guessing them. For a while Patton had been assigned to border duty in the rugged Texas town of Sierra Blanca, eighty miles southeast of El Paso. It retained a wild frontier atmosphere, and was populated by swaggering cowboys who tucked pistols in their belts. Patton, enthralled, did the same until his gun accidentally discharged one day as he sat down; the bullet missed wounding him and removing his private parts by only a few inches. After that, Patton used a holster, but maintained flamboyance by replacing his standard Colt .45 automatic with an ivory-handled Colt 1873 single-action .45 revolver, always keeping the chamber opposite the hammer empty to avoid inadvertent gelding. Subsequently assigned to Fort Bliss, Patton yearned for action, and, when his unit was left off the expedition roster, he begged Pershing for a place on his personal staff. Pershing said he'd consider it.

Besides Patton's obvious talents, another factor was in play. The lieutenant's twenty-nine-year-old sister Anne, "Nita" to family and friends, had come to Fort Bliss to stay for a time with Patton and his wife, Beatrice. Pershing, a lonely widower, soon noticed Nita, a striking woman of considerable charm, and began a formal courtship that included attending local cultural events as well as frequent horseback and automobile rides. This was a rare professional risk on Pershing's part—disparaging personal gossip derailed many promising Army careers, and even a hint of scandal suggesting that a commanding officer in any way compromised a subordinate's sister could have been disastrous. To assure propriety, whenever he "stepped out" with Nita, Pershing brought along chaperones, often including the lady's ambitious brother. Patton had mixed feelings about the budding romance. He understood the advantage of Pershing as a potential in-law, but worried that he'd inevitably be accused of benefiting from nepotism. To his credit, Patton's pleas to join Pershing's staff on the expedition apparently never alluded to how happy his selection would make Nita, though Pershing was surely aware of it.

Patton's incessant requests only added to the multitude of other demands being made on the general, who finally snapped at the younger man, "Everyone wants to go. Why should I favor you?" Patton replied, "Because I want to go more than anyone else." Pershing tested him with a predawn call the following day: "How long will it take you to get ready?" Patton said he'd already packed, just in case, so he could report on the double. Pershing muttered, "I'll be goddamned," then added, "You are appointed aide." While the general's other aides performed critical duties such as supervising the ordering and loading of munitions and supplies, Patton handled his boss's personal chores, like picking up Pershing's laundry. He cheerfully performed these menial duties while keeping a sharp eye out for more substantial opportunities.

>-+-◦-+-◦-+-<

Late on Monday, March 13, the Punitive Expedition totaled 4,800 men and 4,175 animals including cavalry mounts, packhorses, and mules. Every available Army truck was on hand. Several passenger cars were reserved for use by Pershing and his staff. The general put a plan in place for the first few days. By now, Villa must be deep into Chihuahua, but had to have passed through villages along the way—surely people there would offer the expedition helpful information about Villa's general direction and the number and condition of his remaining troops. Despite warnings from veteran American diplomats that, in their experience, many Mexicans, especially the rural poor, hated gringos above all others, it was assumed by Pershing, his military superiors, and the U.S. press that Villa's pursuers would be welcome everywhere. An editorial in the March 11 *El Paso Herald* predicted that the U.S. troops would "be assisted in every possible way by the decent and law-abiding Mexicans."

But on the night of the 13th, the commander of Mexican federal forces at the Palomas border gate sent a stern message to the American forces in Columbus: he had orders to oppose any attempted crossing by the expedition. In a return message, Pershing argued that the U.S. and Mexican governments had agreed that the expedition should come south, and certainly the small federal garrison in Palomas could never prevail against the overwhelming American force. The Mexican commander repeated that his orders were to fight, and he would.

Washington fired off cables to Mexico City; Carranza made no immediate reply. His resistance to the expedition was clear in the Palomas commander's order to oppose its entry into Mexico. The U.S. government realized it would look bad for the expedition to begin its mission by fighting soldiers of the Mexican government, but it would be worse for Pershing to be stalled in Columbus as Villa fled farther by the day. Funston ordered Pershing to begin marching south.

Anticipating a bottleneck at the Palomas crossing gate even under peaceful circumstances, Pershing split his forces in two, one wing in Columbus and the other fifty miles west at Culberson's Ranch, another border crossing point. Pershing personally led the Culberson's Ranch contingent. In honor of his pursuit of the Villistas immediately after their March 9 raid, Major Frank Tompkins was assigned to ride point on the Columbus wing. The two U.S. forces would rendezvous at Nuevo Casas Grandes, about seventy-five miles deep into Mexico. Pershing's group crossed the border unopposed shortly after midnight on Thursday, March 16. Tompkins, anticipating trouble, rode for Palomas about noon on Wednesday. The American troops had their guns ready, but as Tompkins wrote later, "The command entered as planned and found that the Mexican troops had vanished."

The U.S. troops from Columbus camped for the night just outside Palomas. An unexpected cold front blew in. The soldiers shivered in their blankets and awoke to find their canteen water was frozen solid. This mild inconvenience was only the first of many unpleasant surprises awaiting the Punitive Expedition in Mexico.

CHAPTER FIFTEEN

Elusive Prey

After Columbus, Villa led his remaining forces back south into Chihuahua. He was certain that Tompkins's aborted pursuit was preliminary to what would soon follow. Villa's challenge was to evade capture by the gringos while not so completely eluding them that they quickly abandoned the chase and returned to their side of the border. The irresistible provocation Villa intended was accomplished, but at far greater cost than intended. He'd come to Columbus with almost five hundred men, and now retreated with more than a hundred fewer, plus dozens of badly wounded who could hardly stay on their horses. Even most of the horses were in deplorable condition; they were already worn down from the arduous trip to Columbus before expending their limited remaining strength galloping away from Tompkins and his cavalry. So many *yanqui* soldiers had been in that Army camp—Villa fumed about the bad information from his spies and, especially, the entreaties from his subordinates that persuaded him to go against his own instincts and carry out the attack as planned. As soon as he dared call for a brief stop to rest, Villa castigated these officers, snarling, "I gave way to please all of you."

Even in bad temper, Villa realized there was no time for lengthy recriminations. His badly wounded men slowed the brisk pace necessary to put sufficient space between the Villistas and gringo pursuit. They must be left behind, but hopefully someplace where their injuries could be tended. Villa's healthy troops needed fresh mounts; supplies of food and water were required for the men, and forage for the animals— there was little grass for the horses to crop in the desert or the mountains. Above all, Villa needed more *soldados*. For all these reasons, his flight began with stops at the scattered villages south of the border. In each, Villa asked to leave some of his wounded to be cared for; he warned that the *yanquis* would be coming, but promised that if his people were hidden until they healed, he would remember the favor and see that their protectors were rewarded. Whatever horses and supplies these peasants could spare were handed over. But to Villa's surprise, even after he swore that war with the gringos had finally broken out, very few men volunteered to join his forces. He resorted again to conscription, reminding his reluctant new *soldados* that attempted desertion meant death.

On March 15, Villa reached El Valle, about 120 miles south of Palomas. This was the most substantial village the Villistas entered since the Columbus raid, and Villa ordered that everyone there gather to hear him speak. His message remained the same: "The Americans are about to come to Mexico to fight us. War has already been declared and I desire to see how many of you will join me." To Villa's great pleasure, forty men stepped forward. These willing volunteers swelled the Villista ranks back to about four hundred—perhaps enough, their leader thought, to make surprise attacks on isolated outposts of Carranza's federal troops in hopes of getting the guns and ammunition they'd failed to acquire from Camp Furlong. Now Villa continued south with more than retreat on his mind, though his overriding concern remained American pursuit. Surely their chase after him had begun. Where were they? How fast were they coming?

＞・＜＞・○・＜＞・＞・＜

It was March 17 before the two wings of the Punitive Expedition managed to converge eighty-five miles south of the border at Colonia

Dublán, a mostly deserted Mormon enclave. They had tremendous difficulty getting even that far. No one had extensive experience traveling in Chihuahua, and the Army had no maps of the region. This portion of the northern Mexican state was miles of desert buried especially deep in sand because of drought. Winds kicked up thick plumes of dust that choked men and horses. The expedition's precious trucks, hauling water and animal forage and other essential supplies, had even harder going. There was nothing resembling even the most rudimentary American road. The expedition report noted, "The difficulties of the situation . . . can hardly be imagined. The wheels of heavily loaded trucks sank deep into the friable alkali soil and cut deep furrows that filled with dust ground fine as powder. New tracks were laid out [by engineers] only to have the operation repeated, requiring these ruts to be filled with gravel whenever possible as the only recourse left."

Even moving at a snail's pace, expedition men and animals were soon exhausted. But Pershing, commanding from the passenger seat of a Buick, pushed them on. After arriving at Colonia Dublán, he expected to promptly engage local informers to provide information on the Villistas' location, and guides to lead his forces there to attack them. His first informants indicated Villa was now about sixty miles to the southwest, near the town of San Miguel de Babícora. Pershing promptly dispatched a substantial portion of troops to the area, but they did not find Villa. Pershing telegraphed Funston that he'd learned a lesson: "The report that Villa was at San Miguel was unfounded. Practically every Mexican so far encountered has questioned our right to be in Mexico, and claimed there was no authority for our presence. . . . If this campaign should eventually prove successful, it will be without the real assistance of any natives this side [of the border]."

That was a source of significant frustration, but not the only one. Pershing wanted the eight planes at his disposal flown immediately to Colonia Dublán. If Mexicans wouldn't inform on Villa, then at least the pilots could scour the region from the air—they'd locate him that way. But the planes were underpowered, barely able to maintain minimal flying height, and their pilots had no experience with the crosswinds of northern Mexico. Within weeks, all eight either crashed or broke down. Supposedly more durable replacements arrived, but these soon proved inadequate even for basic airborne observation and conveying messages between Pershing and his commanders in the field. Pershing concluded, "They were of little use."

Funston was angry with Pershing, notifying Army chief of staff Scott that the expedition's leader's field reports were "very meager and unsatisfactory. Today I sent him a very sharp telegram on the subject." Funston's criticism failed to reflect the process necessary for Pershing to stay in touch with him. Expedition communications specialists had to maintain ground wire between Columbus and every remote spot in Mexico where Pershing made temporary headquarters. Soldiers were required to guard long stretches of wire, which would otherwise be cut by Villistas or Villa sympathizers. Weather ranging from sandstorms to blizzards could snap the wires at any time, requiring lengthy hunts to locate and repair the damage before communication could resume. But Pershing refused to offer excuses, and Funston, still seething from being passed over for expedition command, gladly assumed that the problems were Pershing's fault.

Carranza further complicated the situation. On March 18, Lansing received formal notification that the Mexican government "is studying with the urgency the case demands" whether the expedition would be allowed to remain in Mexico. The message warned that any previous communication between the two countries should not be interpreted by the U.S. as Mexico "tolerating any expeditions into [our] national territory." Two days later, Lansing replied that he "sincerely regretted" any misunderstanding. But haste was necessary. America would be "glad to receive" suggestions about mutual efforts to catch Villa.

Mexico City's immediate response was that until a formal agreement with America was in place—impossible under current circumstances—the government would not allow American occupation or entry into any Mexican towns, "much less such towns as are occupied by our own troops, as this might give rise to frequent conflicts." The implication was clear: Mexican federal troops were ready to fight the intruders. Carranza also required full disclosure regarding the number of troops in the expedition, their exact locations, and detailed explanations of "the causes which occasioned their crossing" as though his government had not been previously aware of the Columbus raid. Lansing feebly responded that the expedition was "a friendly endeavor." Pershing was informed that if his troops approached towns occupied by federal forces, they must ask and receive permission before entering, either to pass through or buy supplies.

More than a dozen journalists who came into Mexico with the expedition waited impatiently with Pershing in Colonia Dublán for something to happen. Denied any appreciable action to describe, and hounded by their editors to provide publishable material, their stories varied from frantic ("Must Catch Villa Before He Reaches Hiding Place in Mountain Fastness," in the March 20 El Paso Times) to dryly factual ("Radio and Telegraph to Pershing Fail: Communication with Army in Field Cut Off," in the March 22 New York Times). Every day newspapers across the U.S. speculated about when the expedition would catch Villa, which most reporters and readers still assumed was a foregone conclusion. Then Villa went into action, and the journalists had plenty to write about.

> ⊱──◇──⊰

On March 19 the Villistas rode into Namiquipa, about thirty miles south of San Miguel de Babícora. They'd hardly climbed off their horses when word came that a substantial force of Mexican federal troops was coming to occupy the town. Villa ordered an immediate retreat, but a few hours later an informer found the Villistas about four miles out of Namiquipa and reported that there weren't many *federales* after all, perhaps two hundred. Villa had twice that number; he turned his men around and attacked. The federals broke and ran, leaving behind a hundred rifles, two machine guns, and about a hundred horses. The victory convinced Villa that additional attacks on the federals might be equally fruitful. After some thought, he set his sights on a federal garrison in Guerrero thirty miles to the southwest. According to Villa's informants, the gringos chasing him still dithered around Colonia Dublán. Even if word reached them that the Villistas were on their way to Guerrero, the *yanquis* would have to traverse high mountain ranges coming after him there, taking so many days that their quarry would be long gone, carrying with them many more guns and other critical supplies.

Colonel George Dodd commanded a 7th Cavalry contingent scouting near El Valle, a town fifty miles north of Namiquipa. *Federales* currently occupied the town, so the Americans could not enter. But the Mexican commander rode out to exchange formal greetings, and warmed sufficiently to tell Dodd that Villa was rumored to be in Namiquipa, along with many men who'd participated in the Columbus raid. Dodd had his forces there the next day, only to learn that the Villistas were gone—no one admitted knowing where. Pershing had ordered Dodd to reconnoiter toward the southwest, so he moved on in that direction. The American cavalry and their horses suffered badly as they ascended into the Sierra Madre range. The cold was intense, the air was thin, and much of the time they were lashed by a storm of mixed sand and ice. But sometimes they came upon indications—dead horses in particular—that another large company had come this way before them.

The Villistas, equally hampered by rough terrain, did not realize that Dodd was coming up behind them. They even rested in a village for a day. But on March 27, they overlooked a valley containing not only Guerrero but two smaller towns, Miñaca and San Ysidro. *Federales* were supposedly present in all three, with Guerrero having the largest garrison. Villa divided his forces accordingly, personally leading the Guerrero assault. Miñaca fell fast, but there were many more federals than anticipated in San Ysidro. They withstood the Villista assault, then began driving the attackers across the valley toward Guerrero. Villa had won an easy victory there. When he heard the sound of retreating Villistas and pursuing *federales* outside town, he ordered his men to rush to the aid of their comrades. As he frequently did, Villa led the charge himself. Often, it inspired his devoted followers. This time, it presented opportunity to some reluctant conscripts.

Modesto Nevares remembered later that he and a few other conscripts decided to kill Villa and "go over to the Carrancistas" during the ensuing confusion. They fired at Villa; though the conscripts were terrible shots, one of their bullets tore into the back of Villa's right leg, angling down from behind the knee and shattering the shinbone. Villa shrieked, then fell. At almost the same moment, the *federales* abandoned their counterattack and fled, leaving the Villistas in possession of Guerrero and the entire valley.

Villa's commanders had their leader carried back into town. Nevares and some of the other would-be defectors were among those ordered to assist. Villa's wound was grievous; bone splinters flecked the gaping exit wound on the front of his leg. Only rudimentary care was available in Guerrero; Villa would have to be taken somewhere away from any fighting so he could heal without risk of capture by his enemies. Villa remained coherent enough to participate as his subordinates came up with a plan. About one hundred Villistas would escort the leader 125 miles farther south, with the eventual goal of settling him in Parral, a town near the border between Chihuahua and Durango and where residents were especially pro-Villa. The Villista officers would hold briefly in Guerrero, then begin leading their troops south as well. To his dismay, Nevares was one of the *soldados* assigned to take Villa to Parral. Since most of the others in the party were Villista loyalists, he believed his chance to desert was gone. Just after midnight on

March 29, Villa was placed in a wagon that was led away in the dark by his escort. It was a slow-moving procession; Villa screamed every time the wagon wheels jounced over the slightest bump. Behind him in Guerrero, the Villista officers allowed their men some much needed rest. The *federales* were probably still running, and the gringos were on the other side of the Sierra Madre. For at least a little while, there would be no danger.

On March 28, a Mexican alerted Dodd that Villa was in Guerrero. The Army colonel had just received orders from Pershing to return with his worn-out troops to Namiquipa. Now he replied that instead of turning back, he would lead his 7th Cavalry troops, about 370 in all, the rest of the way through the mountains and attack Villa—the opportunity could not be lost. Dodd had no maps; he hired a native guide to lead his troops through the winding mountain passes between the Americans and the Villistas at Guerrero.

Had Dodd been taken by the most direct route, the 7th might have arrived and attacked just before Villa was taken south. But as Pershing later wrote, "[Dodd's] Mexican guide, no doubt purposely . . . led him over a circuitous route" that added several miles to the march and ended on the morning of March 29 with the expedition troops "on a high bluff to the east of town" requiring them to painstakingly work their way down into position to attack. By then the sun was up. Instead of surrounding Guerrero under cover of darkness, Dodd was forced to make a direct charge. The Villistas held for several hours, then fled, not in one large unit but three smaller groups, scattering out and defying the 7th Cavalry and their exhausted horses to catch them. Dodd soon called off the chase. Besides handing the Villistas a decisive defeat that cost the enemy thirty dead, the Americans freed several captive *federales* who had been scheduled for execution, which might placate the Mexican government. Dodd learned that Villa had been hurt in earlier fighting, badly wounded by the sound of it, and carried from the field. Dodd's own troops had marched 225 miles in only a week, and needed time to recuperate. But if Pershing rushed more troops south, Villa might be taken without much resistance.

Dodd sent a triumphant wire to Pershing: "With Villa probably permanently disabled . . . and the blow administered this morning, the Villista party would seem pretty well disintegrated." The U.S. president and Senate were convinced: Wilson nominated Dodd for promotion to brigadier general and senators immediately voted approval. But Pershing was doubtful. Though crippled, Villa remained at large. By breaking into smaller groups, the Villistas had multiplied the challenge of tracking them down. The Mexican government still insisted that the expedition immediately leave their country. Pershing composed and posted a memo to his troops: "All officers and enlisted men of the command are cautioned against a feeling of over confidence as to the final result to be achieved by this expedition."

Villa's entourage inched their way toward Parral, sometimes stopping in small villages to get water and supplies, but spending nights away from any habitations. In his coherent moments, Villa feared betrayal by villagers. Sometimes the ground being traveled was too rocky to leave Villa in the wagon—the pain would have been too much. In these places, a litter was fixed using blankets and poles. Men took turns as bearers. Alternating extremes of cold and heat, typical of Chihuahua in the spring, exacerbated the difficulty. Villa suffered terribly. Modesto Nevares was able to desert, but before he did, he observed that the flesh around Villa's leg wound had grown black. Villa, previously a teetotaler, gulped raw gin in hopes of dulling the pain. He often pleaded with his protectors to kill him—he couldn't stand the agony anymore. Some days the grim procession managed only a few miles. Informants apprised the group that the gringos were in full pursuit; it was never safe to stay in one place very long. It seemed possible, even likely, that Villa would die from infection to his leg. But the men caring for him were devoted, and kept bearing their leader south in the general direction of Parral.

The Punitive Expedition had its own difficulties moving farther south. They were after not only Villa but the smaller bands of Villistas heading in the same direction. The farther the Americans went, the harder it was to maintain their lines of supply. Even occasional use of Mexican trains would have solved the problem, but Carranza continued forbidding it. Trucks stuck in the sand, and when occasional rain blessedly provided some relief for the troops, the resulting mud literally glued the trucks in place. The wide-ranging cavalry patrols sent out by Pershing tried purchasing food and animal forage from villages, but were usually unsuccessful. The Army expected expedition officers to pay for supplies with certificates redeemable for cash at distant U.S. military bases and embassies rather than providing Mexican currency. Villagers demanded cash payment. Some of the better-heeled expedition officers used their own money to make the purchases, hoping for subsequent reimbursement from their government. Even so, rations and forage were limited; men and animals alike were hungry.

At night, rest was elusive. Even when the days were hot, temperatures dropped precipitously after dark. Soldiers dug shallow ditches, built fires in them, removed the coals, and, after wrapping up in their blankets, crawled in to sleep on the heated dirt. And, always, Mexican federal troops skulked nearby, often in view of the Americans, a few times firing in their direction. When American officers approached them to ask for news of Villa, their Mexican counterparts usually professed complete ignorance, suggesting sometimes that Villa was hiding in some completely different region, and at least once declaring that Villa had died from complications of his wound, so the Americans should go home.

Pershing did his best to rally his troops, moving from place to place in one of several staff cars. The others were used by his staff to convey the commander's orders. Lieutenant Patton especially delighted in roaring up and informing more senior officers of what they must do next. On the morning of March 31, Major Tompkins and his contingent of 13th Cavalry believed they were close to a Villista band of about two hundred that had been reported to the east. They were about to begin pursuit when Patton arrived and told them to look for the Villistas farther north—that was what Pershing wanted. With the expedition commander many miles away and with no means of contacting him directly, Tompkins argued with Patton—they had it on good authority that the Villistas were to the east. Patton insisted that Pershing's order must be followed, promising to take responsibility if things went wrong. They did. Only cattle were found in the north, and afterward, Tompkins recalled, Pershing was "provoked with me" for letting the bandits escape. But Patton, who was present, interrupted the commander's tirade and, as promised, "assumed full responsibility." Tompkins was impressed; perhaps there was more to the swaggering Patton than ambition and an ivory-handled gun.

Pershing suspected that most of the Villistas, as well as their wounded leader, were making their winding way south, taking advantage of the rough terrain to keep safe distance between themselves and the American patrols. It was obvious that Mexican federal troops were more concerned with thwarting the U.S. expedition than capturing Villa. A real concern was that Villa and his forces would slip into Durango. If the Americans followed, they would be more than five hundred miles deep into Mexico, stretching supply lines long past breaking point and allowing the Mexican government to claim that the so-called U.S. intervention was a full-fledged invasion.

Pershing had recently received additional troops, doubling his forces. That provided him sufficient personnel to launch a widespread pursuit south, several wings of cavalry sweeping down in roughly parallel routes, keeping in as close contact as possible with each other and, ideally, swinging in to surround their quarry just above the Chihuahua-Durango border. Villa himself might be among those captured. The expedition commander consulted with some of his officers, who reinforced his opinion. Tompkins told Pershing that "the history of Villa's bandit days shows that when hard-pressed he invariably holes up in the mountains in the vicinity of Parral. He ha[s] friends in that region." Tompkins pleaded for the supplies necessary to sustain his hundred-man troop of 13th Cavalry during a fast-paced rush 150 miles south to Parral. Pershing agreed, and assigned him the central route, with Colonel William Brown and the Buffalo Soldiers of 10th Cavalry on the right and Major Robert Howze and the 11th Cavalry on the left. The American forces departed on April 2.

A few loyal Villistas kept moving their wounded leader south. Villa barely clung to life. Their object was to get him somewhere he could get the weeks of rest and recuperation necessary for recovery. For a few days they sheltered in a cave northwest of Parral; Villa would later claim that, as he lay near its mouth, he saw Howze's cavalry sweeping past in their search for him. Then, on April 10, Villa was provided refuge on a small ranch outside the town of Santa Cruz thirty miles northwest of Parral. His host was a loyalist; most townspeople were unaware that Villa was nearby. Days later, Howze's troops scoured the area around Santa Cruz, but missed Villa again. Safe for the moment, Villa began a slow recovery.

>─┼─◀▷─○─◁▶─┼─◄

Tompkins, homed in on Parral, outpaced the other U.S. cavalry wings. On April 10 they skirmished with a few dozen Villistas in the town of Valle de Zaragoza, about twenty-five miles north of Parral. The Villistas ran. For a change, the townspeople proved helpful to the Americans, telling them that ninety Villistas had come through on the day before, and another hundred had been seen moving south. Tompkins was exhilarated; with luck, his forces would have the honor of delivering the final blow that annihilated the Villistas—it was a matter of moving quickly enough to get between them and the Durango state border.

At his camp that night, Tompkins was surprised when a Mexican rode in and identified himself as Captain Antonio Mesa of the federal garrison in Parral. Tompkins told Mesa that he and his men badly needed supplies; they hoped to provision themselves in Parral, then ride on in pursuit of the Villistas. Mesa assured the American major that this could be done; in fact, Mesa would send messages ahead to smooth the way. The captain spent the night in the U.S. camp. After joining his hosts for breakfast the next morning, Mesa said that he would ride ahead to Parral and ensure that all was ready when Tompkins and the cavalrymen of the 13th arrived.

On April 11, Tompkins's force covered thirty hard miles, rushing now, eager to refresh themselves in Parral, and soon afterward, with any luck, engage in a fight that would redound to their glory. They stopped for the night at a ranch in Santa Cruz, luxuriating in an unusually warm evening that didn't require digging sleeping holes and burning fires in them to heat the dirt. There was even an irrigation ditch where the thirsty cavalry mounts could drink their fill. The next morning Tompkins led his men along the final eighteen miles to Parral, confident of a friendly welcome there. The soldiers couldn't stop speculating, the major later recalled, about "the good time we should have" in a town of twenty thousand and the much anticipated availability of "long cool drinks."

Tompkins was puzzled when no federal officers rode out from Parral to greet the Americans—Captain Mesa had promised that this courtesy would be observed. Along with a few troops, Tompkins trotted up to a guard post and requested permission to enter town, as well as someone to escort him to the garrison commander. This was granted, but instead of welcoming Tompkins, General Ismael Lozano asked what the U.S. troops were doing in Parral; everyone knew Villa was fifty miles north in the village of Satevó. No message about the Americans' imminent arrival had been received from Captain Mesa, whose current whereabouts were unknown. Lozano speculated that he'd been captured by Villistas. In any event, the Americans should not have come to Parral, and must leave at once. Tompkins said they'd leave as soon as they'd purchased supplies; after that, would Lozano direct them to a place outside town where they could camp? Lozano summoned a man introduced as Mr. Scott, "an American merchant," though Tompkins was suspicious of his "strong Mexican accent." Scott promised he'd sell the Americans whatever they needed.

Meanwhile, the rest of the 13th Cavalry had arrived in town, waiting for their commander in the street below the room where Lozano and Tompkins conferred. "A great racket" outside drew Tompkins to the window; he saw that "a big crowd" had formed, chanting "Viva Villa" and "Viva Mexico . . . a small, compactly built man . . . seemed to be trying to stir the people to violence. He was well-dressed and looked like a German." Tompkins went down to the street and shouted "Viva Villa" himself, causing some of the mob to laugh. The merriment was momentary.

Lozano led the American troops north of town to what Tompkins described as "a gap between two hills [and] into a hollow behind." The mob followed, and suddenly shots were fired at the Americans. Some federal troops ascended another nearby hill; they shot at the U.S. troops, too. Tompkins saw about a hundred more Mexicans moving to his right, and ordered his men to ride for the road between Parral and Santa Cruz. The mob, now a mix of civilians and *federales*, charged after them. A rear guard of American soldiers kept pursuers at bay, shooting to kill—Tompkins afterward claimed twenty-five fatalities among the Mexicans.

It took more than three hours for the Americans to fight their way back to the same Santa Cruz ranch where they'd spent the previous night. Two U.S. cavalrymen were killed, another died soon afterward, one was missing, and six were wounded, including Tompkins, who was hit in the left shoulder but continued in command. The fight slowed to a stalemate. The Americans held their ground; the Mexicans closed within a half mile and waited. When U.S. sharpshooters still found their targets, the mob backed another half mile away.

A federal waving a white flag of truce brought Tompkins a note from Lozano. The Mexican general said he was able to restrain his troops for "a little bit," but "supplicate[d]" Tompkins to leave the area at once; otherwise "I shall be obliged to charge [with] the greatest part of my forces." If Tompkins promised to leave, Lozano would withdraw his troops. Tompkins wrote back that he was prepared to go if Lozano could assure him the Americans would not be "molested." Otherwise, he'd hold his ground until reinforcements arrived. There was no immediate response from the Mexican general.

Tompkins sent riders to find the other cavalry wings he knew were in the area. After riding about eight miles, three made contact with the 10th Cavalry. By early evening the Buffalo Soldiers thundered into Santa Cruz; the Mexican forces lingered, only dispersing two days later when Howze and the 11th Cavalry arrived.

⊱──◦──⊰

On April 13, the Mexican government dispatched two vehement telegrams to the U.S. State Department, both claiming that Major Tompkins precipitated a violent confrontation at Parral. Besides this unforgivable affront, Mexican troops should be "entirely in control" of Villa's pursuit and inevitable capture. Accordingly, it was time for "the withdrawal of [U.S.] forces from our country." Secretary of State Lansing, scrambling to learn what happened, replied that the Punitive Expedition's purpose—an "endeavor to take the bandit Villa"—remained. Lansing suggested that the best way for this to be accomplished, and the American troops subsequently ordered home, would be "for commanders in the field for both countries to cooperate." If the American forces left now, it could only encourage other revolts against the Mexican government—surely President Carranza didn't want that.

While Lansing counseled cooperation, Pershing urged the opposite. It had been bad enough that the Mexican government had hampered his mission by refusing the use of trains and forbidding entry into towns. *Federales* and civilians had lied incessantly about Villa's whereabouts. Now American soldiers scrupulously adhering to ridiculous stipulations had still been attacked by troops of the Mexican government. On April 18 Pershing wired Funston that "in order to prosecute our mission with any promise of success it is therefore absolutely necessary for us to assume complete possession for the time being of the country through which we must operate. . . . Therefore [I] recommend immediate capture by this command of [the] city and state of Chihuahua [and] also the seizure of all railroads therein, as preliminary to further military operations."

Funston wired back from the Army Southern Department headquarters in Texas that "war with [Mexico] is almost inevitable." He predicted that if the expedition stayed in southern Chihuahua, it would soon be attacked "by a large force . . . from Central Mexico, as well as Sonora troops." Pershing's supply line would prove too long to maintain, and because the expedition was five hundred miles deep in Mexico, when the Mexican attack came "we cannot support you."

Then came a thunderbolt: Funston ordered Pershing to fall back "with a view to concentration of [your] entire force at Colonia Dublan. Such action imperative." Funston acknowledged that, following the events at Parral, Pershing and his forces wanted to defend American honor by fighting, but "no question of prestige can be entertained as military considerations must govern. Acknowledge and report daily."

To the delight of the Villistas lingering around the Chihuahua-Sonora border, their gringo pursuers turned back north. It appeared to be abject retreat. Some Villista officers printed and distributed posters urging fellow citizens to join their cause at this auspicious moment: "Now is the opportune time for every Mexican to answer the call to arms in order to combat these intruders."

On March 12, three days after the Columbus raid, U.S. border agent George Carothers had warned Secretary Lansing that any U.S. pursuit of Villa lasting "over a month" would result in all of Mexico uniting against America. The month was up, and Carothers had apparently been right.

CHAPTER SIXTEEN

"Responsibility for the Consequences"

Funston's unwelcome order to Pershing originated in the White House. After Parral, Woodrow Wilson's anger with Carranza matched Pershing's fury. If the American president chose to strike back, he had all the political support necessary. Most of Congress advocated military retaliation for Parral even if war with Mexico resulted. Secretary of War Baker, previously an advocate for restraint, now urged Wilson to "put an end to the pusillanimous rule of Carranza and clean up Mexico."

Yet the president hesitated. U-boats continued torpedoing unarmed civilian vessels in the Atlantic. Wilson sharply reminded Germany's leaders that these acts were unacceptable, continuing to leave unsaid but unmistakably implied that unless the Germans desisted, America was ready to join the war against them. That threat would be greatly reduced if much of America's army was fighting Carranza. If Congress and some of Wilson's closest advisors didn't realize this, Germany did. Following Parral, Count Johann von Bernstorff, Germany's ambassador to the U.S., gleefully wired his government that "it seems increasingly probable that the punitive expedition against Villa will lead to a full-dress intervention. . . . So long as Mexico holds the stage here, we are, I believe, safe from an act of aggression on the part of the American government."

Immediately after Parral, Wilson instructed Army chief of staff Scott and Funston to bring him options. On April 22, they presented three: the expedition could advance in force, taking over Mexico's railroads to expedite delivery of reinforcements and supplies; Pershing and his troops could withdraw to northern Chihuahua and remain there as incentive for Carranza to capture Villa; the expedition could be entirely withdrawn back across the border. Wilson chose the second option. There was considerable humiliation in pulling the U.S. forces back at all, but at least some movement toward the border might mollify Carranza, while still allowing Wilson to insist that the expedition was staying in Mexico until its mission was accomplished. That the purpose of this mission remained nebulous—Pershing still was charged with eliminating the Villistas as a viable threat, while most of the American public expected Villa to be captured and held to account for the Columbus raid—added an additional element of discomfort. But as Funston now instructed Pershing, "military considerations must govern," and Wilson's main concern was thwarting Germany.

While Wilson, Scott, and Funston focused on military options, Secretary of State Lansing attempted diplomacy, sending a private message to Carranza suggesting a meeting between Scott, Funston, and General Obregón, who American leaders believed was the voice of reason within the Carranza administration. Perhaps they could agree on some means of avoiding more "misunderstandings" like Parral. Carranza initially balked, but on April 28 Obregón and the two American generals met in Juárez; it was required by Carranza that the location be below the border, allowing him to claim that the gringos came as supplicants. After the first meeting, Funston informed Lansing that it was a waste of time. Obregón was disappointing; all he did was insist that Villa was dead, so the Punitive Expedition had no reason to remain in Mexico. This completely contradicted Lansing's instructions to Scott and Funston, which were to secure an agreement that Mexico and the U.S. would be equal partners in pursuing Villa, or, even better, that Pershing's forces would furnish support to an all-out Mexican effort to capture him.

Obregón was accompanied by General Jacinto Treviño, and for the next few days the two Mexicans refused to budge: before any other issues were addressed, the U.S. must set a specific date when the expedition would leave their country. Scott and Funston were further concerned after learning that a substantial Mexican federal force was beginning to move slowly north toward the border. Apparently, Carranza was positioning his military eventually to surround Pershing's troops. It seemed to Scott that Obregón was deliberately stalling to give the *federales* time to advance.

Scott wired Washington that the expedition must not be withdrawn. That would represent "a complete victory for Mexicans over the United States in the eyes of the Mexican people [who are] already arrogant, and encourage further aggression." Scott wrote in his memoirs that he privately advised President Wilson this Mexican aggression might very well include an attempted invasion of the United States: "The people of Mexico are ignorant and untraveled; they see a thin line . . . and believe they can break through it, as they easily can, but they have no idea of what will happen afterward." If Wilson ordered the expedition completely withdrawn, Scott predicted, "You are tempting them, through their ignorance." Wilson took Scott's advice to heart, instructing him to tell Obregón that the expedition would not be withdrawn until the U.S. was convinced there was no more danger to its citizens along the border. Until then, Pershing's troops would fall back, but not out of Mexico—and, if attacked, they would defend themselves.

There was another possible approach—Wilson could have attempted personal negotiations with Carranza, an offer to meet face-to-face, two presidents pragmatically bypassing convoluted bureaucratic maneuvering to prevent further escalation of an already volatile situation. Though Carranza would almost certainly have refused an invitation to the White House—his mistrust of Americans would never have permitted placing himself in their hands, or appearing in any way to be a supplicant—he might have been receptive to an unexpected suggestion from Wilson that the American president would be pleased to visit Mexico City, tacit acknowledgment of Carranza's stature as his country's leader, and a gesture of respect toward all Mexicans. Pride alone would have required Carranza to act as a perfect host; the only previous meeting between the two countries' leaders occurred when Taft and Díaz briefly met at the border in October 1909. The gesture by Wilson might have made a difference—it would at least have demonstrated America's commitment to a peaceful, reasoned solution with Mexico.

Yet there's no record that Wilson ever considered a Carranza summit in Mexico. It wasn't because the American president demanded that foreign leaders come to him—following World War I, Wilson spent most of December 1918 to July 1919 in France, working with presidents and prime ministers on details of the Treaty of Versailles and the proposed League of Nations. That he made no similar journey two and a half years earlier to meet with the leader of America's geographic next-door neighbor is evidence that Wilson didn't consider Carranza worthy enough. (In April 1943, Franklin Roosevelt became the second American president to enter Mexico during a brief visit to Monterrey. Four years later, Harry Truman made the first formal state visit by an American president to Mexico City.)

On May 2, it appeared that the stalemate was broken. Scott informed Washington that he and Obregón had hammered out an agreement. Carranza would commit to aggressively pursuing Villa and his forces. In return, the Punitive Expedition would be gradually withdrawn from Mexico, with the first withdrawals taking place immediately. The presidents of both countries would save face. Wilson agreed, but there was no immediate response from Carranza. Meanwhile, events swept their nations even closer to war.

After receiving a direct order from his superiors to move his forces back north to Colonia Dublán, Pershing obeyed. But he argued for and was granted a concession—the withdrawal would be moderately paced rather than rushed. This allowed the expedition to watch for Villistas even as it retreated, and, should any be encountered, there were no orders forbidding the Americans from attacking them. On May 4, passing close to Cusihuiriachi in central Chihuahua, the U.S. troops were warned by representatives from the American silver mines nearby that an estimated 120 Villistas were occupying the town. Pershing sent Colonel Howze and the 11th Cavalry, and the U.S. forces routed the raiders. Sixty-one Villistas died; it was a major victory, one that greatly improved expedition morale. It also reminded Mexico's people that, despite their government promising the Americans were on their way out, the gringos remained, and were killing Mexicans.

On May 5, almost two months after Villa's raid on Columbus, America received a jarring reminder that settlements on the U.S. side of the border remained in danger. A band of about sixty raiders crossed the Rio Grande in the rugged Big Bend region of southwest Texas and attacked two small communities there, a wax factory and some housing in Glenn Springs and a mining company/trading post in Boquillas. Three American soldiers died in Glenn Springs as well as a civilian child; a Boquillas merchant and his clerk were kidnapped by the raiders as they crossed back into Mexico, presumably to be ransomed later.

The Punitive Expedition was hundreds of miles away to the west, too far to ride after the perpetrators, who included Villistas, a few federal troops, and some nonaffiliated bandits acting in disturbing alliance. Big Bend was part of Funston's Southern Department territory; the general cobbled together portions of the 8th and 14th Cavalry, units that hadn't been previously assigned to Pershing's expedition, about 375 men in all. Some of the commanders and soldiers rode in cars, which raced ahead of mounted cavalry and cut down on the raiders' lead. This second Punitive Expedition chased their quarry for three weeks, managing to kill a few without U.S. loss of life. Both hostages were recovered unharmed; their captors released them when pursuit closed in. Funston ordered the American forces to withdraw across the Rio Grande as soon as its commanders considered their assignment "successfully completed."

With the hostages safe and the raiders scattered, the U.S. troops returned to Texas, but not before Carranza protested this latest invasion of his country. The Mexican president informed the U.S. that now no agreement between their governments would be possible, or even considered, until an "early" date was established for Pershing's expedition to be entirely withdrawn. Wilson declined, and further infuriated Carranza by calling the National Guard in Arizona, New Mexico, and Texas to active duty on the border. Additionally, Wilson reimposed the U.S. embargo on arms sales to Mexico. If Carranza did intend at some point for his troops to attack Pershing, they'd have to do it without America supplying the guns and ammunition.

It seemed to Carranza that America had no intention of recalling Pershing's troops anytime soon, if at all. The longer they remained, the greater the risk to Carranza that his people would rise up against him, then turn to Villa to expel the hated *yanquis*. Official demands that the expedition withdraw had no effect on the Americans. Additional pressure might expedite the gringos' departure. The U.S. claimed that the Punitive Expedition remained in northern Mexico to protect American citizens along the border. Very well; they would be overwhelmed with opportunities from a resurrected *Plan de San Diego*.

The original *Plan* was probably not Carranza's, but the Mexican president now used it to achieve his own political ends. Carranza's promise to prevent *Plan* raids into the U.S. had swayed Wilson's decision to grant official recognition to his administration in October 1915. That promise was kept—Carranza had used his federal troops stationed on the border to choke off the raids, as he could have done at any time. If the raids started again, with no apparent connection to the Mexican government, America might look to Carranza for the same critical assistance he'd provided earlier. In return for his cooperation, Carranza's new price would be the immediate withdrawal of the Punitive Expedition from Mexico.

This time there was no organic *Plan de San Diego* movement among Tejanos for Carranza to exploit—he had to quietly assemble some of his own supporters and join them with remaining *Plan de San Diego* militants. Colonel Esteban E. Fierros, a loyal Carrancista, was promoted to brigadier general and placed in command of a 450-man hybrid force of *federales* and *Plan* raid veterans based in Monterrey, a city in northeastern Mexico about 150 miles south of the border and 435 miles east of the Punitive Expedition in Chihuahua—beyond reach of Pershing's cavalry when the new wave of border depredations began. Luis de la Rosa, one of the original *Plan's* leaders, served as a subordinate officer to Fierros. All that remained was to surreptitiously arm and supply the "Fierros Brigade," carefully select its targets, and order raids to begin in the same region terrorized by previous *Plan de San Diego* attacks. Ideally, Texas border communities from Laredo to Brownsville would be caught completely off guard.

But the Americans were alert. Faced with the growing possibility of war with Mexico, the Bureau of Investigation placed more than forty additional agents and informers along the border. Governor James Ferguson increased the Texas Rangers force to fifty. Within a week of the Glenn Springs and Boquillas raids, the ranks of civilian militias in Texas swelled—any Mexican was considered a potential threat. On May 13 the newspaper in Marathon, located on the northern tip of Texas's Big Bend, boasted that its self-appointed militiamen "laugh and joke in the presence of death, and there is no such thing as murder. Every man would think he was honored to be [ordered] to fire the fatal shot that would send some raider to his death . . . heaven help the Mexican that can't show a clean record." National Guardsmen from Arizona, New Mexico, and Texas took up their new border posts, and General Scott argued that these five thousand troops were appallingly insufficient. He urged President Wilson to call up every state's National Guard, some 150,000 men in all; Wilson was considering it.

By the time the Fierros Brigade was in place in Monterrey, Bureau of Investigation agents and other informers had alerted Washington that some revival of the *Plan de San Diego* was apparently in progress. There was concern that Germany might be funding the operation, and certainty that Carranza must in some way be involved. But matters between Mexico and the U.S. were already so volatile that it seemed sensible to remain watchful rather than confrontational as long as possible. It had only been a month since the April 12 debacle at Parral. The second Punitive Expedition remained in Mexico, chasing the raiders of Glenn Springs and Boquillas. Even a few weeks without further incidents or accusations might allow tempers on both sides to cool. But on May 14, an impetuous young officer in the first Punitive Expedition caused additional uproar.

>-◆>-O-<◆-I-<

Pershing led the expedition north as ordered, pausing for a while near Namiquipa, eighty miles below Colonia Dublán. Since he could no longer pursue Villa to the south, he divided the north-central region of Chihuahua into five sectors, and assigned specific cavalry units to scour each sector for Villistas. Several bands, led by prominent Villa officers including Julio Cárdenas and Candelario Cervantes, were known to be in the area. Acquiring supplies in villages and from farms and ranches remained a problem for the American forces. They were still not supplied with Mexican currency, and the native population disdained redeemable U.S. Army chits. Even Mexicans who had previously been helpful now kept their distance. Pershing believed that they "were much aroused in the belief that war was inevitable." Acquiring sufficient food for 10,000 troops and 4,500 animals was a daily challenge.

On May 14, 2nd Lieutenant Patton was assigned to take ten soldiers and two civilian guides on an expedition to locate and purchase corn somewhere in the vicinity of the town of Rubio and the nearby San Miguelito Ranch, reportedly a favorite Villista stopping place. Expedition patrols had searched for Villistas there before, but never had any luck. Patton and his party squeezed into three Dodge touring cars. They drove into Rubio, where they were able to buy some corn. On a hunch, Patton ordered the cars to San Miguelito Ranch. According to the Punitive Expedition Report, when the Americans reached the main ranch house "several Villistas ran out, firing upon the detachment as they went. Lt. Patton and one of our men opened fire in return, killing three of the Villistas, one of whom proved to be Col. [Julio] Cardenas."

Patton's recollection was more colorful. He wrote that during a brisk exchange of gunfire he narrowly missed being hit, gunned down two Villistas, then climbed the ranch house roof for a better look. Part of the roof collapsed under his weight, leaving Patton dangling by his armpits. He hauled himself up and joined in firing at a man fleeing on foot; a shot from one of Patton's guides finished off this third Villista. Afterward no other men were found on the property. Cárdenas's mother, wife, and infant daughter were in the ranch house.

Patton thought Cárdenas was among the three dead. The two guides weren't certain, so Patton decided to take the bodies into the expedition camp and seek confirmation there. The three automobiles were already crammed with Patton, ten soldiers, two guides, and heavy bags of corn, so Patton ordered the Villistas lashed to the cars' roofs and hoods like dead deer. The return route to the expedition camp deliberately went through Rubio, where "inhabitants were much excited by the sight of the dead." One of the bodies was identified as Cárdenas. Pershing was impressed and referred to Patton as "my bandit";

he allowed the young lieutenant to keep Cárdenas's sword and fancy saddle as souvenirs. Patton proudly carved two notches in the handle of his sidearm, and showed them off to reporters. A story in the *New York Times* described a "touch of glory in the thin, reedy-voiced lieutenant." On May 23, Patton was promoted from 2nd to 1st lieutenant, and further promotion to captain soon followed. The shootout at San Miguelito Ranch is considered the first fully motorized combat action by the U.S. military.

﹥─﹢﹡﹢─O─﹢◦﹢─﹤

On May 22, the Mexican government sent a formal, lengthy letter to Lansing. Besides reiterating previous grievances, the message condemned the current border incursion by the second Punitive Expedition, and argued that, after their meeting with Obregón in Juárez, Scott and Funston agreed on behalf of the American government to immediately withdraw Pershing's troops—an alleged promise that was not kept. Taken together, these insults to Mexico caused "new complications for the Mexican government, renders more distant the possibility of a satisfactory solution, and creates a more complicated situation between [our] two countries." The two expeditions must be immediately withdrawn, accompanied by an American promise—kept this time—to never commit "future incursions." America must comply at once: "The Mexican government does not wish war with the United States, and if this should occur it will be as a consequence of the deliberate cause of the United States." The Carranza and Wilson governments had exchanged so many accusations, demands, and ultimatums that it was no longer possible for leaders on either side to discern posturing from genuine threat. But the tone of Mexico's May 22 message was so offensive to Lansing that the secretary deliberately did not reply for several weeks, leaving the governments of both countries uncertain if the other might launch attacks at any time.

Both the U.S. and Mexico had in place basic war plans against the other. America intended charging into northern Mexico and seizing Torreón, a key rail hub. That would leave Carranza unable to move troops expeditiously, while American forces could strike in virtually any direction. Mexico's plan was for its federal army to cross the Texas border and take Laredo; actions after that would be determined by events. At least in numbers, the armies matched up evenly. The Mexicans could field anywhere from 60,000 to 100,000 officers and troops; estimates varied in Mexico City because the federal army's record-keeping was so inadequate. America's Regular Army totaled 107,642 officers and enlisted men, but only about 70,000 were now stationed in the U.S. The rest served in the Philippines, Hawaii, the Panama Canal Zone, and other remote locales. Neither country's forces were sufficiently trained. Raw recruits vastly outnumbered battle-tested veterans. That made it hard for either side to project how effectively its troops would fight.

Still, America held a basic, significant advantage. Up until Wilson's latest embargo, Mexico depended on the U.S. to sell weapons and ammunition to its federal army. Now, beyond its limited stores of guns and bullets, it must rely on overseas suppliers—in the event of war with the U.S., American ships would surely blockade Mexican harbors. Mexico simply could not sustain long-term hostilities with America. Carranza understood this. If war with the U.S. did come, he wanted his army to initially fight so hard and well that the Americans would agree to negotiate peace terms before the Mexican army's limited offensive resources were exhausted. Though Mexico would not gain a foot of land, Carranza might at least receive a formal, public guarantee against future *yanqui* military incursions—enough, perhaps, to secure his presidency by finally earning the respect of the Mexican people.

Pershing could not understand why his superiors were so concerned about war with Mexico and the safety of his troops while they remained below the border. His firsthand impression of the Mexican military left him with little respect for its soldiers or its leaders. In his memoir Pershing recalled assuring the War Department that "any considerable body of Mexican troops" would be "little better than a rabble without training or discipline and not seriously to be feared." While Washington fretted, Pershing's troops continued finding and eliminating Villistas. On May 25 a small force of American soldiers was sent out from camp near Namiquipa to scout and map local terrain. They were attacked by Villistas but effectively drove them back, killing two. One of the Villista dead was Candelario Cervantes—along with Julio Cárdenas, the expedition had eliminated two of Villa's most trusted officers in a span of eleven days.

But May ended on an unsettling note for the Punitive Expedition. Mexican troops began massing around them on three sides, leaving only the north open. American civilians remaining in Chihuahua fled across the border. One told a reporter from the *San Antonio Express* that "I never dreamed before that there was all that artillery in Mexico. But I saw enough of it with my own eyes to be convinced." Mexican civilians panicked, too; two thousand destitute refugees camped outside Juárez, hoping officials on the U.S. side of the river would allow them to cross the International Bridge before fighting engulfed the region. An American consul in Mexico reported a rumor that Germany offered Carranza the services of thirty-two military advisors in return for the right to build a submarine base near Veracruz. A Bureau of Investigation agent contacted Washington with urgent news: Carranza was offering amnesty to all political prisoners and former soldiers of the Díaz regime who volunteered to participate in an invasion of America. Secretary of War Baker responded by moving almost every U.S. soldier not already in the vicinity down to the U.S. side of the border.

June was worse, beginning with a series of violent anti-American demonstrations in Chihuahua and Durango; by mid-month there were additional riots in Sonora. Officials in Washington suspected that German influence and financing were involved. Lansing and Baker privately advised Wilson to withdraw the Punitive Expedition; Germany wanted to provide the final impetus that provoked war between America and Mexico. Extracting the expedition would thwart that. Wilson refused; like Carranza, he realized that his presidency was at stake. Nineteen sixteen was an election year. If Wilson appeared to back down from Mexico in June, voters would remember in November. Wilson believed that only he could keep America out of a larger overseas war. Whatever happened in Mexico was secondary.

On June 10, Bureau of Investigation agents learned of Mexico's war plan to capture Laredo. Lansing still had not made an official reply to Carranza's insulting message of May 22, but now he sent a private message to the Mexican president: America was ready to fight. Carranza pulled back troops from Nuevo Laredo just across the Rio Grande, but this was less capitulation than calculation. If necessary, the full Mexican war plan could be implemented later; instead, Carranza unleashed his small, secret force in Monterrey.

On the night of June 10, eighty horses were stolen from a ranch forty-five miles north of Laredo. In itself, this was relatively insignificant, but the next night a U.S. Army patrol encountered armed Mexicans burning a railroad bridge in the same vicinity. A running fight ensued; three raiders were killed and six captured before the rest escaped across the river. One of the dead was in full Mexican army uniform. It was no disguise; he was later positively identified as a federal lieutenant colonel. Four nights later, one hundred Mexican raiders attacked San Ygnacio, a small town south of Laredo. A squadron of American troops was unexpectedly bivouacked there. A pitched battle left eight raiders and three U.S. soldiers dead. Panic began spreading among South Texas border towns—it was the *Plan de San Diego* all over again. The Punitive Expedition and increased American military presence on the border were supposed to prevent things like this. Apprehension grew as the raids continued, always around and between Laredo and Brownsville, prime attack locations during the 1915 raids.

Pershing, more than four hundred miles away to the west, was in no position to bring his forces and help. General Jacinto B. Treviño, commander of Carranza's forces in the Chihuahua City region, had the Punitive Expedition hemmed in on three sides, with more Mexican troops massing at key border towns like Juárez. On June 16, Treviño wired a stark warning to the American commander: "I have orders from my government to prevent, by the use of arms, new invasions of my country by American troops, and also to prevent the American forces that are now in this state from moving to the south, east or west of the places they now occupy. I communicate this to you for your knowledge for the reason that your forces will be attacked by the Mexican forces if these indications are not heeded."

Pershing responded that the American government placed no restrictions on the expedition's movements. "I shall therefore use my own judgment as to when and in what direction I shall move my forces in pursuit of bandits or in seeking information regarding bandits. If, under these circumstances, the Mexican forces attack any of my columns, the responsibility for the consequences will lie with the Mexican government." Still, Pershing moved the expedition to Casas Grandes, adjacent to Colonia Dublán and eighty miles closer to the border if he required additional reinforcements. Treviño and his troops followed.

On June 17, after more raids around Brownsville, Brigadier General James Parker sent troops after the fleeing Mexicans with instructions to follow them wherever they went. This immediately required crossing the Rio Grande into Mexico; Parker's orders were clear, and Lieutenant A. D. Newman and fifty cavalrymen swam their horses over to the south bank. More cavalry and a machine gun squad crossed slightly farther downriver, and the American forces trailed the raiders toward Matamoros. General Alfredo Ricaut, the Mexican commander there, wired Parker that his *federales* were prepared to drive the Americans away unless the U.S. troops immediately returned to Texas. They didn't, and instead of fighting the Mexican forces abandoned the town. Satisfied, the Americans began withdrawing toward the Rio Grande. As they did, there was gunfire from lingering Mexican troops. The U.S. troops fired back, killing two of the snipers and scattering the rest before returning to Brownsville. Ricaut wired Mexico City that "my troops advanced under orders to fight the invaders and had a sharp encounter with them, making them recross to American territory."

On June 18, Wilson announced that he was calling the entire National Guard to the border, more than 100,000 men in all. Two days later, Secretary Lansing finally sent an official reply to Carranza's message of May 22. In terms as offensively formal as those used by the Mexican president, the U.S. secretary of state declared that the Punitive Expedition's presence in Mexico was necessary as "the only check on further bandit outrages and the only efficient means of protecting American lives and homes—safeguards which [President] Carranza, though internationally obligated to supply, is manifestly unable or unwilling to give." Accordingly, Carranza's demand to withdraw the expedition "cannot now be entertained."

Carranza had given an ultimatum, and America defied it. It seemed only a matter of time before some new incident precipitated war. On June 21, the day after Lansing's reply to Carranza, it happened.

CHAPTER SEVENTEEN

Carrizal

Several events on June 18, 1916, seemed to confirm that America and Mexico were about to declare war. The U.S. positioned warships to line both Mexican coasts and blockade key ports the moment hostilities began. General Obregón made a public plea for able-bodied men to enlist in Mexico's federal army and help repel foreign invaders. The governor of the Mexican west coast state of Sinaloa announced that war against the U.S. was imminent, and anti-American riots ensued. In northern Chihuahua, General Pershing decided to probe the ranks of Mexican federal troops hemming in the Punitive Expedition on the east.

Pershing had brooded for two days about the message from Treviño warning him that his forces would be attacked if they ventured in any direction other than north to the border. The expedition commander was confident that his troops would prevail, but his combat experience against Indians on the American frontier and rebels in the Philippines taught him that calculating the strength of the enemy was essential. Mexican forces were arrayed to the expedition's west, south, and east; Pershing, expecting at any moment to either be attacked or else receive orders to attack, wanted to know how many. Though he was disdainful of the Mexican commanders, he assumed even they would know enough to control the railroad lines that lay to the east and west, which would provide them easy access to supplies and reinforcements. When war commenced, Pershing's first move would probably be to capture railroad hubs and gain the rail access advantage for his own forces. He was troubled by rumors that as many as ten thousand Mexican federal troops were positioned seventy-five miles to the east at Villa Ahumada, a key hub on the rail line linking Juárez to the Chihuahua capital. Pershing needed an accurate count of the enemy there to determine his own best strategy. Since he no longer trusted native informers, Pershing's only option was to send a scouting party of American troops. The risk was enormous. Though all Pershing sought for the moment was information, the Mexicans might assume the scouts were coming east to fight, and react accordingly.

Even with that potential consequence, Pershing decided to go ahead. He summoned Captain Charles T. Boyd, commander of Company C, 10th Cavalry. The two men had known each other ever since Pershing himself served as an officer in the 10th. Pershing, who considered Boyd to be a levelheaded veteran, ordered him to take the forty-one Buffalo Soldiers comprising Company C, along with Boyd's subordinate, Lieutenant Henry Adair, east to "reconnoiter in the direction of Ahumada." Pershing explained to Boyd that his scouting party was "not expected to fight . . . but if wantonly attacked, use your judgment as to what you should do." Later, in a memorandum to Washington, Pershing insisted he also told Boyd "that the Mexican situation was very tense, and that a clash with Mexican troops would probably bring on war and for this reason was to be avoided. . . . I felt confident that Captain Boyd fully understood the importance and delicacy of his mission."

That confidence was misplaced. After leaving Pershing, Boyd called Company C's noncommissioned officers together, explained the assignment, and reminded them, "It is reported that the Mexicans say that they will attack us if we move in any direction except to the north. We are going to test that." After gathering gear, Company C set out east, led by Lemuel Spillsbury, a Mormon from Colonia

Dublán who volunteered as a guide. Boyd was unaware that after his meeting with Pershing, the expedition commander, for reasons never explained, ordered Captain Louis S. Morey and Company K of the 10th to go on the same mission. Company K was camped a few miles above Pershing's headquarters at Casas Grandes; they left a few hours later than Company C and took a slightly different route. Morey, who did not know about Boyd's similar assignment, was the only officer in his company, which otherwise comprised thirty-nine enlisted men. Both Buffalo Soldier companies rode toward the same destination: Rancho Santo Domingo, about ten miles west of the town of Carrizal, which in turn was a few miles west of Villa Ahumada. Both Boyd and Morey hoped that the Americans who operated the ranch might be able to provide eyewitness estimates of the number of Mexican troops in the area.

When Morey and Company K arrived at Rancho Santo Domingo early on the evening of June 20, they were surprised to find Boyd and Company C already there. The two officers conferred and decided they would combine their forces; since Boyd had seniority over Morey, he would be in command. Ranch foreman W. P. McCabe agreed to let the U.S. troops spend the night on his property. McCabe said that a troop of a few hundred Mexican cavalrymen had occupied the ranch for a time, but recently moved to Carrizal, nine miles east and roughly midway between the ranch and Villa Ahumada. Reports of ten thousand Mexican troops in Villa Ahumada were highly exaggerated, McCabe added. Perhaps three hundred were there. This was precisely the information Pershing wanted; the Buffalo Soldiers could have returned to the expedition camp at Dublán with their mission accomplished. But Boyd wanted to see for himself; in the morning, Companies C and K would ride through Carrizal and on to Villa Ahumada. If the Mexican soldiers there wanted to fight, Boyd predicted, the Americans would "clean them up."

McCabe, Morey, and civilian guide Spillsbury all argued against it. If the Mexicans in Carrizal opened fire while the Americans rode through town, the narrow streets would prove deadly. McCabe volunteered to show the cavalrymen two other roads from the ranch to Villa Ahumada that bypassed Carrizal completely. Boyd insisted on riding through town. The Americans would be watching for any sneak attacks: "We are not going to have a repetition of the Parral incident." Morey wasn't convinced, but Boyd was senior officer and his decision had to be obeyed. To save time the next day, Boyd wrote notes that he would send to the Mexican commanders from the outskirts of Carrizal and Villa Ahumada, assuring them that the Americans were on a peaceful mission and asking permission to pass through the towns. Morey doubted that the Mexicans would be persuaded. Before the Americans rode out at 4 a.m. on the 21st, he left his wallet and pocket watch with McCabe, along with instructions about what to do with them if he never came back.

The three American officers, civilian guide, and eighty enlisted men approached Carrizal at 6:30 a.m. They paused at an irrigation ditch about six hundred yards away to water their horses. The ground was flat until a low ridge jutted up along the west side of town. The ridge was lined with cottonwood trees, and just behind the trees was another deep irrigation ditch. The Mexican troops in Carrizal had seen the gringos coming; they began positioning themselves along the ridge, using the cottonwoods for cover. More *federales* set up along the lip of the irrigation ditch.

Boyd sent a messenger ahead with one of the notes he'd written the night before, requesting permission to pass through town. A few minutes later a Mexican lieutenant colonel and some guards trotted out, waving a white flag. When the officer asked Boyd why the Americans had come, he replied that they were pursuing a deserter who was supposedly in the area. The Mexican wasn't fooled. He said that any *yanqui* deserter would undoubtedly run north to El Paso, not farther east; meanwhile, he had orders "to stop your advance."

At that moment another federal rode up from Carrizal with the message that General Félix Gómez, the commander there, invited Boyd to ride in with his troops; they'd discuss the situation. Boyd declined—if the general wanted to talk, let him come out to the Americans. Boyd expected Gómez to refuse, but within minutes the Mexican general arrived. After being told that the U.S. troops were pursuing a deserter, Gómez said he was under orders from General Treviño not to let American forces go "east, west or south." Boyd replied that he had his own orders to go through Carrizal. If they did, Gómez said, his troops would have to fire on them. Perhaps a fight could be avoided; would Captain Boyd wait while Gómez contacted Treviño to see if an exception might be made? Boyd, who was using Spillsbury as an interpreter, ordered the Mormon civilian to reply that "we're going through." Gómez snapped that the yanquis would have to "walk over the dead bodies of Mexican soldiers," and rode back to town. Within minutes, the Americans could see more Mexican troops lining up along the ridge. Two machine guns were also placed there.

Boyd may have thought Gómez was bluffing. It's more likely that the captain believed no Mexican troops could outfight Americans, even if the U.S. forces were outnumbered by at least three or four to one and had to charge over hundreds of yards of open space against defenders holding high ground. The American retreat at Parral was much on Boyd's mind; he'd mentioned it to McCabe at Rancho Santo Domingo the night before. Here was the chance to avenge that insult, though it seemed likelier that once the Mexicans saw the Americans advancing, they'd break and run.

Boyd ordered Morey to take Company K to the right side of the road while he led Company C on the left. As the Americans began to advance, all of them on horseback, some Mexican troops fanned down from the ridge to flank them. Boyd kept his troops moving forward for about three hundred yards, constantly reminding them not to fire the first shots. Then he ordered everyone to dismount. They'd go the rest of the way on foot. Surely, any moment, the Mexicans would pull back.

They didn't. When the Americans were two hundred yards from town, the Mexicans opened fire. The U.S. troops had no cover. Boyd drove Company C straight into the mouths of the machine guns; survivors later recalled their captain was urging them on when he was killed by a bullet through the eye. On the right side of the road, Morey and Company K were pinned down in a crossfire. They found a slight depression in the ground and tried unsuccessfully to make a stand there. Morey was badly wounded but remained conscious. The Buffalo Soldiers fought valiantly; a few even reached the cottonwoods on the ridge before being cut down. Others, realizing the fight was lost, turned and ran back toward Rancho Santo Domingo, taking with them whatever wounded comrades they could. Though they could have surrounded and shot down the fleeing gringos, the Mexican forces chose not to pursue. Instead, they rounded up twenty-four prisoners—twenty-three Buffalo Soldiers and Lem Spillsbury. Twelve Americans lay dead west of town and along the ridge. Their bodies were collected and taken into Carrizal along with the prisoners, who were not treated well. At least thirty Mexican troops had died, including General Gómez, and more were wounded—Mexico never acknowledged how many. They took the captured Americans' rifles, ammunition, and valuables before herding them farther east to Ahumada; there they were placed on a train and shipped to the prison in Chihuahua City, where they were left to wonder what would be done with them.

⊱──◆─○─◆──⊰

In the time it took the surviving Buffalo Soldiers to stagger back to Rancho Santo Domingo and send near-incoherent word to expedition headquarters in Dublán about what happened, news of the battle had already been disseminated to reporters by exultant officials in Mexico City. Wilson learned the terrible news about eight hours after the last shot at Carrizal was fired; newsboys outside the White House shouted about an extra edition, and the president sent someone to buy a copy. Pershing was first informed a few hours later in a telegram from El Paso, where the Mexican consul had shared the news with an officer at Fort Bliss. Pershing assumed that Mexican troops attacked his peaceful scouting party, effectively precipitating war between America and Mexico. He immediately wired Funston requesting permission to seize Mexican railroads and assault Chihuahua City—would Funston also order troops from Fort Bliss to move south and reinforce Pershing?

About the same time Pershing's unexpected message arrived, Funston was staggered by a telegram from the War Department in Washington: according to the Mexican government, forty American troops had just been killed at Carrizal. No other details were provided. Washington wanted to know exactly what had happened, and so did Funston. Early on June 22 he dispatched a blistering message to Pershing:

> Why in the name of God do I hear nothing from you the whole country has known for ten hours through Mexican sources that a considerable force of your command was apparently defeated yesterday with heavy loss at Carrizal. Under existing order to you why were they so far from your line being at such distance that I assume that now nearly twenty-four hours after affair news has not reached you who was responsible for what appears on its face to be a terrible blunder.

Pershing was less certain. He'd told Boyd, a veteran officer, to avoid confrontations with Mexican troops. Since the Carrizal survivors weren't yet back in the main expedition camp to provide eyewitness accounts, Pershing assumed that his peaceful scouting party was decimated by an unprovoked attack. Early newspaper reports indicated a number of prisoners had been taken at Carrizal, too—if the Mexicans did not release them, they must be rescued. Pershing readied his troops to launch retaliatory attacks—surely that order would arrive soon.

In Washington, General Scott drew up plans for capturing specific railroad hubs in northern Mexican states as a first step toward fighting all the way south to Mexico City. Then Pershing contacted Funston suggesting that the government "should suspend the movement contemplated." Carrizal witnesses including Captain Morey and Rancho Santo Domingo foreman McCabe had informed Pershing that Boyd insisted on riding through Carrizal even though he was aware of other, safer routes to Villa Ahumada. They explained that the Mexican commander at Carrizal tried to avoid any confrontation; it was Boyd who refused to wait while General Gómez contacted his superiors, and Boyd who ordered Companies C and K to advance against the superior Mexican force. In a later memorandum Pershing insisted that the real fault at Carrizal still lay with Mexico, since Mexican troops fired first. But "there is little that can be said in approval" regarding Boyd's decision to force the issue. Pershing wanted his superiors to understand that "no one could have been more surprised than I was" about Boyd's poor decisions.

Wilson still contemplated war. American soldiers were Mexican prisoners, and instead of agreeing to U.S. demands that they be returned immediately, the Mexican government sent a terse note reminding American leaders that they'd been warned expedition forces would be attacked if they moved in any direction other than north. Because the U.S. didn't listen, at Carrizal "several men on both sides were killed." The note made no mention of the prisoners. Secretary Lansing responded that America interpreted the note as "a formal avowal of deliberately hostile action." He insisted that the prisoners be released at once. On June 28, another note arrived from Mexico City; it falsely accused the Punitive Expedition of committing atrocities, including arresting hundreds of innocent Mexican civilians. Again, there was no mention of the American prisoners. Wilson instructed

Secretary of War Baker to draft a presidential address requesting congressional permission to use all necessary force against Mexico and bring about the replacement of the Carranza government. Then Wilson waited to see what Carranza did next; anything less than conciliatory would finally precipitate war.

For the first few days after Carrizal, Venustiano Carranza was exultant. American soldiers defied his ultimatum and were soundly thrashed as a result. U.S. forces might routinely rout Villistas, but now they knew that Mexican federal troops were sterner stuff. Carranza made certain that his insulting post-Carrizal messages to the American government were widely reported in Mexico's press. Here was further proof to the Mexican people that they finally had a president with the mettle to stand up to the *yanquis*. Perhaps war would come. General Obregón assured Carranza that if it did, he would take the important American town of San Antonio in Texas. The Punitive Expedition camp in Dublán was surrounded on three sides. Mexican forces from Juárez could be moved to block them off to the north. At least for the present, circumstances favored Mexico.

But Carranza was not a fool. On reflection, any advantages held by his country would not last long. Arms and ammunition would quickly run low for Mexican forces, while American troops had plenty. Even if Carranza could make deals with other foreign suppliers, the Mexican economy was so shaky that payment on delivery would surely be demanded, and Carranza didn't have sufficient funds available. There were other daunting facts to consider. If Mexico and America went to war, the number of soldiers available to each side would soon tilt toward the U.S. Presently, their armies were approximately equal in size. But the twenty million men in America of appropriate age for military service exceeded the entire Mexican population of fifteen to sixteen million. Wilson could draft dozens of additional soldiers for every one currently enlisted. Carranza could conscript every postpubescent male in Mexico, from fuzzy-cheeked teenagers to tottery old men, and still run out of troops long before America did. And when war did break out, the U.S. would send waves of well-armed forces across the border into Mexico. Because Emiliano Zapata still fought against him south of Mexico City, Carranza couldn't order all his troops north to oppose the additional American invaders. Unless he retained a sufficient force in the south, Zapata would take the Mexican capital.

On June 29, a train from Chihuahua City chugged into Juárez. Soon afterward, twenty-four men dressed in rags were marched to the International Bridge and directed to cross over into the U.S. Crowds cheered as a few of the battered Buffalo Soldiers dropped to their knees and kissed American soil. There was no accompanying Mexican message of apology for imprisoning them, but neither were there threats that any future return of prisoners would involve coffins. President Wilson delayed addressing Congress. Then, on July 4, the Mexican government contacted Secretary Lansing, suggesting that both countries appoint negotiators to resolve ongoing issues. Mexico would allow these negotiations to be held in the United States. Wilson and Lansing were enthusiastic; it was agreed that the first meeting of a Joint High Commission would take place in New London, Connecticut, on September 6.

Each nation was to be represented by three negotiators. Wilson selected Secretary of the Interior Franklin K. Lane to chair the American delegation. Congressional leaders offered an oblivious suggestion: ask Mexico's representatives to sell Baja California and some of Mexico's northern states to the U.S. Lansing tactfully responded that such a request might have "an unfortunate effect on Mexican public sentiment." But word of it apparently reached Mexico City; Carranza was convinced that at some point American delegates would either make the offensive purchase offer or simply demand cession of these territories. This resulted in the negotiations bogging down from the outset. The Americans wanted to address border security; the Mexicans refused discussing anything until the Punitive Expedition was withdrawn. Lane guessed the reason for their intransigence: "They will not believe that we do not want to take some of their territory." The U.S. might have broken the stalemate by agreeing to withdraw the expedition. After all, American troops no longer left camp at Casas Grandes in pursuit of Villistas; the risk of clashing with Mexican federal troops was too great. But November's presidential election was just two months away; polls indicated the race between Wilson and Supreme Court justice Charles Evans Hughes was close. Wilson couldn't afford even a small percentage of voters believing he'd been run out of Mexico, as his Republican challenger would surely allege.

Through much of September, the Mexican delegation to the Joint High Commission relentlessly insisted there was no reason for the Punitive Expedition to remain; Villa was either dead or reduced to insignificance. Even the recent wave of *Plan de San Diego* raids in South Texas had lessened considerably (on orders from Carranza, though the Mexican delegates didn't realize this). As the U.S. well knew, there were now plenty of Mexican federal forces stationed along the border and in northern Mexican states, available if needed to protect American citizens there. So much for the threat that brought the Punitive Expedition into Mexico.

That argument was negated by shocking news from Chihuahua: Pancho Villa was back.

CHAPTER EIGHTEEN

>─┤◆├─○─◄┤├─◄

The Return of Villa

Two months after being wounded at Guerrero, Pancho Villa finally reached a place where he felt safe enough to rest and heal—a ranch near San Juan in Durango, a few dozen miles south of the state's border with Chihuahua. Villa's recovery was frustratingly incremental. The wounds on his leg oozed pus and bone splinters; it was weeks before Villa could stumble even a few agonized steps, and longer before he could tolerate briefly riding a horse. Care for his injury was primitive—leaves and matted grasses to absorb leakage, and bandages fashioned from calico cloth. Villa could not risk summoning a doctor who might subsequently reveal his location, and he had little faith in modern medicine anyway. But the pain gradually lessened, allowing Villa to anticipate the time, probably in midsummer, when he'd be sufficiently healed to resume full activity. The question then would be what to do next.

By late June, the bulk of Carranza's federal army was in central and northern Chihuahua, surrounding Pershing's American troops and reinforcing garrisons along the border. Most of the rest were occupied battling Zapata south of Mexico City. The *federales* undoubtedly had a good idea of Villa's probable location if he still lived, but not enough available forces to mount a manhunt and sweep the Chihuahua-Durango border area. Villa could, if he chose, slip away, losing himself in the jungles of Yucatán or sailing to Cuba, where he had family and friends. Then, with Carranza and the gringos preoccupied with each other, Villa could, at least for a while, live peacefully in self-exile.

But there is no indication Villa even contemplated this option. He wanted to survive; his struggle to recover was proof. But death, hopefully a heroic one, was still preferable to self-imposed anonymity. Since his battlefield exploits against the forces of Porfirio Díaz raised him from obscurity, Villa reveled in his notoriety as the fearless champion of Mexico's common people. He'd lost that reputation for a time, but, as he recuperated at the ranch near San Juan, word spread around the area that Villa was there and men began arriving, asking for the honor of joining him. By late June there were perhaps six hundred, and Villa was certain that, when he reemerged with this new Villista force, many more would follow. But who should he lead them against?

It was one thing to raid a small American border town, catching the gringo soldiers there by surprise. Pershing, however, had ten thousand well-armed, vigilant troops at Dublán. Until Villa could match the *yanquis* in numbers, any attack there would surely fail. And even though it lacked the capacity to fight Pershing, the current Villista iteration was already too large to sneak across the border and attack a likely target on the American side. The National Guard call-up, plus the reinforcements sent by Funston to block any attempt at invasion by the Mexican federal army, eliminated that threat. Villa still hated Americans, but it was not a propitious time to attack them.

That left Carranza and the *federales*. Months earlier, Villa publicly swore on several occasions that he would no longer use bullets against fellow Mexicans, but circumstances had changed. Carranza was increasingly unpopular, not only for his inability to expel the gringo invaders, but for failure to do anything to ease the plight of Mexico's peasants and working class. Villa still had informers, who agreed that morale was terrible among Carranza's forces. Let Villa return and win a battle or two; then disgruntled *federales* would eagerly change sides and become Villistas. If enough did, Carranza would effectively be driven from office. But who would succeed him? Not Villa, who'd insisted for years he didn't want to be president, and meant it. Obregón was the obvious choice, but he not only hated Villa, he'd defeated him every time they met in battle. Obregón would be a greater threat to Villa than Carranza ever was.

In the end, Villa reverted to form. He conveniently forgot his earlier vows never to fight countrymen again, and assumed anyone pledging loyalty to him would do the same. Mexican federal troops were the closest potential foes, and their garrisons in and around the Durango-Chihuahua state line were small. He'd defeat them first, build a larger army, and then march north, reestablishing himself as a regional force. After that, who could tell? *Federales*, Americans—the foe mattered less than public belief that once again Pancho Villa fought for Mexico's common people.

In July and August, Villistas attacked and overran several towns, easily overcoming opposition by outnumbered *federales*. The Mexican government took notice, but did not feel special concern. The losses were irritating, but the military priority remained maintaining pressure on Pershing at Dublán. The Villistas could be dealt with later. There was no sighting of Villa himself at any of these minor skirmishes, leading the *federales* to assume that either the persistent rumors of his death were correct, or else he was still hiding. Either way, Carranza and his generals believed that Villa himself was gone for good. They were shocked on the night of September 15 when an undeniably living Villa and a force of over two thousand stormed Chihuahua City, temporarily capturing the state capital and driving General Treviño and his supposedly elite troops into the hills outside the city.

Like Colonel Slocum in Columbus six months earlier, Treviño discounted rumors of Villistas lurking in the vicinity and was caught unprepared. While the federal general and his *soldados* regrouped, Villa freed penitentiary inmates—many gratefully joined him—piled wagons high with captured artillery, munitions, and other military gear, and escaped before the nine thousand *federales* could counterattack. The sheer audacity of the raid thrilled many of his countrymen, and in large part restored Villa's earlier reputation for invincibility. Mexican officials were stunned to have Villa back as an active, effective enemy again, but not as much as General Pershing, 150 miles away at the expedition camp in Dublán. He believed that Villa was probably dead because he'd sent secret agents to Durango to murder him.

><+>·O·<+><

In April 1916, Pershing assigned "special service officers" to recruit agents in Chihuahua to locate Villa and, if possible, infiltrate his camp and send back reports. Pershing had already learned that information from native Mexicans couldn't be trusted. His subordinates turned instead to several Japanese. Villa hated the Chinese, but his prejudice did not extend to other Asians. Four Japanese previously known to Villa were hired and promised $5 in gold as daily wages; they are identified in various documents as Tsutomo Dyo, Fuzita, Sato, and Suzuki. After Parral, expedition troops could no longer range widely in search of Villa. Pershing's orders specified destroying the Villistas, not capturing their leader, but he was well aware that the majority of the American public would be dissatisfied with anything other than Villa's apprehension and execution. They might very well blame Pershing, either not realizing or caring that, in restraining his troops at Dublán, he was obeying orders. Pershing was a loyal officer, but he also valued his pristine public reputation. With his already minimal odds of nabbing Villa reduced even further by the limits imposed on his pursuit, Pershing decided that if he couldn't catch his slippery quarry, perhaps he could arrange his assassination.

Dyo and Sato heard rumors that a badly wounded Villa was hiding near the state line between Chihuahua and Durango. They eventually found their way to where Villa recuperated outside San Juan; once they were in the area, they had only to ask locals where he was.

Everyone seemed to know, and no one considered two Japanese to be any threat. Dyo ingratiated himself with Villa by mentioning he'd seen the fugitive's wife; she'd heard that her husband was injured, and asked Dyo to bring him some good bandages. Villa allowed Dyo to change the dressings on his still seeping wound, and afterward permitted both Japanese to accompany him and his men as they began their series of initial attacks on small federal garrisons in Durango and southern Chihuahua. The two Japanese sent word to their expedition spymasters that Villa still lived, and they'd successfully infiltrated his camp. Fuzita and Suzuki soon arrived with new instructions. On July 8, they gave Dyo and Sato three tubes of poison pellets supplied by Pershing's special service officers, and explained that thirteen pills ought to be enough to kill Villa. Dyo, who was now helping prepare Villa's meals, should dissolve the pills in Villa's morning coffee. The slow-acting poison wouldn't take its full, lethal effect for three days, giving the assassins plenty of time to sneak away before their victim expired.

Dyo and Sato returned to the Villista camp, where they tested the tablets on a dog. The poison evidently worked faster on animals; the dog died almost immediately. On the morning of July 9, Dyo served Villa poisoned coffee. Villa sipped some, then passed the cup to one of his officers, who drank the rest. The Villistas set off, heading northwest, and after a few miles the Japanese slipped away. They reported to their army bosses that, though it wasn't quite certain, Villa was probably dead. To Pershing's dismay, Villa's dramatic mid-September attack on Chihuahua City proved that he wasn't. Either the estimation of a sufficient dose had been too low, or else Villa hadn't drunk enough of the poisoned coffee.

Pershing was disappointed, but had other things on his mind. *Federales* still surrounded him, and Pershing had just applied to the War Department for promotion to major general. But the Bureau of Investigation, which had also hired Japanese agents and set them on Villa's trail, learned of the failed assassination attempt and reported it to the War Department; Pershing apparently had not informed his superiors there about the murder plan. The news caused great consternation in the War Department, and with President Wilson and Secretary Lansing. It would be greatly embarrassing if the world learned of America's inept attempt to assassinate an enemy. Attorney General Thomas Gregory ordered the Army to investigate. Much to Pershing's relief, the investigation was perfunctory. The public never learned of the bungled plot, and investigators accepted Pershing's statement that neither he nor any members of this staff "had any knowledge or any connection with any such plan as these Japanese report. It is entirely possible that these Japanese had some such plan of their own." But the Punitive Expedition's "Report of Operations of 'General' Francisco Villa Since November 1915," sent from its Dublán headquarters on July 31, 1916, six weeks before Villa reappeared at Chihuahua City, included a nine-page section written by Tsutomo Dyo about joining the Villistas, treating Villa's wounded leg, and preparing and serving him coffee on the morning of July 9 ("he drank about one eighth of the total") before fleeing the Villista camp with Sato. The poison was not mentioned. The report describes this information as "told in a diary of one of our confidential agents." Pershing received his promotion to major general. There is no further record of Dyo and Sato, or of the Punitive Expedition subsequently employing any other Japanese "confidential agents."

⊱─◆─○─◆─⊰

Villa continued attacking Mexican federal troops in Chihuahua, hitting hard, taking munitions and supplies whenever he could, then racing away before reinforcements could arrive. Though the rejuvenated Villistas didn't assault or even threaten U.S. forces in Dublán, Pershing believed that it was only a matter of time; Villa would attack the expedition as soon as he had enough volunteers and sufficient arms and ammunition. By late fall more than five thousand Villistas were active in Chihuahua; perhaps one-third were *federales* who switched sides. In late October Pershing warned Funston that Villistas rather than Carranza's forces now controlled most of Chihuahua. With the *federales* battered and demoralized, Pershing suggested, it was time for the Punitive Expedition to leave Dublán and take Chihuahua City, which would offer a better base for renewed American operations against Villa. Funston concurred, but Woodrow Wilson didn't. Pershing's assurances that his troops would overwhelm the three thousand *federales* currently holding the city failed to change Wilson's mind. The U.S. presidential election was just days away; if an expedition attack on Chihuahua City resulted in an unexpected American defeat or Carranza declaring war, it might tip the balance in favor of Wilson's opponent.

On Tuesday, November 7, American voters went to the polls. The vote was so close that a result wasn't announced for three days, when it was determined that Wilson had won California by fewer than four thousand votes, giving him a narrow 277–254 electoral college margin over Justice Hughes. With his second White House term secured, Wilson was determined to settle conflicts in Mexico; war with Germany seemed increasingly inevitable, and all of America's limited military might would be needed across the Atlantic. American delegates to the Joint High Commission were informed that the president expected a prompt agreement that included a Mexican commitment to protect American lives and property above and below the border. Mexico's delegates were also eager to conclude the extended negotiations. On December 24, the delegations jointly announced a breakthrough: both governments could pursue bandits for one hundred miles on either side of the other's border, and the Punitive Expedition would be withdrawn within forty days of the agreement's ratification so long as the American government considered its citizens and their property in northern Mexico to be safe from Villa. Wilson and Lansing immediately declared their support. All that remained was for Carranza to agree.

Venustiano Carranza still had little empathy for Mexico's poorer classes, but he understood that Villa's recent victories reestablished him as their champion against both the gringos and a Mexican government that failed to eject America's insulting expedition. Carranza's federal troops could probably defeat the Villistas in evenly contested battles, but Villa was wily and kept attacking where and when he was least expected. In late November Villa briefly captured Chihuahua City for the second time, and on December 22 the Villistas temporarily occupied Torreón. In both cases Villa roused public spirit against the *yanquis* and Carranza, and gained hundreds of enthusiastic recruits. Reports estimated Villista strength at six thousand and increasing daily. Mexico's leader knew Villa's flaws; at some point he was likely to lead his forces into unnecessary annihilation, as he had thirteen months earlier at Agua Prieta. But for the present he stayed a step ahead of Carranza's forces.

In October, Villa published a grand "Manifesto to the Nation," advocating the overthrow of Carranza and "the most corrupt Government we have ever had." Villa promised that a new Mexican government would never allow Americans to purchase property in Mexico for the next twenty-five years, and all current gringo railroad and mining operations would be absorbed by the Mexican nation— everyone would share in these riches. To prevent further gringo insults to the motherland, an eighteen-league (fifty-four-mile) buffer would be established south of the border; patrols would prevent future *yanqui* invasions. These appeals to national pride were effective. British vice consul Patrick O'Hea, who owned a Chihuahua soap factory that was ransacked during a Villa raid, wrote that "the army that now follows him, Villa has called to his standard like a mad mullah preaching a holy war, a crusade against the foreigner. . . . Every speech of his is a raving on the same topic." There was a drawback: over the next months, a significant portion of Villa's most enthusiastic recruits who'd been attracted by his nationalist demagoguery grew disenchanted when they only fought fellow Mexicans rather than gringos. But for the moment, Villa's anti-American rhetoric was effective.

Carranza countered in early December with the announcement of plans for a new constitution that, once written and enacted sometime in 1917, would mandate the appropriation or nationalization of "all privately owned lands, waters and resources . . . as necessary for the public interest." No foreign ownership of property or industry would be allowed within one hundred miles of the border, and Mexico would own everything in its subsoil, such as precious metals and oil. Further, all citizens regardless of background would have access to public education, health care, fair wages, and the right to organize unions. But these enticing promises didn't have the effect Carranza hoped. Villa's popularity—and confidence—continued growing. Villa predicted to a reporter from the *New York World* that his forces would soon do what Carranza's federal troops could not—attack the Punitive Expedition troops and "drive them out, or make them fight, and after they are gone I will make a gap between the two countries so wide and deep that no *Americano* will ever be able to steal Mexican land, oil or gold."

If Villa was somehow credited with forcing the Punitive Expedition out of Mexico, Carranza's government would almost certainly collapse. So far as Carranza was concerned, the agreement reached on December 24 by the Joint High Commission worked to Villa's advantage. The qualification that Pershing and his troops would withdraw within forty days of ratification only so long as northern Mexico was considered safe from Villa was a particular sticking point. To Carranza, it meant that America claimed the right to leave the expedition in place at Dublán indefinitely—and every day the Americans remained there, more Mexicans were likely to support Villa.

Carranza was determined to be perceived by his people as the man who rid Mexico of the Punitive Expedition. His government, and perhaps his life, depended on it. Three days after the Joint High

Commission announced the tentative agreement, Carranza rejected it, declaring that Mexico would no longer negotiate with America on any security issues so long as the expedition remained in Mexican territory. Almost ten months after Villa's raid on Columbus, nothing was resolved.

CHAPTER NINETEEN

Withdrawal

By the end of 1916, the Punitive Expedition had been bottled up in Dublán for five months. After the debacle at Carrizal, Pershing was forbidden by the War Department to move even a few troops in any direction and risk another confrontation with the Mexican federal forces surrounding him on three sides. Even after his November reelection, President Wilson remained reluctant to order a withdrawal. War with Mexico was still possible, and in that event having a substantial U.S. force already below the border would be advantageous. That its ten thousand troops had to remain indefinitely in frustrating limbo was an unfortunate consequence.

The U.S. soldiers in Dublán were frustrated by the orders to stand in place. They wanted revenge for Carrizal, and for Parral, too. Those incidents failed to shake the expedition's belief that Mexican forces were inherently inferior to the U.S. Army, something the American troops would prove if given the opportunity. Tompkins and his cavalry retreated at Parral because the Mexican commander there tricked them. At Carrizal, the Americans lost because Morey and Company K didn't coordinate properly with Captain Boyd and Company C in the charge against entrenched *federales*. Pershing and Tompkins believed this so strongly that they included the opinion in their memoirs. Woodrow Wilson was the object of frequent criticism—in a letter to a friend, George Patton wrote that the U.S. president had "not the soul of a louse nor the mind of a worm or the backbone of a jellyfish." But most of the expedition's anger was directed at the Mexican people, who they believed had proven themselves unworthy of American support. Patton wrote that "one must be a fool indeed to think that people half savage and wholly ignorant will ever form a republic. It is a joke." In his July 31, 1916, report on Villa, Pershing declared that "the native Mexican is utterly unreliable . . . his characteristics are to practice deception at all times."

Yet at Dublán, Pershing still rose above resentment and frustration. He realized that the expedition's immobility offered an opportunity for much needed instruction. Basic training in the peacetime Army had not adequately prepared most of his troops for wartime. Pershing ordered that everyone participate in rigorous daily drills, from field maneuvers to target practice. The soldiers' fumbling early efforts proved Pershing was correct. Patton observed that "in the matter of fire tactics, involving fire direction, control and discipline, as well as in the designation of targets and signaling, we were woefully deficient." Pershing drove everyone hard, himself most of all. The expedition commander was a hands-on instructor. If the order to fight in Mexico ever came, Pershing was determined that his men would be prepared to make short work of both Villistas and *federales*.

Pershing expected his officers to set disciplined examples; when they didn't, he administered harsh private reprimands, or, in a few extreme instances, sent scathing reports to the Army's Southern Department headquarters in San Antonio. Colonel Herbert Slocum was a particular object of Pershing's written wrath. After Slocum's questionable actions before and during the Columbus raid, Pershing still allowed him to command the expedition's 13th Cavalry contingent, at least in part to give the colonel an opportunity to atone. But on September 18, Pershing wrote to Southern Department command that "I was very much disappointed in Colonel Slocum . . . his attitude soon convinced me that he could accomplish nothing." Pershing accused

Slocum of being "old for his years, and [he] thinks too much of his comfort." The criticism was noted by the War Department. Though Slocum remained in the Army until he reached the mandatory retirement age of sixty-four in 1919, after his service in the Punitive Expedition he was relegated to minor assignments that left no opportunity for promotion to general.

Pershing's concern for his men extended beyond training. Dublán was in the middle of flat country, baked by the sun in summer and freezing in winter. The canvas pup tents supplied by the Army provided little shelter. But a handful of Villista prisoners was coerced into teaching the American soldiers how to make adobe bricks, and soon the U.S. troops sheltered in two-man adobe huts, with roofs rigged from the canvas tents. Trucks arrived daily from Columbus, hauling meat and fresh produce; the soldiers ate well. Fields were prepared, and teams played baseball and football—participation was encouraged. For the most restless, there was boxing. Another area was reserved for prostitutes. Pershing understood the sexual needs of young men. The women allowed in camp were checked by doctors to ensure they were disease-free, and paid an agreed-upon wage for their services. Additional amenities were provided by a flood of Chinese, who fled their villages and begged the expedition's protection when Villa returned and resumed his casual slaughter of any Chinese he encountered. Once allowed in the Dublán camp, they set up small businesses, offering laundry services and food to the American soldiers at modest prices.

The commander himself enjoyed periodic recreation, usually in the form of visits to Columbus, which had temporarily blossomed into a center of frenetic activity. Merchants flocked there to help supply the expedition. Trucks and equipment passed through in transit to Dublán. There were new cafés and shops offering pleasant diversion for Pershing and Nita Patton, whom he invited to come from Fort Bliss to join him. Lieutenant Patton and his wife, Beatrice, again served as somewhat reluctant chaperones. At some point Pershing and Nita came to what was then called an "understanding"; as soon as his duties permitted, he would go to California and formally ask her father for her hand.

＞－◆＞－○－◇－◆－◄

During the same months that the Punitive Expedition trained in Dublán, Carranza explored global alliances. There seemed little chance that Mexico's dysfunctional relationship with the United States could be mended. Carranza was certain that America would always treat Mexico as an inferior nation to be simultaneously disdained and exploited, rather than as a valued neighbor. He realized that his country needed outside investment and loans to support its economy, and agreements with stronger nations to ensure national security. But Carranza refused to acknowledge permanent secondary status; any partner must offer respectful assistance with the intention of eventually accepting Mexico as an equal. That was not possible with America, a country convinced of its own overweening moral and cultural superiority. Carranza wanted to avoid war with the gringos, and would, from geographic necessity, negotiate with them when he must, but only when any agreement would benefit both nations equally or, ideally, in some way provide an advantage to Mexico. This would be appropriate, since America had, for so long, pressed one-sided agreements on Mexican leaders less determined, less *principled*, than Venustiano Carranza. And, in the summer and fall of 1916, America was not Mexico's only potential ally.

Though the United States was Mexico's dominant economic partner, Britain, Germany, Japan, and France all had investments in the country. America's Monroe Doctrine usually barred anything of a potentially military nature; in recent years Germany and Japan had been warned off by the U.S. when they explored establishing bases on the Mexican coast. But in those cases, Mexico's leaders didn't insist on their country's right to form whatever military alliances it pleased, for fear of alienating the United States. Now Carranza was willing to flout America's offensive paternalism, though only after first discreetly exploring options. France was not a prospective partner; its money was always welcome, but the invasion and occupation of the 1860s precluded inviting any French military presence a half century later. With World War I in progress, Britain needed Mexican oil more than ever, but its dependence on America for munitions prevented any agreements with Mexico that would antagonize the U.S.

Japan began the war as an active participant allied with England and France, but ceased most operations after capturing German holdings in the Pacific. In late July 1916, Carranza quietly sent representatives to Tokyo, hoping to purchase arms and ammunition, plus the equipment needed for Mexico to manufacture its own gunpowder and cartridges. Japan had promised that, during the war, it would not make munitions available to anyone other than Allied nations, and Mexico was neutral. The Japanese Foreign Ministry abided by the agreement and would not receive Carranza's agent, but officials of the Japanese navy did, and arranged the sale. In November, Japan's envoy in Mexico City hosted a series of parties proclaiming his country's regard for Mexico; Japanese ordnance experts crossed the Pacific to help get a Mexican munitions plant up and operating. American officials noticed—the *New York Times* printed a story about Japan's assistance— but Wilson and Lansing chose not to make an issue of it. The Joint High Commission was meeting in Connecticut, and resolving current issues seemed more important than adding another. Carranza now believed he had a burgeoning friendship with Japan that might well grow into a wider alliance. He turned next to Germany.

On October 16, Carranza suggested to German officials that Mexico might be willing, under certain undefined circumstances, to provide assistance to German submarines in "Mexican waters"— a potential invitation for U-boats to freely hunt British oil tankers off the coast near Tampico. Carranza stressed that Germany was the "only great power" with which Mexico desired "stronger economic and political ties." He also wondered if Germany would be opposed to any further armed American "interventions" into Mexico; if so, might the German government consider issuing a public statement to that effect? Germany wouldn't commit, but expressed enough pleasure at Mexico's offer of a closer relationship that, three weeks later, the Mexican envoy to Berlin followed up with a short list of suggestions. Besides supplying additional military advisors, Germany might assist with the building of a munitions plant in Mexico, and sell submarines to the Mexican military. Again, the Germans were noncommittal. But Germany's military leadership in particular felt encouraged. Carranza was not only open to, but eager for, a deal. Under appropriate circumstances, Germany might make a counteroffer.

But in the final months of 1916, the Germans feared that the Joint High Commission might negotiate an agreement for the U.S. to withdraw the Punitive Expedition, lessening the potential for war between the U.S. and Mexico and allowing America to position its military to enter World War I. Another means of maintaining tension between the two countries was required. A German consul in Mexico contacted Pancho Villa.

Villa's recent string of victories was impressive. He felt close to the point where his forces would be strong enough to take on the *yanquis* as well as Carranza—it was a matter of getting more arms and ammunition. The Germans had a suggestion. Villa and his troops should attack the oil fields around Tampico, and also the port city itself. Once Villa took Tampico, German ships would dock there and supply him with all the guns and ammunition he wanted. In return, Germany would be allowed to cut off Britain's access to Mexican oil. Left unexpressed was the near certainty that if Villa occupied Tampico, America would launch another expedition into Mexico to drive him out. That might begin an American-Mexican war, or at least make it harder for the U.S. to enter the war overseas. Either outcome would please the Germans. Villa was initially receptive, but eventually declined after considering the risk in attacking an area so well defended by federal troops. If Germany was to continue using Mexico against America, its partner would have to be Carranza.

>-+*>-o-<*+-<

In early January 1917, Wilson decided to bring the Punitive Expedition home. In the end, he and Carranza were too much alike. Each believed himself to be morally and intellectually superior, and that compromise was a concession to inferiors. It irked the American president to give Carranza the satisfaction of agreeing to his demand for its unconditional withdrawal, but preparing for war with Germany took precedence. On January 12, three days before the members of the Joint High Commission abandoned negotiations, Wilson privately instructed Secretary of War Baker to begin the process of extracting Pershing and his troops. On January 21 Pershing wired Army chief of staff Scott that "everything is in readiness," but cautioned that Villa would undoubtedly begin a new series of aggressive attacks in Chihuahua as soon as "we are well across the border." On February 5, Pershing arrived in Columbus just ahead of the rest of the expedition so he could formally salute his troops as they crossed back into the United States.

The withdrawal column included 10,690 soldiers, 9,307 horses, more than 300 wagons, trucks, and passenger cars, 2,030 Mexican refugees, 21 Villista prisoners, and 533 Chinese. The latter posed a problem—under current immigration restrictions, they were not allowed into the U.S. Pershing risked insubordination by insisting that they be permitted to enter. While the Mexicans were processed in Columbus, the Chinese were transferred to Fort Bliss, where most worked as cooks and handymen. Some found employment at civilian businesses and ranches. In 1921, as a gesture of gratitude toward the expedition commander, Congress granted special permanent residence dispensation to "Pershing's Chinese."

Across America, there was debate over whether the Punitive Expedition succeeded or failed. Critics correctly pointed out that Villa remained at large in Chihuahua. The expedition's "Report of Operations of 'General' Francisco Villa Since November 1915," submitted to the War Department on July 21, 1916, estimated that in its first five months of operations, 281 Villistas were "killed and captured by the U.S. Troops and *Carranzistas*." Heading the list was "General Francisco Villa, wounded at Guerrero, March 27th," without the qualification that he was shot by one of his own recruits. The estimated cost to taxpayers for the expedition's eleven months in Mexico ranged from $130 to $340 million.

The controversy didn't damage Pershing's military career; his superiors appreciated the pragmatism he demonstrated under extraordinarily difficult conditions. Two weeks after he brought his troops safely back to Columbus, Pershing received an important new assignment. Fifty-one-year-old Major General Frederick Funston dropped dead from a massive heart attack, and Pershing succeeded him as commander of the Southern Department at Fort Sam Houston in San Antonio. This was the Army's primary field position. It had been a foregone conclusion that, if America entered the European war, Funston would command the U.S. troops. Now it would be Pershing.

News of the expedition's pending exit from Mexico dismayed German leaders. Not only would Pershing's troops now be primed for overseas combat, the National Guard troops on patrol at the border had also been recalled, meaning all 150,000 of them were also available for foreign service. Based on their own imminent plans, German officials realized that America's entry into the war was virtually a foregone conclusion. It was time for Germany to offer a deal to Mexico's leader, one going far beyond anything previously contemplated.

On February 5, 1917, at almost the same moment that the Punitive Expedition crossed back into the United States, German imperial minister to Mexico Heinrich von Eckhardt was instructed to observe the highest level of secrecy as he passed an urgent message to Venustiano Carranza.

▷·◁▷·○·◁▷·◁

CHAPTER TWENTY

Germany Makes Its Move

On January 9, 1917, German government and military leaders met in the city of Pless to determine a new plan for winning World War I. After thirty agonizing months, the conflict remained a bloody stalemate marked by near-interminable trench warfare costing thousands of lives on both sides for every yard of ground gained or lost. British blockades of Germany's ports caused food shortages; if the blockades remained in place, German citizens might soon be reduced to eating dogs and cats. Always, there was the threat that America, with its bottomless supply of war matériel, would enter the conflict on the side of the Allies. Some change of strategy was needed for Germany to win before momentum irrevocably favored the enemy. The military leaders at Pless believed they had such a plan.

In the early months of the war, German U-boats practicing unrestricted submarine warfare terrorized the seas. But the May 1915 sinking of the British luxury liner *Lusitania* ended that. To Germany, it was a clean, necessary kill—besides nearly 2,000 passengers, the *Lusitania* conveyed a cache of munitions. But 128 Americans were among the 1,198 who died, and U.S. protests were so heated that the German high command reluctantly ordered its U-boats to attack more selectively, endangering the lives of fewer citizens of neutral nations. This meant more supply ships slipped through to the enemy.

Now, German military commanders wanted a return to unrestricted submarine warfare. Once the U-boats were free to sink any targets deemed suspicious, England could be effectively closed off as a source of supplies and reinforcements to the Allied forces in Europe. Britain's warships would have to defend its own coasts instead of harassing German ports. If unrestricted submarine attacks resumed soon, perhaps by February 1, Germany would regain a significant advantage and, in a matter of months, might achieve a well-deserved victory. To the military leaders, this logic seemed unassailable.

Kaiser Wilhelm II and the civilian leaders at Pless weren't convinced. What if America reacted by joining the Allies? This was something Germany had tried to prevent since the outset of the war. U.S. forces pouring into Europe, bringing with them a bristling arsenal of weapons, fleets of tanks and trucks—wouldn't that more than offset any additional ship sinkings by the U-boats? The military commanders offered a surprising assurance: American entry into the war wouldn't make an immediate difference. It was obvious that the current U.S. military was woefully inadequate. It would be at least six months before America could draft, train, and deploy forces capable of fighting effectively in Europe. The same six months was all it would take for the U-boats to choke off enemy shipping and force the Allies to capitulate, or at least negotiate peace terms favorable to Germany. Additionally, what if, even after raising up a more competent military, the U.S. had to keep most of it home to fight on its own southern front? Only a few months earlier, Mexico had come to Germany suggesting an alliance. Surely Carranza, the Mexican leader, still remained eager to ally. It was well known he hated America. Perhaps he would be amenable to an agreement that opened the way for Mexico to regain territory lost to the United States. After further discussion, the civilians concurred.

One week later, on January 16, German foreign secretary Arthur Zimmermann encoded and sent a telegram to Count Johann von Bernstorff, Germany's ambassador to the United States. Bernstorff, at the embassy in Washington, was instructed to pass the message on via another telegram to Heinrich von Eckhardt, Germany's minister in Mexico City.

> *We intend to begin unrestricted submarine warfare on the first of February. We shall endeavor in spite of this to keep the United States neutral. In the event of this not succeeding, we make Mexico a proposal of alliance on the following basis: make war together, make peace together, generous financial support, and an understanding on our part that Mexico is to reconquer the lost territory in Texas, New Mexico, and Arizona. The settlement in detail is left to you.*
>
> *You will inform the President [Carranza] of the above most secretly as soon as the outbreak of war with the United States is certain and add the suggestion that he should, on his own initiative, invite Japan to immediate alliance and at the same time mediate between Japan and ourselves.*
>
> *Please call the President's attention to the fact that the unrestricted employment of our submarines now offers the prospect of compelling England to make peace within a few months. Acknowledge receipt.*
>
> ZIMMERMANN

The message combined a pragmatic offer with shrewd manipulation. Acting on his own, Carranza repeatedly risked war with the United States. Mexico's chances against the U.S. would be incalculably greater if America fought a two-front war with a significant portion of U.S. forces engaged across the Atlantic. But nowhere in the telegram did Germany commit any of its own troops to fight *alongside* Mexicans. Carranza might make that assumption; it would be useful if he did. But beyond "generous financial support," Germany promised only "an understanding" that "*Mexico* is to reconquer the lost territory in Texas, New Mexico, and Arizona" (my emphasis). How much of that territory—all three states, parts of them, or even a tiny strip of land above the border—would depend on Mexico's ability to take it back. German leaders were privately even more disdainful of Mexico's present military proficiency than they were of America's. They did not believe Mexico could ever defeat the U.S., only that Mexico would tie up a portion of the American forces that would otherwise oppose Germans in Europe.

The German suggestion to Mexico of reclaimed land deliberately didn't include California. That great prize was intended to lure Japan into a German alliance. Those two nations remained in an official state of war, but it would be ideal for the Germans if, as their unrestricted warfare throttled the Allies in Britain and Europe, Japan attacked California while Mexico assaulted Texas, New Mexico, and Arizona. Japanese officials would be reluctant to meet with representatives of Germany, but Mexico and Japan were friendly. Mediation by Carranza could help restore communications between Germany and the Japanese; from there, Japan might be convinced to change sides, especially if the Germans dangled California as a potential reward. The Germans considered Japan's chances of taking California far superior to Mexico's odds of regaining any portion of the other three states, but in any event those outcomes would not be Germany's concern. It all hinged on Carranza, and, if the United States declared war on Germany, whether his enmity for America would incline him to accept the German offer.

Two missteps, both stemming at least in part from German arrogance, doomed first the intended secrecy, then the effectiveness of the proposal. In August 1914, during the early weeks of the war, England cut Germany's transatlantic cables, making it impossible for the Germans to make direct telegraphic connection to Mexico. There were other options: Sweden, a neutral country, offered the use of its cables. So did the U.S.; President Wilson saw extending this courtesy as a means of demonstrating America's neutrality. Germany took regular advantage of both nations' generosity. American diplomats in Germany routinely accepted messages, including those in code, addressed from German officials to their nation's diplomats in Mexico. These telegrams were initially sent to the State Department in Washington; officials there passed them along to the German ambassador and his staff, who used America's Western Union to make the final transmissions to the German embassy in Mexico City. Zimmermann's telegram was sent through both the Swedish and U.S. transatlantic cable systems.

German leaders enjoyed the irony of the U.S. helpfully transmitting a message intended against America's best interests. Though that meant the U.S. government as well as Western Union would have a copy, it seemed to make no difference—from the outset of the war Germany used the same secret codes, confident they couldn't be deciphered. The Germans did not know that British intelligence regularly intercepted all telegrams sent over Swedish and American cables— and that Britain's agents had cracked the German code. By the time on January 17 that Minister Eckhardt in Mexico City received and deciphered Zimmermann's instructions, England already had a partial translation. English intelligence officials chose to withhold what they knew from American leaders until they had a full translation, which might take a few weeks. A time element was involved—Germany intended resuming unrestricted submarine warfare on February 1, but the German offer was not to be made to Carranza until the U.S. entered the war. There apparently was time for British codebreakers to decipher the full message and provide it to the U.S. without allowing Germany to discover that England had broken its code.

On January 22, Wilson addressed the Senate. His message was that it was possible for warring nations to achieve "peace without victory." The Allies and Germany should meet in negotiations, not battle, and America would gladly mediate. The Allies, who'd hoped for an announcement of unconditional American support, were disappointed, but Ambassador Bernstorff was also concerned. He had orders to inform the U.S. State Department on the afternoon of January 31 that Germany would unleash its U-boats again the next morning. If President Wilson really intended to press peace negotiations on both sides without favoring the Allies, perhaps it would be better to delay the enhanced U-boat action. But Bernstorff's suggestion to the German military was rejected: the U-boats were already out to sea, positioning themselves to wreak maximum carnage the moment restrictions were lifted. They could not be recalled.

At 4 p.m. on January 31, Bernstorff called on Secretary Lansing at the State Department and officially notified him of Germany's intention to resume all-out U-boat activity. Lansing apprised Wilson. German leaders anticipated an immediate announcement that American was entering the war. Instead, Wilson mused to White House staff that it might still be wrong for the U.S. to abandon its role as peacemaker by joining the fight. It was February 3 before the president offered a public reaction. In an address to Congress, he announced that America would break off diplomatic relations with Germany, but added that he was not convinced Germany was resuming unrestricted submarine warfare. Officials in Berlin were dumbfounded. On February 5, Zimmermann sent another wire to Mexico City via Washington: though the U.S. had not declared war as expected, Imperial Minister Eckhardt should take the German alliance proposal to Carranza "even now."

Had Germany made its offer to Carranza late in 1916, when the Punitive Expedition remained at Dublán and he was desperate to be rid of the Americans, it might have been accepted. But on February 5, the same day that Pershing and his troops crossed back to the U.S., Carranza felt triumphant. He'd stood up to the Americans, and they backed down. The Mexican people could not credit anyone other than himself for this glorious achievement. All the Mexican federal forces that surrounded the expedition at Dublán could now be unleashed on Villa. A recent convention had ratified Mexico's new, progressive constitution, another reason for the nation's working class and poor to feel grateful to him. After almost eighteen months in de facto power, Carranza announced a May election, in which he'd run unopposed and win the single four-year presidential term permitted under Mexican law. When Eckhardt presented Germany's proposal, Carranza was intrigued but felt no need to quickly respond. In due time, Germany would be notified of his decision.

The Germans were alarmed. Neither Wilson nor Carranza had acted as anticipated. On February 20, Eckhardt requested a meeting with the Mexican leader. Carranza was conveniently unavailable; Foreign Minister Cándido Aguilar met with Eckhardt and assured him that Germany's proposal was being carefully considered. Four days later, Aguilar visited Japan's mission in Mexico City, where he asked a Japanese minister how his nation would theoretically react to American entry into the war. The minister was noncommittal, though he personally believed Japan would continue standing with the Allies. Aguilar apparently did not mention the possibility of Mexico mediating between Japan and Germany.

Germany had to wait, but Britain didn't. On February 23, British intelligence shared the decoded Zimmermann Telegram with Walter Page, the American ambassador in London. Page sent the translated telegram on to the State Department with a covering note explaining that Britain shared the information with the stipulation that the U.S. not reveal the British had cracked Germany's war code. When the explosive material arrived at the State Department on Saturday morning, February 24, Lansing was away on vacation. Acting Secretary Frank L. Polk rushed the decoded telegram and Ambassador Page's note to the White House. Even after reading it, Wilson still wasn't ready to accept the telegram as authentic. He wanted to see the Western Union copy, too. Western Union balked, claiming that U.S. federal law protected the contents of the telegrams it relayed. State Department lawyers were dispatched to argue the government's case with the company. For the moment, Wilson continued working on an address to Congress scheduled for Monday; the president planned to request passage of an Armed Ship bill that would place Navy gunners on U.S. merchant ships with orders to shoot German U-boats on sight. Wilson wanted a vote before Congress adjourned on March 4 for a break through the summer. Wilson made his Monday address, and as he spoke news arrived that the *Laconia*, a British passenger ship, had just been torpedoed and sunk by U-boats; two Americans were killed.

On Tuesday, Western Union delivered its copy of the Zimmermann Telegram to the White House, and Wilson determined that the message was genuine. After wiring his thanks to British intelligence for providing the U.S. with information "of inestimable value," Wilson ordered Lansing, who was back from vacation, to contact Carranza in Mexico City. Lansing was informed that Carranza was out of town; Aguilar, again responding in his place, denied any knowledge of the telegram or its contents. On Wednesday evening, a reporter for the Associated Press was invited to meet with Wilson and Lansing at the White House. He was briefed on the telegram only after agreeing to keep the secret of how it was obtained. On Thursday, March 1, front pages of newspapers across America blazoned the same story, which began, "The A.P. is enabled to reveal . . ." The headline in the *New York World* was representative: "*MEXICO AND JAPAN ASKED BY GERMANY TO ATTACK U.S. IF IT ENTERED THE WAR.*"

Carranza offered no public response, but the March 2 edition of *El Pueblo*, a government newspaper, insisted that Mexico had never received the German offer. Japan's foreign minister issued a statement that his country would never betray its friendship with the United States. Zimmermann, the telegram's signatory, was besieged by requests for comment. On March 2 he challenged America to prove that the telegram was authentic. But the next day, when a friendly journalist coaxed, "Of course, Your Excellency will deny this story," Zimmermann blurted, "I cannot deny it. It is true."

The U.S. House of Representatives overwhelmingly passed the Armed Ship bill, but the Senate adjourned without voting. On March 9, President Wilson signed an executive order putting the same terms into effect. He also announced that the National Guard would remain on active call, since the Regular Army was not currently sufficient to "prevent interference by German agents with the postal, commercial and military channels and other instrumentalities of the United States." Wilson was somewhat more flexible regarding Mexico. In mid-March, an unopposed Carranza was elected president, and in recognition Wilson appointed Harry P. Fletcher to serve as the U.S. ambassador in Mexico City. This gesture of full diplomatic recognition failed to thaw Carranza's attitude toward America. When Ambassador Fletcher asked him to formally repudiate the Zimmermann Telegram, Carranza would admit only that the offer had been made. Germany remained hopeful that Mexico might still become its war partner.

On March 18, with the U.S. still officially neutral, German U-boats sank three American ships. President Wilson announced that he would recall Congress on April 2, and when the president addressed the combined House and Senate, he declared that neutrality was no longer possible; Germany sought allies against America "at our very doors." The Zimmermann Telegram proved it. The United States must "accept this challenge of hostile purpose." Four days later, Congress approved American entry into World War I.

Minister Eckhardt pleaded with Carranza to ally with Germany and declare war on America. When these entreaties failed to elicit a response, Zimmermann ordered Eckhardt to attempt bribery: "Arrangements are being made on this side to transfer considerable sums." It was April 14 before Eckhardt could notify Berlin of Carranza's decision: "He says the alliance has been wrecked by premature publication but might become necessary at a later stage."

>─+◆>─O─<◆+─<

German military leadership was certain it would take the United States six months to draft, train, and transport forces across the Atlantic, but Pershing and the first wave of American troops reached France in three. By November 11, 1918, when fighting ended, 1.3 million U.S. servicemen were engaged. Prominent among them were more than five thousand former members of the Punitive Expedition, whose intensive training in their dusty camp at Dublán in northern Mexico honed the combat skills necessary to batter Germany into ignominious defeat.

From the moment their country entered World War I, many Americans forgot about Mexico. But anti-American sentiment among Mexicans remained strong; at Carranza's inauguration in Mexico City on May 1, 1917, the gathered crowd cheered German minister Eckhardt and jeered U.S. ambassador Fletcher. With most of the American Army and National Guard away in Europe, the border was relatively unguarded and, especially in South and West Texas, Mexican raiders took advantage. When the Texas Rangers responded in savage, indiscriminate fashion, one of the bloodiest eras in border history ensued.

CHAPTER TWENTY-ONE

The Rangers Go Too Far

I n August 1916, nineteen-year-old Laird Engle joined a growing number of Texans moving south to the state's border with Mexico. The proliferation of Army camps along the border in the wake of the *Plan de San Diego* raids and the summer attacks on Glenn Springs and Boquillas created new civilian business opportunities—the military needed supplies of every sort, as well as cafés, bars, and shops for off-duty recreation. Engle, a native of Beeville, moved two hundred miles south to Llano Grande, a town on the north bank of the Rio Grande forty-five miles west of Brownsville. There he found a wide choice of relatively lucrative employment, writing to his fiancée in Beeville that "there is nothing here but soldiers and money but there is a lot of both of those." The drawback was constant danger. Within weeks of arriving, "a Mexican hidden in the brush" shot at Engle, and narrowly missed. When his fiancée complained in a letter about drought in Bee-ville, he chided her: besides their own extended drought, Americans on the South Texas border endured "bandit raids . . . they get their houses shot to pieces, their cattle killed and they are lucky not to get killed themselves."

These raids, historians Charles Harris III and Louis R. Sadler write in *The Plan de San Diego*, contributed to an already ongoing "legacy of racial tension in South Texas." That tension increased after America's entry into World War I. While the Punitive Expedition and all of the

National Guard were transferred away from the border, Americans living there still endured raids. Some were committed by rustlers, taking advantage of the opportunity to cross the river, snatch cattle, and retreat back into Mexico relatively unimpeded. As *federales* and Villistas fought each other along the border after the Punitive Expedition withdrew, hungry *soldados* from both sides stole from American herds. Carranza's control over his forces along the border was limited; commanding officers there operated as regional warlords, certain that their government couldn't risk them defecting to the Villistas. But to the border residents of South Texas, and particularly to the politically influential owners of the region's sprawling ranches and farms, the marauders' affiliations made less difference than their nationality. The U.S. Army forces remaining on the Texas border were inadequate to contain the ongoing Mexican threat; once again, the state must rely on itself for border protection rather than the federal government. That meant the Texas Rangers, and the Rangers were ready for more action.

In September 1916, there were sixty-four Texas Rangers paid for their service by the state. But now these "Regular" Rangers were often supplemented by "Special" Rangers, totaling perhaps five hundred from the first *Plan de San Diego* raids in 1915 through the end of the decade. Commissioned on an as-needed basis, Special Rangers were unpaid, but wielded the same authority as members of the regular force. Their civilian employment backgrounds mattered less than their willingness to adopt the Rangers' aggressive methods of law enforcement. According to an investigation by the *Fort Worth Star-Telegram* in 1920, Special Ranger ranks included "an undertaker, a stereotyper, a rock mason, a painter, a chamber of commerce manager, an oil mill operator, an electrical advertiser, a dentist, a barber, a wrestling referee and a retail liquor dealer." The Army had been reactive on the border, chasing raiders after they attacked. The Rangers were proactive; to them, any Mexican on the American side of the Rio Grande was always suspect. Tejano communities were especially mistrusted; even if the inhabitants weren't raiding themselves, they were probably harboring raiders, or at least had some knowledge of their whereabouts.

By the fall of 1916, Tejanos felt compelled to place lookouts outside their villages to signal if Rangers were approaching. Then everyone would scatter until the Rangers went away. But by September 28, 1916, there were still sufficient arbitrary killings for a memo to be issued from headquarters in Austin reminding Ranger captains that "a necessary qualification for a Ranger is bravery, but the killing of a man is not necessarily proof of the possession of that quality." Accordingly, known killers could no longer be recruited as Rangers without special permission from the adjutant general himself. Another memo from Austin in November ordered the Ranger captains "to prevent the execution of all Mexicans except by process of law." But Ranger companies continued administering vigilante justice, relying on their own assumptions of guilt rather than turning prisoners over to local courts for trial.

In May 1917, the Texas legislature approved expanding Regular and Special Ranger ranks to a total of one thousand. Regular Ranger salary was increased—$125 each month for captains, $60 for sergeants, $50 for privates—in hopes of attracting a better grade of recruits. Though Ranger headquarters in Austin was inundated with applications, better pay was only one attraction. Regular Rangers, and unpaid Special Rangers, too, were exempt from the wartime military draft. Beyond protecting Texas citizens, the Rangers also were charged with ferreting out German agents along the border. By early 1918, a new category of unpaid "Loyalty" Rangers was established; some five hundred fervent patriots around the state were additionally commissioned to inform on anyone they suspected to be German sympathizers.

But the Rangers' primary responsibility remained border protection. In September 1917, after Governor James Ferguson was removed from office for corruption, Lieutenant Governor William Hobby assumed the state's top office. He promptly appointed a new Ranger adjutant general—James A. Harley, a lawyer and former state senator. Hobby, concerned about ongoing reports of border brutality toward Mexicans, directed Harley to bring the Rangers under control. One of Harley's first acts was to appoint William Martin Hanson, a former deputy sheriff in South Texas and businessman in Tampico and Veracruz, as "Special Investigator for the Adjutant General of Texas." In one of his first reports about Ranger conduct on the border, Hanson, commissioned as a full-fledged Regular Rangers captain, assured his boss that "the Rangers may have made some mistakes in the past, but the conditions were such that any red-blooded human would have done just as they did in a majority of cases." But subsequent events challenged that conclusion.

><+>-0-<+><

On Christmas Day 1917, a band of Mexican raiders attacked the Lucas C. Brite Ranch thirty miles from the town of Marfa in southwest Texas. The 125,000-acre ranch boasted its own post office and the Busy Bee general store. The raiders ransacked the Busy Bee and savagely murdered an employee by hanging him from the ceiling and cutting his throat. Several other workers were wounded before the attackers gathered their stolen goods and rode away. Army cavalry and civilian posses trailed the raiders but failed to catch them. But on December 29, Ranger Captain J. M. Fox sent a message to headquarters in Austin reporting a joint Ranger-Army pursuit with better results: "I have just returned from the River where we have been chasing a bunch of 30 bandits that made raids on Mr. Bright's [sic] Ranch on the 25th and we had good luck. Got about 25 of them, and everything quite [sic] at this time. One soldier got shot but only a slight wound. With best wishes and a happy and Prosperous New Year." Fox did not offer any evidence linking the dead Mexicans to the raid, and his superiors in Austin did not ask, let alone insist, that he provide it.

But "about 25" Mexican deaths on December 29th weren't the end of it. The alleged raiders were caught and killed a few miles from two small villages separated by the Rio Grande—Pilares on the south bank and Porvenir on the north. Porvenir had about 150 inhabitants, many of them itinerant male laborers who were away for weeks or months at a time working on area ranches and farms. Some Ranger and Army officers believed that villagers of Porvenir spied on behalf of Mexican raiders, suggesting American targets for attack. Purging these suspected abettors of raids would intimidate other similarly minded Tejanos.

About 4 p.m. on January 28, eight Company B Rangers and four civilian guides rode into the southwest Texas camp of a U.S. Army cavalry contingent led by Captain Henry H. Anderson. They handed Anderson a message from Colonel George T. Langhorne, his commander at the main 14th Cavalry base in Marfa. Langhorne's note instructed his subordinate to assist the Rangers in surrounding and searching the village of Porvenir. It wasn't unusual for the Army to support the Rangers, but Anderson still called Langhorne to confirm the order. Then, while the Rangers and their guides ground-hitched their mounts and rested, Anderson summoned his men and explained their assignment. The Rangers believed a prominent border outlaw named Chico Cano was hiding in Porvenir; Anderson and some of the cavalry were to ride there with them, arriving around midnight to take Cano and any other lurking bandits by surprise. Several of the cavalrymen believed the Rangers were mistaken. Robert Keil wrote later that "some of us" had just returned from the village, where they bought six dozen fresh eggs for their camp mess: "We knew the people in Porvenir . . . we were sure they wouldn't harbor outlaws." Keil told the Rangers they would probably find only eight to ten males in Porvenir, all of them young boys or old men. The grown, able-bodied men were all away doing ranch work.

As they approached Porvenir, the soldiers were instructed to surround the village, rouse the people sleeping there, search their thatched-roof mud huts, then bring the villagers and any discovered contraband to a nearby rock bluff where the Rangers waited. The cavalrymen followed orders; the villagers insisted that no outlaws were among them, and the Americans assured them that the Rangers only wanted to talk. Keil wrote that a search of the huts yielded an old shotgun and a few butcher knives. As he'd predicted, the few males in Porvenir were either boys or old men. When the villagers were brought to them on the bluff, the Rangers told the soldiers to leave "so we can talk to them alone." When the cavalrymen were about three hundred yards away, Keil wrote, they heard "loud talking." After "perhaps ten seconds . . . it seemed that every woman down there screamed at the same time. . . . Then we heard shots, rapid shots, echoing and blending in the dark." The Rangers "tore out of there." The soldiers raced back, clicked on flashlights, and in the beams saw "a mass of bodies, but not a single movement." No women had been killed, but all fifteen boys and old men were ripped apart by gunfire. One of the women asked the soldiers to send for a priest. Captain Anderson swore to the surviving villagers that "we knew nothing of what was going to happen. If we had, we would have stopped them." The Army captain left a detail to guard Porvenir for the rest of the night. In the morning he sent another squad to help bury the dead. Keil wrote that several members of the burial detail became violently ill while handling the mangled corpses: "We only had our hands to work with, you know, and it was a terrible mess."

Henry Warren, a local Anglo schoolteacher who was friendly with the Porvenir villagers, reported the killings to local authorities. Captain Anderson complained to Colonel Langhorne. Warren's allegations were passed along to state officials, who in turn contacted Ranger adjutant general Harley. A few days after the incident, when he learned that complaints had been lodged against him and Company B, Fox sent his account to Ranger headquarters in Austin:

I beg to make a report of a fight with Mexicans on the night of the 28th. Eight Rangers in company with 4 Ranchmen was scouting on the River and found several Mexicans who stays [sic] in Mexico daytime have been coming over [the Rio Grande] and sleeping at night during this cold weather and when we gathered several of them together [we] were fired upon by other Mexicans and had a general fight. Our horses got away during the shooting and it taken some time to get them back it being dark and next morning 15 dead Mexicans were found there. Several artikles [sic] were found in there possession belonging to Mr. Bright [sic] taken when the raid was made Dec. 25th 1917.

Fox's report failed to mention the Army's presence in Porvenir that night, but Warren's complaint did. Contacted by Ranger headquarters in Austin for confirmation, Colonel Langhorne urged Adjutant General Harley to trust Fox rather than Warren, who "lived like Mexicans and urged upon them the advisability of keeping all other white men out of the community." On the other hand, Langhorne praised Ranger Captain Fox for "loyally co-operating with the troops and the civil authorities in the Big Bend, and [he] has rendered excellent service."

Harley wasn't convinced. He continued his investigation, and Warren brought his complaints to other state officials. Besides accusations about Porvenir, Warren described additional allegedly unprovoked Ranger attacks on innocent Tejanos. A few others felt encouraged to make their own complaints, and among them were individuals with impeccable records of public service. Emilio C. Forto, a former sheriff and county judge in Brownsville, wrote to Army officials that "insofar as I know, the Ranger force has never been a pacifying element among these border Countries," and that the Rangers and many Anglo citizens "do not seem to care to learn or to respect the ideals of the Mexican population." It initially seemed that the state government was unmoved by such statements: in mid-February, just two weeks after the killings in Porvenir, the ranks of Regular Rangers were increased to 165. On April 1, Ranger captain Hanson, Harley's "special agent," informed his boss that, according to Hanson's extensive network of Mexican informants, German agents were obtaining vital information "through several half-bad Mexican girls and women who come and go from Texas, and who are paid . . . with German money." Further, the possibility remained of a military alliance between Germany and Mexico: "Carranza has many German officers in his army." Strong Ranger presence on the border was deemed more vital than ever.

But Harley ordered Hanson to visit Porvenir and obtain affidavits from witnesses there, and the Army confirmed that a dozen of its cavalry troops had heard about if not directly witnessed the killings. Captain Anderson made it clear that he had believed the Rangers planned to make arrests only if any proof of collaboration with the Brite Ranch raiders was discovered in Porvenir. Fox was summoned to Austin for a mid-May meeting with Harley. Afterward, Harley fired some of the Rangers involved at Porvenir, reassigned the others, disbanded Company B, and transferred Fox to desk duty in Austin. If Harley expected the remaining Ranger captains to notice and adjust their interaction with Mexicans, he was soon disabused. On May 29 General W. A. Holsworth at the Army Southern Department in San Antonio wrote to Ranger special agent Hanson that he'd learned that W. W. Davis, captain of the Ranger company based near El Paso, planned "to post his men at two fords near Ysleta Friday night and open fire on all Mexicans in the vicinity, whether on our side or the Mexican side, on the plan that by that method he would stop what he characterizes as wholesale horse and cattle stealing. . . . He admitted that he might kill a few innocent Mexicans, but he proposed to stop stock stealing at the cost of innocent lives, if necessary. . . . Of course, I stopped that kind of nonsense, for the time being at least."

Hanson forwarded Holsworth's letter to Harley. A June 5 memo to Davis from Harley's assistant admonished the Ranger captain with the gentlest possible words: "Information has reached this office which would incline the department to believe that you were going to take heroic measures even to the shedding of innocent blood in an endeavor to stop wholesale horse and cattle stealing. . . . I trust that this information is not altogether correct. . . . In the past, some Rangers have assumed the attitude of court and jury in addition to their duties as peace officers. This is the wrong attitude absolutely. I know you will appreciate the spirit in which this letter is written."

Harley had to be circumspect in reproving Davis. J. M. Fox had responded to his Porvenir-related demotion by resigning from the Rangers and publishing a widely read open letter to Governor Hobby in a local newspaper, claiming he and the other Rangers were unfairly penalized for doing their jobs: "We have stood guard to prevent Mexican bandits from murdering the ranchmen, the women and children along this border while you slept on your feather bed of ease." A Presidio grand jury, whose jurisdiction included Porvenir, found no evidence of wrongdoing by Fox or his Ranger company. Many Texans living along or near the border were outraged at what they considered unconscionable treatment of a Ranger officer who was only protecting American citizens from Mexican predators. Most believed Fox's statement that at least some of the Porvenir dead were involved in the Brite Ranch raid, and that the Rangers only defended themselves after being attacked. Pecos County sheriff Dudley S. Barker wrote to Hobby that "for those sort of greasers you have seen fit to fire the rangers. I do not deem it a crime to kill those kind of sneaking thieves, especially when they are resisting arrest." The backlash caused political concerns for Hobby, who after taking office following his predecessor's removal was running for his own full term as governor. After winning by a comfortable margin in November, Hobby may have believed that the Ranger-related controversy was concluded. But in December, fresh complaints from a state legislator forced an even broader public examination of Ranger conduct.

José Tomás Canales, a Texas native and graduate of the University of Michigan School of Law, represented District 77 in the state legislature. Canales's district encompassed the far southern tip of Texas; during 1915–1916, he led a group of Mexican American scouts who served as agents for the U.S. Army. Canales heard often from constituents who received rough treatment from the Rangers; on one occasion when Canales felt a Ranger captain harassing Mexicans went too far, he used political connections to have the offending officer transferred to another part of the state. Then in October 1918, a relative of Canales named Santiago Tijerina was taken into custody by several Rangers and accused of participation in a border smuggling ring. Tijerina told Canales that before the Rangers released him, they tried to provoke him into fighting, so he could be shot for resisting arrest. One of the Rangers was a hulking young man named Frank Hamer, who in 1934 became part of American true crime lore for leading the ambush that killed Clyde Barrow and Bonnie Parker. When Canales complained to the local sheriff on his relative's behalf, Hamer warned Canales that he would get hurt if he criticized the Rangers again. Canales took the threat seriously enough to write Governor Hobby, asking for protection from "Haymer." Hobby passed Canales's letter on to Adjutant General Harley, who, after questioning Hamer, wrote to Canales in mid-December suggesting that everyone, including Texas Rangers like Hamer, sometimes made mistakes. Canales replied that no mistake had been made, and he would see Harley when the state legislature reconvened in Austin after the first of the year.

In January 1919, Canales introduced a bill reducing Ranger ranks to twenty-four regulars "in time of peace" and requiring recruits to have at least two years of previous experience as lawmen. Rangers would also be required to immediately turn over all prisoners to local county sheriffs. Rangers would be liable to civil suits for abuse of authority, and post individual surety bonds ranging from $5,000 to $15,000, depending on rank. In a dramatic floor speech, Canales

declared that Ranger misconduct was equivalent to German war
atrocities, "spilling the blood of innocent men who were accorded no
right under the law while in their hands." It was unlikely that the bill
would pass, at least as initially written; most of Canales's fellow legislators shared their Anglo constituents' support of the Rangers' extreme
methods of law enforcement. Canales's best hope was that the process
of debate would bring to light enough unsavory facts so that his col-
leagues would be impelled to impose at least some checks on the Rangers. He was pleased when, at the end of the month, legislators agreed
on a joint House-Senate investigative committee—now Canales could
call witnesses to tell their gruesome stories before his bill came up for
vote. Opponents of the proposed legislation were equally enthusiastic.
There were plenty of Texans eager to testify on the Rangers' behalf.

Committee hearings began on January 31. Newspaper ads invited
anyone claiming pertinent information to come forward and testify.
Eighty did; afterward, there were over 1,600 pages of hearing tran-
scripts. Canales introduced nineteen incidents of alleged Ranger
misconduct, which ranged from intimidation to cold-blooded murder,
including the killings at Porvenir. But in every instance, it came down
to witnesses' testimony versus the Rangers'. On February 19, only Canales seemed surprised when the five-member committee announced
its ambiguous conclusion: On occasion, "gross violation of both civil
and criminal laws" were committed, but the Rangers had also provided
"exemplary service. . . . From its inception, the policies of the Ranger
force have been the same, and these are now accepted as traditional,
'Get your man and keep no records except of the final results.'" The
committee report also lauded Adjutant General Harley for his efforts
to eliminate law enforcement excess by his forces. The Texas House of
Representatives endorsed the committee's findings by a vote of 87–10,
then passed a watered-down variation of the original Canales bill requiring stricter guidelines for appointing Special Rangers and that any
Ranger prisoner be immediately remanded to officials of the county

where the arrest was made. The revamped bill concluded by proposing that Ranger salaries be raised: $200 a month for captains, $125 for sergeants, and $100 for privates. On March 8, the Texas House approved the bill by a vote of 95–5. Nine days later the state senate concurred 27–1, and on March 31 Governor Hobby signed the bill into law.

There is no way to be certain how many innocent Mexicans and Tejanos were killed along the border by Texas Rangers, only that the number is gruesome. Estimates range from around 350 to 5,000 or more, though the lower number is probably more accurate. Even allowing for frequent application of their lethal brand of justice, there simply weren't enough full-time Rangers to murder thousands. But unpaid Special Rangers, who often outnumbered the Regulars, certainly killed at least as many, and civilian militias emulating the Rangers added to the awful toll. In contrast, during the dozens of border attacks attributed to the *Plan de San Diego*, Anglo raid victims are estimated at seventeen dead and twenty-five wounded.

Texas state representative José Canales did not seek reelection after his term expired in 1920, and the Rangers went back to work—though not as many. Harley disbanded three Ranger companies "due to the fact that the war emergency for Border protection no longer exists," reducing the Regular Rangers to about seventy. It was a convenient excuse to pare back the Ranger roster, both to eliminate undesirable members and ease the strain imposed on the state budget by increased salaries. But Harley was mistaken if he believed that Armistice Day in November 1918 ended tension along the southern U.S. border. If anything, conditions there were even more volatile; America still faced potential war with Mexico.

Showdown at Nogales

Venustiano Carranza's long-sought time of political triumph began in January 1917 with the grudging departure from Mexico of the Punitive Expedition, extended through the adoption of a new Mexican constitution that mandated progressive policies, and climaxed in May 1917 when crowds filled the Mexico City streets, celebrating his inauguration as their democratically elected president. Then it ended. The ragged supporters who cheered Carranza as he took the oath of office expected immediate change in their lives, the land redistribution and higher wages and health care and education that the new constitution mandated and the new president promised to deliver. But Carranza didn't. Mexico's economy was in particular disarray; loan payments to foreign lenders were due, but the government had no money to meet them, or to pay, feed, and supply the soldiers still fighting Emiliano Zapata in the south and Pancho Villa in the north. The only reliable source of government income was taxes paid by the same wealthy *hacendados* whose lands Carranza pledged to seize and redistribute among the working class and poor. Carranza needed their money, so he couldn't take their land. Like Porfirio Díaz before him, Carranza sought the support of Mexico's wealthy upper class, earning it by guaranteeing they could keep their vast holdings so long as they paid their taxes and vowed to increase crop production, since some of Mexico's more arid regions were suffering food shortages.

A more empathetic leader might have explained to the masses why economic concerns must take temporary precedence over social reform. But Carranza never felt obligated to explain himself; he was president, he knew best, and dissent would not be tolerated. The *hacendados*, appreciative of their reprieve, made certain that Carranza never lacked assurances of his sagacity. The poor found their hard lives unchanged; the sweet promises had come to nothing. Their sense of betrayal was shared by Álvaro Obregón, newly retired from government service and living as a gentleman farmer in his home state of Sonora. Unlike the aristocratic Carranza, Obregón was descended from peasants. Early in life he was a farm laborer, a millworker, and a door-to-door salesman before entering local politics and eventually rising to lead Sonora state forces in the rebellion against Victoriano Huerta before aligning with Carranza. Ever mindful of his own background, Obregón wholeheartedly embraced the new constitution's promise of land reform, and believed it should be carried out no matter what initial economic havoc might result. Obregón had proven himself to be perhaps Mexico's most gifted general, but he did not choose to rebel against Carranza as Villa and Zapata had done. He preferred nonviolent means; Carranza's presidency was constitutionally limited to a single four-year term. Obregón decided that he would run for president in 1920, and, if elected, fulfill the progressive pledges that Carranza ignored.

If Carranza had any notion of Obregón's plan, it wasn't among his immediate concerns. Besides salvaging the national economy, Carranza was focused on finishing off Villa. So long as the scoundrel remained at large in northern Mexico, a significant number of the country's poor would embrace him as their champion. Had he known how much outside sources were encouraging his enemy, Carranza would have been even more obsessed with ridding himself of Villa.

The Punitive Expedition's withdrawal in January 1917 was a setback for Villa. It was his plan that originally lured the gringos into Mexico; their ongoing presence was his best propaganda tool against Carranza. When the Americans left, Villa could no longer use them as an example of Carranza's alleged toadyism toward the hated *yanquis*. The proposed new constitution was another blow. It promised peace, land, and relative prosperity for all Mexicans—how would the common people perceive Villa as a hero if he opposed a national government giving them all that? But Villa couldn't stop fighting Carranza, or even quietly lay down his arms in the belief that his hated foe would allow him to retire to some distant place and live in peace. The enmity between them was too great. Given any opportunity, Villa would kill Carranza, and he realized that Carranza would do the same.

Villa always lashed out when frustrated, and this time was no different. With his army still numbering several thousand, he fought a large federal force led by General Francisco Murguía in central Chihuahua. The battle seemed to favor the *federales* when Villa's cavalry retreated, but it was a ruse. As the government forces raced in pursuit, they were flanked by other onrushing Villistas; Murguía barely escaped. Six hundred federal troops were captured; Villa had them executed. To conserve ammunition, he ordered the condemned men to be lined up in tightly packed rows, so that as many as five at a time would be killed with each shot.

Germany was impressed by his bloody success. When Carranza didn't immediately accept their alliance offer of money, munitions, and potentially regained territory in exchange for joining them in war against America, the Germans approached Villa with substantially the same proposal. Border intelligence agent Zach Lamar Cobb wired the U.S. State Department on March 1, 1917, that he had troubling information from Mexican informers. They warned that during February, Villa had claimed he was going to help the Germans "whip the U.S.," and in return "obtain Texas, Arizona and California back for Mexico."

Nothing ever came of Villa's boast, and it's not known whether Germany made a firm offer or simply sounded him out. But during the first months of 1917, the Germans clearly considered Villa to be a possible alternative to Carranza.

So did powerful Americans. Carranza's new alliance with Mexican *hacendados* did not extend to U.S. ranchers, farmers, and bankers with substantial investments south of the border. Their loans to Mexico were not repaid, but they were dunned for taxes on their holdings by the Mexican government. American business leaders had supported Carranza over more rough-edged revolutionaries, and felt betrayed after he became president and, in their opinion, turned against them. In early 1917, Villa was contacted by Charles Hunt, an American cattle dealer along both sides of the border: U.S. senator Albert Fall of New Mexico wished to discreetly get in touch with him. Fall, who called for American intervention in Mexico even before the Punitive Expedition was dispatched, constantly badgered President Wilson and his administration to take a firmer hand with Carranza. Once assured Villa was open to contact, Fall gave Hunt a lengthy letter to deliver to the Villista leader. It described Carranza as "a tyrant dragging down the Mexican nation and people" and offered a proposition: If Villa would promise to protect all American lives and property in the region, Fall and certain associates would provide Villa with the financing necessary to establish "a stable government especially in northern Mexico," specifically a new nation including the Mexican states of Baja California, Sonora, Chihuahua, Coahuila, Nuevo León, Tamaulipas, and at least portions of Veracruz. One of the financial backers would be America's Standard Oil Company.

Villa would almost certainly have been interested, but the letter never reached him. Hunt asked an intermediary to take Villa the letter, but the go-between passed it along instead to an agent of the American government. It was soon reprinted in the *New York Times*, and Fall was left to explain to Secretary of State Lansing that all he'd intended was to ascertain if Villa no longer considered himself an enemy of America.

It was fortunate for Fall and his co-conspirators that their plans fell through so quickly; only a few weeks after the letter was published in the *Times*, Villa clashed again with General Murguía, and this time it was the Villistas who were routed. Villa escaped with only a few hundred followers. It was hard finding volunteers or forcing conscriptions to rebuild his forces. When Villa approached villages, men ran away and hid, in part because he could no longer claim they would fight Americans instead of fellow Mexicans, and also because of his growing reputation for needless cruelty. By early 1918, Villa's rebellion against Carranza was reduced to a grudging standoff. The *federales* couldn't catch him so long as he stayed north in Chihuahua, and Villa wasn't strong enough to move south on Mexico City. Carranza still intended to eliminate Villa, but there was a more pressing military concern along the border: American troops were crossing into Mexico again.

⯈⊷⊶○⊷⊶⯇

Edwin Neville's ranch on the north bank of the Rio Grande was a low-budget operation. Neville and his family worked the land along with a few Mexicans. Their closest neighbors were the impoverished villagers of Porvenir six miles to the south. On March 25, 1918, it was probably the ranch's location that attracted an attack by some fifty Mexican raiders eager to avenge January's slaughter in Porvenir by the Texas Rangers. The Nevilles were the closest American target. The fight was one-sided and brief. Though Edwin Neville escaped, the raiders killed his son and the family housekeeper. Ranch livestock was taken, and everything in the ranch house as well—cans of food, clothing, even sheets and blankets from the beds. Then the raiders rode back across the river into Mexico.

On March 27, Captain Henry Anderson, the same officer who was present at the Porvenir massacre, took ninety-six members of the

8th Cavalry across the river, following the tracks left by the bandits. Unsurprisingly, they led to the village of Pilares; in his official report, Anderson noted that Pilares "long had the reputation of being a bandit stronghold." Rather than typical adobe huts, most of the shelters comprising the village were "canvas, old boards, and other odds and ends, and were scarcely habitable." As the U.S. cavalry approached, they came under fire from Mexicans they assumed to be the Neville raiders. The superior firepower of the Americans drove the Mexicans back. They were soon in full retreat with the cavalry hard on their heels. The chase went eleven miles farther into Mexico before a few of the Americans riding in front wheeled, raced back to Anderson, and reported at least "five hundred Mexicans"—*federales*—were approaching. There seemed no question that they were ready to fight. Anderson pulled his men back to Pilares. There they found "approximately two hundred rounds of ammunition . . . arms known to be taken from the American side of the river in the [Neville] and previous raids, dynamite, some of it in the form of a grenade, saddles and other horse equipment. Clothing was found which was known to have belonged to Mr. Neville and other Americans." There were also items stolen during the December 25, 1917, raid on the Brite Ranch.

With the *federales* closing in, Anderson ordered that Pilares be burned, "excepting one hut occupied by an old Mexican woman." With the hovels in flames, the American troops retreated across the Rio Grande. Anderson estimated that between thirty and thirty-five bandits were killed, with U.S. losses limited to "one private killed, two horses slightly injured."

The Mexican government made immediate, vigorous protests—this was another example of American forces invading Mexico without permission, arbitrarily killing citizens, razing an entire village, and then running away from Mexican federal troops who understandably wanted to stop the carnage. In light of previous U.S. offenses, the Mexican government believed the assault to be a preliminary to yet another American incursion similar to the Punitive Expedition. Mexico demanded an apology, and assurances that such an unauthorized attack would never happen again.

Secretary of War Baker ordered a full investigation. On May 20, Colonel W. J. Glasgow concluded that the 8th Cavalry's mission into Mexico and subsequent burning of Pilares "was a measure of military necessity." With World War I still raging, Baker particularly wanted to avoid additional problems with Mexico. He issued a new order: All Army pursuit of Mexican bandits must terminate at the border "except in cases involving the rescue of American citizens who have been captured by bandits and whose rescue by the forces of the Mexican government is open to serious doubt." Mexico wasn't satisfied. Its border forces stayed on alert; even the presence of a few American troops anywhere on the north side of the border was considered evidence of impending invasion. Whether with Carranza's approval or on their own volition, *soldados* began taking potshots at American soldiers on the other side of the river or anywhere else within range. Often, the Americans fired back. Besides individual safety, a greater threat was obvious; if, at any point and place, sniping evolved into full-fledged fighting, then outright war between the U.S. and Mexico still might erupt.

By July 10, the problem escalated to the point that Secretary of State Lansing felt obliged to make a formal, written request of Secretary of War Baker. Mexican officials continued complaining to the State Department about American soldiers firing on Mexican troops, and Lansing was tired of it: "I have the honor to suggest that the orders given to the officers in command of the forces along the Mexican border be so modified as to prevent American soldiers from . . . firing across the border into Mexico, without specific orders from the War Department." Five days later, Baker sent his equally formal reply: "With regard to the question of preventing soldiers firing across the border into Mexico without specific orders in each case from the War

Department, it would be most undesirable from a military standpoint to instruct our men that when they are being shot at themselves from the Mexican border they were not to return fire, but to ask the War Department for permission to do so."

Cross-border sniping continued by both armies. During August, tension mounted. American border agents reported rumors of German military advisors joining Mexican troops in Sonora, just below the border with Arizona. In Europe, Germany was losing ground against the Allies; the Sonoran reports might indicate a last-ditch German agreement with Carranza and an imminent attack by Mexico on the U.S. Mexican leaders had fresh concerns of their own. Villa was known to have somehow gained enough recruits to launch yet another campaign against the government. Villa's most likely first strike would be against Chihuahua City, since he'd had previous success there. In anticipation of that attack, substantial numbers of *federales* in northern Mexico were sent to central Chihuahua, and to other places where resurgent Villistas might attack. This left greatly depleted ranks of *soldados* in place on Mexico's immediate side of the border. These remaining defenders understood that they must resist any attempted American incursion with particular ferocity. On August 27, the inevitable clash occurred, at one of the few places remaining on the border where Mexicans and Americans coexisted in relative friendship and peace.

<hr />

Nogales, Sonora, and Nogales, Arizona, were two of the many adjacent, "bifurcated" cities dotting the 1,900-mile border, and it was appropriate that they shared a name. The two communities mingled so freely, sharing not only a hybrid economy but culture, that they became jointly known as Ambos Nogales, "Both Nogales." The border itself ran along a main downtown street, with customs officials kept busy inspecting shipments of goods and produce crossing in both directions. When widespread Mexican revolution erupted in 1910, many refugees sought sanctuary on Nogales's American side, where residents were so welcoming that the basement of its Masonic Temple was converted at local expense into a school for the newly arrived Mexican children.

Twice, Ambos Nogales was rocked by revolutionary battle. In March 1913, Constitutionalists led by Sonora native Álvaro Obregón soundly defeated federal troops; rather than give themselves over to the rebels, the losers simply stepped across the border and surrendered to the American military, which had established a camp there. In November 1915, Pancho Villa and his battered forces, in full flight after their defeat at Agua Prieta, passed near Nogales and fired at U.S. troops on the American side of the border. The U.S. soldiers shot back, and the Mexican federal troops controlling Nogales also opened fire. In the confusion, the Mexicans killed one American soldier and the U.S. forces killed two *federales*. After the Villistas were driven off, commanders of the American and Mexican federal troops expressed mutual regret for the accidental deaths.

Over the next few years, relations between the twin cities deteriorated somewhat, strained less by unhappiness among neighbors than by Mexico's national resentment of the Punitive Expedition and regional border tensions. Ambos Nogales crossings remained frequent, and occasionally life-threatening; after three incidents when American guards shot and killed Mexican nationals for allegedly ignoring orders to halt (December 1917, March and June 1918), the two cities' mayors agreed to temporarily supplement widely separated border markers with a short length of chain link fence in the busiest downtown area, less as a barrier than a reminder to anyone leaving one country for the other to immediately heed instructions from guards on either side.

On August 27, 1918, about 850 American soldiers were stationed on the Arizona side of the Nogales border, members of either the 35th Infantry or the 10th Cavalry, the famed Buffalo Soldiers. The Americans estimated that between six and seven hundred *federales* guarded the Mexican side, not realizing that most of those troops had recently been transferred to other parts of Sonora in anticipation of raids by Villa. As usual, both armies had minimal downtown presence, a few soldiers on duty at the downtown crossings and customs points. Until midafternoon, everything was normal. The typically broiling summer weather was enervating; customs officers sweated as they inspected the contents of wagons, estimating the value of their contents and totting up the border tax that was due. A handful of American and Mexican soldiers on guard, separated by the border markers and perhaps fifty yards, observed from patches of minimal shade. There had been recent stories in Nogales's American newspapers that German agents were suspected of using a downtown crossing to move back and forth between the U.S. and Mexico, but such rumors had been rife for months. According to a local historian, that summer on the American side of Nogales "everything was war and Germans." The American soldiers were on the alert for spies.

The unidentified man who shuffled toward the downtown crossing from the U.S. side just after 4 p.m. was clearly Mexican, not German, but he wore a coat despite the terrible heat and seemed suspicious to the Americans. When U.S. immigration inspector Arthur Barber shouted, "*Alto!* Stop," the pedestrian hesitated, apparently uncertain what to do. Francisco Gallegos, an immigration official on the Mexican side, gestured for him to keep coming. When the man did, border guard W. H. Klint, an Army private, raised his rifle and fired a warning shot into the air. Several Mexican guards fired in response, aiming at the American soldier rather than the sky. Klint was hit several times and died soon afterward. Barber had a revolver and returned fire at the federal soldiers, while the man attempting to cross fled down the street. He was never seen again. No one on either side attempted to catch him; they were too busy shooting at each other.

Félix Peñaloza, the mayor of Nogales, Sonora, was in his office a few blocks from the scene. When he heard the first shots, he tied a white handkerchief to his walking cane, which he brandished as he approached the crossing point, shouting at every step for his Mexican compatriots to stop firing. The mayor was still fifty yards away when he was killed by a shot from the American side. For the next hour, the volume of fire from both sides increased. As more American soldiers arrived, they assumed the foes shooting from windows in downtown buildings were *federales*. In fact, most were Mexican civilians, utilizing whatever arms they had on hand to reinforce the handful of government troops on their side of Nogales. They shot enthusiastically, but not accurately. Three U.S. soldiers and one civilian died. The fire from American troops mowed down many Mexicans, killing thirty and wounding seventy according to later reports from Mexico, but accounting for at least five times that many dead by subsequent U.S. estimates.

The body count climbed until about 5 p.m., when a Mexican official sent a message suggesting a truce—he would raise a white flag on his side of the line if the Americans would do the same. Lieutenant Colonel Fred Herman, commanding the American troops, replied that if the Mexicans didn't raise a white flag within ten minutes, his forces would burn the Mexican side of Nogales. Soon afterward, the white flag waved from a window in the Mexican customs house and firing on both sides gradually died down. At 6:30 negotiators met at the U.S. consul's office on the Mexican side. They agreed to a cease-fire until the next morning; by then Plutarco Elías Calles, governor of Sonora, and General DeRosey Cabell, commander of the U.S. Army's camp at Fort Huachuca, Arizona, would have arrived. Hopefully the governor and general could keep the bloody fight from resuming.

The U.S. troops spent the night replenishing ammunition and resting; the civilians who comprised most of their opposition felt themselves less restrained by the cease-fire agreement. Sporadic shots peppered the American side until sunrise. Calles and Cabell met at dawn; probably because the Sonoran governor acknowledged that overreaction from Mexican border guards initiated the fighting, he and Cabell quickly agreed that firing on both sides would stop immediately. The misunderstanding, no matter how regrettable and deadly, must not be allowed to escalate into something wider. Then Calles and Cabell ordered their respective sides to stand down but not fall back; each was not entirely certain the other could be trusted. The cease-fire held until 10 p.m., when thirty to forty shots were fired at some American troops standing watch on a hill. Though one of the soldiers, a private, was slightly wounded, the U.S. forces held their fire. By the next afternoon, the injured private was sufficiently recovered to retaliate by shooting and wounding a Mexican border guard. He was disciplined, and each side assured the other that the gunfire was unauthorized and would be contained. Afterward, Ambos Nogales was quiet.

Calles and Cabell agreed that they must resolve the crisis before their national governments stepped in and began issuing provocative ultimatums. Their solution was to replace the short, temporary border fence through downtown Ambos Nogales with a sturdy two-mile-long, six-foot-high fence bristling with barbed wire. Work began immediately, and the structure was in place by fall. There is no record of who paid the $5,000 construction costs. There were no more significant border clashes until the following summer, when Pancho Villa attempted his most audacious assault since the March 1916 raid on Columbus.

CHAPTER TWENTY-THREE

➤–◆➤–○–◄◆–◄

Villa's Last Attack

Summer 1917 found Pancho Villa's fortunes at an especially low ebb. Defeats had reduced his followers from several thousand to a few hundred. This remaining force was too sparse to fight major battles, yet Villa couldn't attract new recruits to rebuild his army without significant victories that reestablished his reputation as the common people's invincible champion. No one willingly joined a loser. But if Villa was no longer formidable, he was still resilient and willing to take great risks. The *federales* believed they had Villa bottled up in Chihuahua; he would strike where they least expected him, and in a surprising manner.

Two months after being sworn in as Mexico's president, Venustiano Carranza fell into a daily routine. This included frequent horseback rides in one of Mexico City's public parks, accompanied by a single aide. Villa hatched a plan to sneak almost one thousand miles south with one hundred of his men, snatch Carranza from the saddle, and rush his prisoner to the state of Morelos just below the capital, where Zapata remained in rebellion. Mexican federal troops were notoriously disorganized; in the days, perhaps weeks, it would take them to mount a rescue attempt, Villa would put Carranza on public trial for betraying the Mexican people. The one-sided process would conclude with a predictable verdict and execution. Mexicans would be reminded that Pancho Villa was unconquerable. Thousands of patriots would clamor for the privilege of joining him. Despite his other flaws, Villa never aimed low. He never reached Mexico City, either. Even with a limited entourage, Villa couldn't travel anonymously. Everyone knew what he looked like, and Villa was too vain to don a disguise or at least shave his trademark mustache. He and his Villistas had to pick their way along back roads, avoiding federal troops and villages dominated by Carranza sympathizers. This wasn't difficult in Chihuahua, where they knew every mountain and valley, but became increasingly difficult as they moved farther south. Many villages had *defenses sociales*, armed militias that fended off unwelcome intruders. Villa's progress slowed to a crawl. Some of his men grew discouraged and deserted. After a few frustrating weeks, Villa gave up and returned to Chihuahua.

He was despondent enough to write to Francisco Murguía, the federal general who'd reduced him to his current depleted state, and whose forces now hounded Villa's all across Chihuahua. The letters were a mishmash of recycled propaganda, self-pity, accusations, and self-aggrandizement. Villa asked his rival "to listen to the voice of your conscience" and switch sides. Serving Carranza was the equivalent of vassalage to the gringos: "Ask yourself what the tremendous influx of American money into our country means." Alternatively, Villa suggested he might be willing to join Murguía: "I could be of use to my country, if not as a general, even as a soldier." When Murguía didn't respond, Villa taunted that the general was "incapable of capturing me. . . . I will not write to you more."

It was November before Villa stirred himself into action. With winter approaching, his forces needed access to supplies. The Villistas couldn't take any substantial Mexican border point of entry, so Villa marched his remaining troops back to Ojinaga, held as usual by an understrength federal garrison since its adjacent Texas town of Presidio was relatively insignificant. Villa had taken Ojinaga before, and did so again on November 14. Rather than defend the town, the *federales* fled across the Rio Grande into Presidio; the U.S. Army forces there sent them on to El Paso, where they were repatriated to Juárez and rejoined the Mexican army. To Villa's surprise, the Americans simply shut down the Presidio entry point instead of trading with him—didn't *yanquis* always want money? But they spurned Villa's, and he didn't have enough *soldados* to fight his way in and take what he wanted. Villa soon abandoned Ojinaga; had he stayed, Murguía's federal forces could have cornered him there.

In the end it was outside events rather than his own initiative that provided Villa fresh opportunity. By the spring of 1918, it became obvious to the common people of Mexico that the vaunted new, progressive constitution meant nothing. Like many of his predecessors, President Carranza aligned himself with the rich *hacendados*. There was no sweeping land reform or new public education programs or health care. Carranza made no attempt to explain why these promises had yet to be kept; he took it as a personal insult that the public didn't trust him. The economy remained stagnant; federal troops sometimes went unpaid and often were hungry. Unrest in the ranks was especially sweeping in Mexico's northern states, distant from the capital and beyond supervision and control by the national government. Many federal officers in the north preyed on peasants, confiscating food and horses and money. Their victims sought a savior, and Villa took advantage. Even the principled Murguía had difficulty controlling his troops, and Villa had little regard for other regional federal commanders, who he believed were more focused on lining their pockets than defending towns.

Villa emerged from the mountains where he'd been hiding, visiting villages, assuring everyone that he shared their outrage and was ready to fight for them. Once again, he began attracting volunteers. Villista ranks grew for the first time in over a year, and during the summer word spread that Villa would soon lead a mighty army back into battle against the corrupt Carrancistas. The possibility concerned military leaders in Mexico City enough to pull troops back from the border to defend the northern state capitals, especially Chihuahua City, which they considered Villa's most obvious target. The numbers were still against him—seventeen thousand federal troops scattered among the northern states against perhaps three thousand Villistas, though that number was growing—but Villa's men were eager to fight and the *federales* weren't. Compared to federal troops, the Villistas were relatively well armed and fed. To raise the necessary money, Villa "taxed" foreign businesses in Chihuahua, whose owners chose payment to him over the remote chance that federal troops would protect their property if Villa attacked them. Villa didn't neglect Mexican-owned *rancheros* and businesses, either—these were dunned for loans that had little prospect of repayment. Villa's new recruits were delighted; they had food and shoes and guns and ammunition, too, the latter in part thanks to the president of Mexico. Carranza, determined to no longer depend on foreign sources of supply, had built his long-desired ammunition factories in northern Mexico. The ammunition manufactured there was issued to federal soldiers; many who'd been too long without pay sold the bullets to agents for Villa.

Villa marched out to fight in November. His early movements indicated an assault on Juárez; federal troops rushed to reinforce the city. As soon as they were there, Villa attacked and occupied key rail hub Villa Ahumada, eighty miles away. He blocked the tracks for a week, then withdrew. The *federales* were left to wonder where he'd strike next. They still expected him to attack Chihuahua City, but in January Villa assaulted Parral, the same town on the Chihuahua-Durango border where Punitive Expedition troops had fled a mob of *federales* and civilians two and a half years earlier. Federal troops defending Parral put up a spirited fight before the better-armed and -fed Villistas wore them down. With the conquests of Villa Ahumada and Parral, Villa again controlled most of Chihuahua.

It wasn't enough. Heroes gain support with victories, but to retain it they must continue winning. The recent news that Emiliano Zapata had been lured into an ambush and assassinated by *federales* in Morelos reminded Villa that letting down his guard could be fatal. Even a short interval of laurel-resting, time taken in the wake of recent success to plot out long-term plans, was risky. An old ally argued otherwise. Three years earlier, Felipe Ángeles had left Villa's service when his leader blamed him for defeats at the hands of Obregón. Now he was back, urging caution as he always had. Ángeles advised Villa to move farther south into Durango, and build a wider rebel coalition than was possible fighting and recruiting exclusively in Chihuahua. Villa wasn't persuaded. There was another tempting target in Chihuahua. In 1914, Villa's victory at Juárez earned him respect throughout Mexico. It would work again.

>·‹•›·O·‹•›·‹

In June 1919, federal troops in Chihuahua were led by General Jesús Agustín Castro, who'd recently replaced General Murguía, and whose chief characteristic as a commander was reluctance to fight. Instead of sending forces to seek out Villa, Castro reinforced a few important towns and ordered their commanders not to venture out. This passive strategy played perfectly into Villa's new plan. He brought his army up toward Juárez without risk of federal attack from the flanks or rear. The Villistas advanced confidently; on June 7 they were spotted southeast of Juárez, bypassing Chihuahua City. Castro knew where they were. So did General James B. Erwin, the American commander in El Paso. Erwin's informants advised him that four thousand Villistas were coming in two groups, with the larger led by Villa and the smaller commanded by Ángeles. By the time the two rebel wings converged seven miles southeast of Juárez on June 12, Erwin had requested instructions from the Army's Southern Department command in San Antonio. An attack on Juárez was imminent; if the fighting threatened to spill across the river into El Paso, how should American forces respond? Would the edict forbidding American troops from crossing into

Mexico remain in place? The reply came mostly in code, which is still part of the official record. But there was no code used for the last line: "Should more troops seem desirable ask for them."

The rebels blocked railroad tracks into Juárez, effectively cutting off the city. All day on June 14 the rebel army maneuvered into place, opposed only by a few skirmishers. Otherwise, General Francisco González, the federal commander in Juárez, followed orders and waited. Just before midnight, the Villistas charged. Within a few hours, most of the *federales* had retreated behind the walls of Fort Hidalgo, a compound on the hills just outside town. The rebels controlled Juárez itself. At 4 a.m., González ordered a counterattack. It was effective; the Villistas were caught unawares because they apparently thought they'd already won. The rebels were driven back to the outskirts of the city, and needed some time to regroup. But at 4:30 p.m. they attacked again; the federal troops stubbornly stood their ground, and the battle became an extended, grinding process of street fighting. Bullets flew everywhere, including across the river into El Paso.

As soon as the first shots of the Villistas' initial attack were fired around 11:30 p.m., General Erwin dispatched troops to the American side of the international bridges and ordered four artillery batteries to prepare to fire across the river. He informed his superiors in San Antonio that "everything [is] ready for crossing the boundary should it be ordered by me." As fighting continued into the early hours of June 15, Erwin began receiving reports that "shots from the other side of the river [are] coming in to El Paso." The American general sent "experienced officers" to determine who was firing these shots—Villistas or *federales*? They reported that it was impossible to tell. But when the fighting slacked off near dawn, so did the bullets into El Paso. Around 7 a.m., Erwin decided the immediate crisis was past and ordered the American soldiers back to their barracks. When the Villistas attacked again that afternoon, the U.S. troops returned to the river crossing points. Erwin received reports of one El Paso civilian being killed by a stray shot, and several wounded; hundreds of citizens perched on downtown roofs, watching the battle a few hundred yards on the other side of the river. Then an officer from an artillery battery sent word one of his troopers had been killed and another wounded by shots from the south. Earlier in the day, General González had sent Erwin assurances that his troops were ordered not to fire in any direction that threatened Americans. Erwin concluded that the American casualties were inflicted by Villistas: "The time had come for me to act and carry out my orders." Erwin notified González that American forces were about to intervene. Then, at 9:23 p.m., he sent 3,600 troops across the river.

The *federales* quickly broke off fighting and moved aside, leaving the Americans a clear path to the Villistas. A wave of U.S. cavalry and infantry rushing across the river forced the rebels back; their retreat quickly escalated into full flight. Some Villistas made a stand at a racetrack on the eastern edge of Juárez. Concentrated fire from American artillery across the river blasted them out, and from there the U.S. cavalry turned the rebels southwest, into what Erwin described as "a barren and desolate country." In the process, the pursuers overran a Villista supply camp, capturing "a large number of horses, mules, saddles, and arms of various kinds, including one machine gun." Only unanticipated difficulty negotiating a warren of irrigation ditches outside town prevented the American forces from completely cutting off the fleeing rebels. Sergeant Thomas Snead, a veteran of the Punitive Expedition, recalled years later that outside Juárez "there was no real engagement. . . . The Villistas jumped off their horses and ran afoot, dropping their guns." Villa himself escaped, choosing self-preservation over a potentially glorious last stand. Erwin reported that he could not provide a reliable enemy casualty count because "many of the dead and most of the wounded [were] removed before day[light] by Villista sympathizers in Juarez." Two American soldiers were killed and ten wounded. Since there was no further threat to El Paso, the U.S. troops marched back across the river, confident, according to General Erwin, that they'd put "the fear of American forces into the hearts of this Villa band."

The intervention lasted only twelve hours and left Juárez in federal hands, but the Americans received no thanks from Mexico. General González insisted that "I did not and do not think the crossing of the American forces was necessary for the defeat of the Villa forces, as my forces defended the town most bravely." President Carranza snarled that America had grossly violated Mexican sovereignty. But rebel General Ángeles, who'd tried to persuade Villa not to attack Juárez, believed that the Villistas would have taken the city within another few hours if U.S. troops hadn't intervened.

➤━◆➤━○━◆━┥◄

Villa was next seen in early July. A railroad manager in Chihuahua reported that Villa "has not more than 350 men, who are badly demoralized, poorly clothed, [and] with practically no ammunition." Most of his surviving followers had deserted after the debacle at Juárez. Recruitment or conscription was virtually impossible—Villa was now a pariah in even the most remote villages of Chihuahua. He led his remaining force south into Durango, hoping for more propitious conditions there. But his reputation was tarnished further by a failed siege of the state's similarly named capital. When Villa ordered some of his troops to destroy railroad tracks outside town, they balked, and, as they hesitated, trainloads of *federales* roared in. The Villistas were routed. Villa and those followers who didn't desert straggled back to Chihuahua, where more federal troops waited. President Carranza knew that this was his best opportunity yet to rid himself of his longtime nemesis. The hesitant General Gómez was bypassed; Carranza ordered General Joaquín Amaro, experienced and aggressive, to pursue Villa wherever he went. Villa didn't have enough remaining forces to stand and fight, or sources of supplies and temporary shelter if he kept running. Amaro was tenacious. By spring 1920, it seemed inevitable that Villa would soon be brought to bay.

Villa had faced the apparent end before—in 1912, standing before Huerta's firing squad; in 1915 at Agua Prieta, when his last-ditch cavalry charge failed; at Guerrero five months later, when, grievously wounded, he was laboriously carried away by loyalists, with American cavalry from the Punitive Expedition in close pursuit. Each time, through some near-miraculous combination of unexpected events and luck, he survived. Now it happened again.

In June 1919, Álvaro Obregón announced his intention to run for the Mexican presidency when Carranza's term expired in 1920. He expected Carranza's support; Obregón's military talents had been crucial to Carranza's gaining office—now the favor must be returned. But Carranza endorsed another candidate, someone who would continue the nonprogressive policies that Obregón opposed. Obregón chose to run anyway. With Zapata dead and Villa disgraced, Mexico's common people rallied to Obregón as their champion. He actively solicited their votes, describing his own hardscrabble background and swearing that, once in office, nothing would prevent him from working diligently to improve their lives. If necessary, he'd fight for them, too—Obregón's empty right sleeve testified to his battlefield experience.

In April 1920, when it seemed likely Carranza would charge Obregón with treason rather than see his policies repudiated at the polls in June, Obregón and his supporters revolted. Many federal troops, recalling Obregón's inspired military leadership, joined the rebellion. Others, however reluctantly, remained loyal to the Carranza government. To Villa's immense relief, the *federales* broke off pursuing him to fight among themselves. He was free to make his next move, whatever it might be.

Pancho Villa always thought of something.

CHAPTER TWENTY-FOUR

Afterward

In May 1920, with Álvaro Obregón's forces bearing down on Mexico City, Venustiano Carranza fled, intending to temporarily reestablish his government in Veracruz as he did in 1914 when Villa and Zapata drove him from the capital. This time it didn't work; on May 21, pursuers overtook Carranza and murdered him in a village along the way. Obregón announced that democratic elections would be held in September; he did not want to assume the presidency by force. In a bow to his inevitable election, Mexico's congress appointed Obregón's fellow Sonoran Adolfo de la Huerta to serve as interim president for four months. One of de la Huerta's objectives was to finally bring peace to Mexico's northern states and the U.S.-Mexico border—this would hopefully incline America to offer full diplomatic recognition to the Obregón administration. A critical step was coming to terms with Pancho Villa.

Villa was ready to stop fighting, and after considerable negotiation agreed in July to lay down his arms in exchange for amnesty, a 25,000-acre hacienda in Durango just below Parral, a generous annual stipend, and a bodyguard of fifty loyalists whose salaries would be paid by the Mexican government. Obregón thought execution would have been more appropriate, but did not overturn the agreement in November after he was sworn in as Mexico's president. Even the twenty-one Villista prisoners brought to the U.S. by the Punitive Expedition regained their freedom; in April 1921 a judge dismissed the charges against them, ruling that at the time of their actions the U.S. and Mexico were in a virtual state of war.

Obregón took office at the end of November 1920 with the intention of doing great things. He announced a plan to nationalize all properties over 100,000 acres, divide them into small parcels, and redistribute these among the common people. But some of the great landowners began breaking their holdings into smaller units, assigning their ownership to family members or business partners, and claiming exemption from nationalization under the Mexican president's own new rule. He was frustrated, but so were the American business leaders whose loans and investments were critical to the Mexican economy. They considered Obregón's plan suspiciously similar to the actions of the new Bolshevik government in Russia. To placate them, Obregón pledged not to nationalize any American oil companies. He had to support the same *hacendados* and U.S. investors in Mexico that he'd just sworn to diminish, since their property taxes remained his government's most consistent source of income. Obregón realized that his presidency was uncomfortably similar to Carranza's, vulnerable to overthrow by a populist rival. He put down a revolt by his finance minister, but in 1923 a familiar antagonist reemerged.

Pancho Villa was unsuited to quiet retirement. He granted interviews to any journalists who requested them, at first bragging about the fine things he was bringing to the peasants living on and around his property, above all good schools so their children would be well educated. Villa soon couldn't resist making more grandiose claims. In early 1923, he mused to reporters that he might run for governor of Durango, or even president of Mexico after Obregón's constitutionally mandated single term expired: "I do not believe that anyone has the support that [I have]." Villa predicted that even old foes in the federal army would take his side, because "I am a real soldier. . . . I can mobilize 40,000 men in 40 minutes." When Villa visited Mexico City

States, an exalted rank he shared only with George Washington. Pershing could have run for, and probably won, any political office, but chose to remain in the military. In 1921 he was appointed Army chief of staff, and served in that capacity until his retirement from active duty in 1924. Pershing did not share this distinguished postwar career with Nita Patton. In early 1919, while still serving overseas, Pershing, overwhelmed by the attentions of starstruck European women, wrote Nita that "the feeling" was gone, and they should not continue their engagement until it rekindled. Nita returned her diamond engagement ring, and rebuffed Pershing's subsequent pleas for reconciliation. She never married. In 1946, Pershing married a painter he'd met nearly thirty years earlier in France. General of the Armies of the United States John J. Pershing died of congestive heart failure on July 15, 1948.

><+>-O-<+>-<

Though national leaders changed, tension on the U.S.-Mexican border remained. Historian Arnoldo de León believes "that by 1920 there were irradicable hard feelings on both sides. There was some middle ground, mostly through interracial marriages. But that didn't stop the Anglo stereotyping of Mexicans as a race, or Mexicans from resenting it." The era of border raids was finally past, but the advent of Prohibition in 1920 initiated a new wave of smuggling. Americans still wanted liquor and Mexicans became primary suppliers, sneaking barrels and bottles across isolated stretches along the border. Incalculable amounts were smuggled. Only about seventy-five U.S. border agents patrolled 1,900 miles; according to historian Miguel Levario, "Whatever [these] officials discovered and confiscated was only a fraction of what was making it through." In 1924, Congress appropriated $1 million to hire 472 additional agents, the genesis of the modern-day U.S. Border Patrol.

The Texas Rangers also hunted smugglers along the Rio Grande, though state budget cuts reduced their ranks first to about fifty, then twenty-five. Their harsh tactics were increasingly challenged in court, and in 1935, the state legislature transferred the Rangers from personal control by the governor to the newly established Texas Department of Public Safety. The March 1935 issue of *Texas Municipalities* noted, "Ranger methods are no longer suited for fighting modern crime."

Border liquor smuggling remained rampant until 1933, when the cash-strapped U.S. government realized that taxes on liquor and beer would provide desperately needed revenue. But repeal of Prohibition didn't eliminate demand for smuggled Mexican products to satisfy illegal American appetites. Drugs eventually replaced alcohol. National government in Mexico City still lacked control in Mexico's northern states. Drug cartels eventually emerged there, operating as virtual fiefdoms. Besides the challenge of surviving in desperate economic times, Mexico's common people, especially in the north, were often in physical danger. For many, life in America had to be better—at least there were jobs helping to raise and harvest crops. Mexican immigrants constantly arrived, some seeking seasonal employment, others determined to stay permanently. During the first nine months of 1929, prior to the October advent of the Great Depression, forty thousand Mexicans crossed the border and were hired to work on farms and ranches. But the collapse of the American economy triggered fresh waves of anti-Mexican sentiment: unemployed Americans needed those jobs. The government responded. Over the next five years, the annual number of Mexicans admitted legally into the U.S. dropped from a high of 61,000 to about 2,000. In 1929, Congress also passed legislation making illegal entry a felony. In 1930, over 500,000 Mexican nationals relocated back across the border, either voluntarily or via deportation. That same year, all Mexican applications for "common labor" entry were denied. Still, immigrants and war refugees kept coming, illegally if necessary. The current solution of confining unwanted border arrivals in bare-bones detention camps exactly replicates the first such camp at Fort Wingate, New Mexico, more than a century ago.

Periodically, the American government has built physical barriers to discourage unauthorized border crossing. Immediately following World War II, U.S. officials used 5.8 miles of chain link fence from a Japanese American internment camp to block a portion of the border below Calexico. In the mid-1990s, Operation Gatekeeper extended San Diego–area border fences and walls for forty-five miles. Within a few years, high metal-concrete hybrid fences began appearing between some bifurcated border cities, including Douglas–Agua Prieta, Ambos Nogales, and El Paso–Juárez. In 2006, the Secure Fence Act mandated seven hundred additional miles of border barriers, and, during his successful campaign for the presidency in 2016, Donald J. Trump guaranteed construction of a "big, beautiful wall" along the entire border, entirely paid for by Mexico. That proved problematic. Long border stretches of rocky heights and steep crevices still physically defy wall construction; in other areas, high winds have blown down supposedly completed sections. In May 2020, the website of U.S. Customs and Border Protection (CBP) noted construction of 170 miles of new wall, funded entirely by the U.S. after Mexico refused. The Mexican economy remains tenuous. Even if Mexico agreed to pay for the wall, it could never do so without bankrupting itself.

Besides many more miles of wall along the border, there has also been a resurgence of American civilian militias, encouraged by inflammatory political rhetoric. Just as in 1915, when heavily armed, self-appointed posses rode out to hunt down Mexicans, these twenty-first-century militias—often attired in camouflage, carrying semiautomatic weapons, and traveling in pickup trucks rather than on horseback—scout the U.S. side, seeking out what they regard as suspicious-looking Hispanics. The American vigilantes and their Mexican prey from over a century ago would nod in recognition: in so many ways on the border, inherent mutual mistrust and hostility remain.

>─┤─◆─0─◆─├─<

Columbus, New Mexico, still looks much like it did when Pancho Villa attacked in 1916. Its 1,600-resident mix of Anglos and Hispanics live in an eclectic array of low-slung houses, and the air is usually thick with dust. Only the ratio of Anglo and Hispanic residents has changed. In March 1916, they were approximately equal. Today, 88 percent of Columbus's population is Hispanic. The last train passed through town in 1961; the boxy depot has been converted into a museum by the Columbus Historical Society. Besides some items representing residents' daily lives generations ago, its exhibits mostly concern Villa's raid, especially a detailed table diorama that dominates one of the two main rooms. Just outside is the depot's sparse memorial garden, where a gazebo stands lonely guard amid constantly swirling winds. There's another museum just across the road; it also has some raid-related exhibits, but focuses mainly on regional history, with special emphasis on the Mexican Revolution. This museum is part of Pancho Villa State Park, established by New Mexico's state legislature in 1959. The name, retired park manager John Read explains, was intended as a gesture "of putting things behind us, of moving forward." Some white Columbus residents have protested the name for years, to no avail. When travelers visit the park, many spend the night in its spacious camp area, often parking RVs near the base of Cootes Hill, where Villa once stood as he ordered his *muchachos* to attack.

Most of the time, Columbus is virtually somnambulant, its only commotion the rumble of eighteen-wheelers hauling freight to and from Palomas, still three miles south just past the U.S.-Mexican border. An exception occurs every year on March 9, when the historical society holds its Raid Day Memorial program at the train depot and the state park hosts a series of lectures on area history. Proceedings are considerably spiced up by the annual *Cabalgata* [Mounted Procession] *Binacional* Ride of Goodwill; hundreds of costumed riders trot snorting horses up from Palomas and down from Deming and points north. They meet on the road between the depot and park, exchanging waves and cheers. For a change, Columbus is bustling—an estimated eight hundred to a thousand visitors come to town for the festivities. There's a low stage where dancers and musicians perform all afternoon, and food trucks sell a variety of treats. Cars park in every direction on dusty streets. During the 2019 festivities, license plates on a single block indicated visitors from Sonora, Chihuahua, Durango, Texas, Maryland, and Virginia.

But there is a sense of division in Columbus, too, as obvious as the towering metal border wall that has replaced the old barbed wire fence at the Palomas crossing point. The Columbus Historical Society memorial program takes place in the morning, and the Pancho Villa State Park events are held in the afternoon. There's no co-hosting or sharing of microphones. The morning program honors those who died in Villa's 1916 raid. At one point, the names of the 13th Cavalry troopers who fell are called by the master of ceremonies, and selected members of the audience reply, "Present," after each one. Representatives of the Border Patrol are introduced and applauded. Afterward octogenarian Richard Dean, the grandson of James Dean, one of the civilians gunned down by Villistas, guides about thirty people on a walking tour of the battle sites, leading the way along the chughole-pocked town streets in his motorized wheelchair before calling a halt halfway through because "the sun's way up and the rattlesnakes are out." Except for the town mayor, who is Hispanic, everyone at the morning program appears to be Anglo, and only Anglos take the walking tour. The crowd at the park programs later in the day is larger and racially mixed. On the afternoon of March 9, 2019, one of the topics was past and present border treatment of refugees, and the changes to that treatment that are needed. As attendees mingle between programs, a few grumble about local mossbacks who can't get over something that happened more than a century ago. There are efforts to move beyond the antagonisms of the past. The September 5, 2019, edition of the *El Paso Times* includes a story describing recent renovations to the actual border crossing point at Palomas ("port of entry" in modern-day terms), including a new wall "the color of the desert," rimmed with "native vegetation [that] freshens the landscape," and topped with solar panels. According to the article, the intent is to "make entry into the United States an inspiring and dignified experience." But to considerable extent, the disdain between Anglos and Hispanics remains ingrained. At the conclusion of the March 9 morning program in Columbus, a member of the historical society responds to a compliment about the size of the crowd in town by observing, "Oh, it's mostly horses and Mexicans."

Notes

PROLOGUE: COLUMBUS, NEW MEXICO, MARCH 8–9, 1916

Much of the information here comes from extensive interviews with historians Arnoldo de León, Miguel Levario, Charles H. Harris III, and Louis R. Sadler; Carlton Stowers, who interviewed one of Villa's purported spies; John Read, retired director of Pancho Villa State Park in Columbus, New Mexico; and the late Richard Dean, longtime Columbus, New Mexico, resident/historian and organizer of the town's annual memorial program held on March 9.

1 *described by one U.S. soldier stationed there:* "Staff Ride AA-07 draft," Fort Bliss Archives.

1 *home to perhaps five hundred hardscrabble civilians:* John S. D. Eisenhower, *Intervention! The United States and the Mexican Revolution, 1913–1917*, pp. 217–18.

1 *But to Villa, desperate after several overwhelming defeats:* Miguel Levario, Charles H. Harris III, Louis R. Sadler, John Read, and Richard Dean interviews.

2 *Woodrow Wilson and his advisors made the decision:* Herbert Malloy Mason Jr., *The Great Pursuit*, p. 62; Eisenhower, *Intervention!*, p. 185; Levario, Harris, and Sadler interviews.

2 *Though a 1900 census indicated:* John Kenneth Turner, *Barbarous Mexico*, p. 311.

3 *summarily executed all seventeen:* Some accounts state eighteen Americans were killed.

4 *Villa was willing to attempt even bloodier provocation:* Historians have long debated Villa's purpose in attacking Columbus. Was it for supplies, or perhaps to avenge himself on a town arms dealer who'd sold him defective goods? I'm in agreement with Miguel Levario, who believes that after failing to incite American intervention after the massacre at Santa Ysabel, Villa decided that the only certain way to arouse American wrath sufficiently for U.S. forces to come into Mexico would be to murder Americans in their own country.

4 *For two dreadful weeks, Villa led his followers:* The best description of this ordeal is found in Eileen Welsome's *The General and the Jaguar: Pershing's Hunt for Pancho Villa,* pp. 62–80.

4 *The conscripts weren't told where they were going:* There's considerable disagreement among experts whether everyone among the Villistas knew the plan or that most did not. In January 1916, Villa turned back on a trip to attack American border towns in Texas because too many conscripts panicked and deserted after learning they would be fighting American soldiers. He would have learned from this and kept the Columbus information from new conscripts on the march to New Mexico.

5 *Villa sent spies ahead to scout Columbus:* Carlton Stowers and Richard Dean interviews.

6 *But Villa was troubled by another observation:* Read interview.

6 *Villa's subordinates rarely disputed their leader's decisions:* Report of the Punitive Expedition, pp. 28–29. Some information in this report was based on interrogations of captured Villistas, some of whom participated in the Columbus raid.

6 *Villa and his captains led their men north:* Report of the Punitive Expedition, pp. 29–31. Portions of this report involving the Columbus attack were based on interrogations of Villista prisoners who had participated.

7 *the temperature was cool but not cold:* Clarence C. Clendenen, *Blood on the Border: The United States Army and the Mexican Irregulars,* p. 200.

7 *A clock hanging outside the train depot:* Read interview; Columbus raid exhibits at Pancho Villa State Park include the depot clock; when a bullet struck the clock, its hands froze at 4:11.

7 *Villa hissed, "Vámonos, muchachos":* Report of the Punitive Expedition, p. 31.

CHAPTER ONE: MEXICO AND AMERICA

For a comprehensive account of Mexico's past, I recommend *Fire and Blood: A History of Mexico* by T. R. Fehrenbach. Sigrid Maitrejean, a retired foreign service officer for the U.S. Department of State, board member of the Pimeria Alta Historical Society in Nogales, Arizona, and U.S.-Mexican border native, was especially insightful during my research into the U.S. land courts.

9 *The first envoys of the United States government arrived:* Arnoldo de León interview; Arnoldo de León, *They Called Them Greasers: Anglo Attitudes Toward Mexicans in Texas, 1821–1900,* p. 4; Rachel St. John, *Line in the Sand: A History of the Western U.S.-Mexican Border,* p. 17.

10 *A newly formed government committee on foreign affairs:* David M. Pletcher, *The Diplomacy of Annexation: Texas, Oregon, and the Mexican War,* pp. 64–67.

10 *colonists in Texas took advantage:* Arthur R. Gomez, *A Most Singular Country: A History of Occupation in the Big Bend*, p. 41.

10 *Within days, Mexico's congress removed him:* T. R. Fehrenbach, *Fire and Blood: A History of Mexico*, pp. 384–93.

11 *Mexican leaders believed:* Miguel Levario, Arnoldo de León, Charles H. Harris III, and Louis R. Sadler interviews.

11 *The New York Herald was more plainspoken:* Greg Grandin, *The End of the Myth: From the Frontier to the Border Wall in the Mind of America*, pp. 151–52.

11 *President James K. Polk offered $25 million:* St. John, *Line in the Sand*, p. 19.

11 *Polk brandished his stick:* Robert W. Merry, *A Country of Vast Designs: James K. Polk, the Mexican War, and the Conquest of the American Continent*, pp. 240–41.

12 *General William T. Sherman subsequently suggested:* Benjamin Heber Johnson, *Revolution in Texas: How a Forgotten Revolution and Its Bloody Suppression Turned Mexicans into Americans*, p. 7.

12 *The U.S. set up a series of "land courts":* Sigrid Maitrejean interview.

12 *It was sixteen months after the peace treaty was signed:* St. John, *Line in the Sand*, p. 2; Lynn R. Bailey, *The "Unwashed Crowd": Stockmen and Ranches of the San Simon and Sulphur Spring Valleys, Arizona Territory, 1878–1900*, p. 57.

14 *Carbajal recruited a troop of American volunteers:* Clendenen, *Blood on the Border*, pp. 18–19.

14 *needed only eight minutes of deliberation to acquit Walker:* The experience didn't faze Walker. In 1855 he recruited another band of mercenaries, invaded Nicaragua, and temporarily installed himself as president before a combined troop of Costa Rican, Honduran, Salvadoran, and Guatemalan soldiers unseated him. Walker escaped to New York City, enjoyed a hero's welcome there, then set out on another attempt to conquer and rule his own country. The third time wasn't the charm. His 1860 attempt to become leader of part of Honduras failed. Walker was captured and executed.

14 *America began pressing Mexico to sell more land:* Fehrenbach, *Fire and Blood*, p. 412; St. John, *Line in the Sand*, p. 35; Louis Bernard Schmidt, "Manifest Opportunity and the Gadsden Purchase," paper presented on March 1960 at the Arizona Historical Convention; Miguel Levario interview.

15 *Thirty-five-year-old Juan Cortina had fought for Mexico:* Harris, Sadler, de León, and Levario interviews; de León, *They Called Them Greasers*, pp. 54–55; Stephen Harrigan, *Big Wonderful Thing: A History of Texas*, pp. 260–62; David Montejano, *Anglos and Mexicans in the Making of Texas, 1836–1986*, pp. 32–33; Clendenen, *Blood on the Border*, p. 53.

17 *Mexico was deeply in debt:* Levario and de León interviews; John Mason Hart, *Empire and Revolution: The Americans in Mexico Since the Civil War*, p. 9; Uni-

versity of El Paso Special Collections, MS 157, Box 26, Folder 64; Grandin, *The End of the Myth*, p. 153; Fehrenbach, *Fire and Blood*, pp. 424–36.

CHAPTER TWO: BORDER FENCES AND REVOLUTION

For a comprehensive account of Porfirio Díaz's business dealings with American financiers, I recommend John Mason Hart's excellent *Empire and Revolution: The Americans in Mexico Since the Civil War.*

19 *A few months later Díaz revolted:* Hart, *Empire and Revolution*, p. 67; Stuart Easterling, *The Mexican Revolution: A Short History, 1910–1920*, pp. 6–15.

20 *Díaz met in New York City with U.S. business leaders:* Hart, *Empire and Revolution*, pp. 1–3.

21 *William Randolph Hearst, delighted with his new, sprawling ranch property:* Ibid., p. 167.

21 *eventually owned between them approximately 95 percent:* Clendenen, *Blood on the Border*, p. 124.

21 *Outside investment in Mexico totaled $1.2 billion:* Friedrich Katz, *The Life and Times of Pancho Villa*, pp. 16–17.

21 *according to a report by the U.S. consul general:* New York Times, 12/23/1903.

21 *The glittering economic successes disguised a contradiction:* Arnoldo de León and Miguel Levario interviews.

22 *had no option other than to work for the rich Mexican hacendados or American landowners:* St. John, *Line in the Sand*, p. 72; John Kenneth Turner, *Barbarous Mexico*, pp. 111, 122; Montejano, *Anglos and Mexicans in the Making of Texas*; Hart, *Empire and Revolution*, pp. 224–25, 253.

22 *an average of about three thousand every year:* Hart, *Empire and Revolution*, pp. 271–72.

23 *they clustered together, refusing to learn Spanish:* Ibid., pp. 235–36.

23 *The reporter noted that it was difficult:* New York Times, 2/9/1902.

23 *Mexicans were often stigmatized as* greasers: Arnoldo de León interview.

24 *Anglos remembered the Alamo and Juan Cortina:* Miguel Levario interview.

24 *They believed that annexation would burden America:* Hart, *Empire and Revolution*, pp. 233–34.

24 *In 1891 he granted a lengthy interview:* Buffalo (New York) Morning Express, 7/12/1891.

24 *one American government survey indicated:* New York Times, 12/23/1902.

24 *a young lawyer named Ricardo Flores Magón published:* Charles H. Harris III and Louis R. Sadler interviews; Charles H. Harris III and Louis R. Sadler, *The Border and the Revolution: Clandestine Activities of the Mexican Revolution, 1910–1920*, p. ix.

25 *The newspaper and fledgling political party gained support:* University of Texas at El Paso Special Collections, MS 157, Box 45, Folder 3.

25 *Magón was soon arrested:* Charles H. Harris III and Louis R. Sadler, *The Texas Rangers and the Mexican Revolution: The Bloodiest Decade, 1910–1920*, p. 27.

25 *Among the first was the 2.4-million-acre Wood Hagenbarth Ranch: El Paso Herald,* 11/4/1903. The Wood Hagenbarth business conglomerate, headquartered in Salt Lake City, acquired the vast Palomas Land and Cattle Company in 1902.

26 *In 1909, the bureau proposed erecting a barbed wire fence:* St. John, *Line in the Sand,* pp. 203–4. In 1910, the California–Baja California fence proposal was approved by both the Mexican and American governments, with construction to begin in 1911. But by then the Mexican Revolution was at such bloody heights that the project was delayed and eventually abandoned.

26 *Díaz granted an interview to a writer from Pearson's Magazine:* Katz, *The Life and Times of Pancho Villa,* p. 52; St. John, *Line in the Sand,* p. 121.

26 *Madero's flowery speeches lacked specific promises:* Harris, Sadler, and Levario interviews; C. M. Mayo, "The Secret Book by Francisco I. Madero, Leader of Mexico's 1910 Revolution," *Journal of Big Bend Studies,* Vol. 29, 2017.

27 *The historic meeting took place in October 1909:* Charles H. Harris III and Louis R. Sadler, *The Secret War in El Paso: Mexican Revolutionary Intrigue, 1906–1920,* pp. 1–16; Harris and Sadler interviews.

27 *In a note to his wife immediately following the meeting:* Paul Horgan, *Great River: The Rio Grande in American History,* p. 907.

27 *compared it to "a microbe's challenge to an elephant":* Welsome, *The General and the Jaguar,* pp. 18–20.

27 *Díaz had his rival arrested:* Jim Tuck, *Pancho Villa and John Reed: Two Faces of Romantic Revolution,* p. 7.

28 *Fewer than a dozen showed up:* Katz, *The Life and Times of Pancho Villa,* p. 54.

28 *Madero sent a formal letter:* Gene Z. Hanrahan, *Documents on the Mexican Revolution,* Archives of the Big Bend, Sul Ross University. Hanrahan compiled copies of missives between the U.S. embassy in Mexico City and the State Department, including private as well as official correspondence. These are divided into several bound volumes, with material presented chronologically. It makes for fascinating reading.

28 *Taft ordered twenty thousand U.S. troops:* Ibid. Excellent information on these "maneuvers" and other aspects of the American military at this time can also be found in two books by Thomas T. Smith, *The Old Army in Texas: A Research Guide to the U.S. Army in Nineteenth Century Texas* and *The Old Army in the Big Bend of Texas: The Last Cavalry Frontier, 1911–1921.*

28 *Taft approved a projected first step:* Charles H. Harris III and Louis R. Sadler, *The Archaeologist Was a Spy,* p. 24.

29 *Madero gathered the bulk of his rebel forces:* University of Texas at El Paso Special Collections, MS 157, Box 5, Folder 5; Katz, *The Life and Times of Pancho Villa,* pp. 103–17; Welsome, *The General and the Jaguar,* p. 25; Tuck, *Pancho Villa and John Reed,* pp. 9–10; Harris and Sadler, *The Border and the Revolution,* p. 30; Harris and Sadler interviews.

29 *sailed off aboard the German steamer* Ypiranga: Tuck, *Pancho Villa and John Reed,* p. 49

CHAPTER THREE: THE AMERICAN PUPPETEER

31 *almost immediately his coalition began disintegrating:* Arnoldo de León, Miguel Levario, Charles H. Harris III, and Louis R. Sadler interviews.

32 *Wilson wrote that he entered diplomatic service:* Henry Lane Wilson, *Diplomatic Episodes in Mexico, Belgium and Chile,* p. 12.

33 *Wilson warned Secretary Knox in a memo:* This, as well as all other quotes from or citation of Wilson's correspondence with Washington, Madero's letter to President Taft, and the resignation statement attributed to Madero and Vice President Suárez, is taken from Gene Z. Hanrahan's invaluable *Documents on the Mexican Revolution,* available to researchers in the Archives of the Big Bend at Sul Ross State University, Alpine, Texas. I urge anyone interested to go see the Hanrahan volumes for yourself. They make for astonishing reading.

33 *Born in 1878 to sharecropper parents:* Katz, *The Life and Times of Pancho Villa,* pp. 64–77; Welsome, *The General and the Jaguar,* pp. 20–22; Tuck, *Pancho Villa and John Reed,* pp. 7–8, 22–29, 41–42; Levario interview.

34 *Villa had a dispute:* Katz, *The Life and Times of Pancho Villa,* pp. 163–64.

35 *Madero wrote to Villa:* Ibid., pp. 161–62.

35 *Villa was promptly placed before a firing squad:* Easterling, *The Mexican Revolution,* pp. 70–71; Tuck, *Pancho Villa and John Reed,* pp. 51–52; Katz, *The Life and Times of Pancho Villa,* pp. 165–67.

35 *Madero sent word:* Katz, *The Life and Times of Pancho Villa,* p. 189.

35 *troops led by federal General Manuel Mondragón:* Eisenhower, *Intervention!,* pp. 10–32; Col. Frank Tompkins, *Chasing Villa: The Last Campaign of the U.S. Cavalry,* p. 5.

CHAPTER FOUR: "I DO NOT KNOW WHAT TO MAKE OF MEXICO"

39 *it wasn't enough, Wilson insisted:* Miguel Levario interview; Max Boot, *The Savage Wars of Peace: Small Wars and the Rise of American Power,* p. xxii.

40 *That changed in 1898 with the Spanish-American War:* Arnoldo de León and Miguel Levario interviews.

42 *Huerta nicknamed him "the Puritan of the North":* Barbara W. Tuchman, *The Zimmermann Telegram*, p. 37.

43 *Carranza sent telegrams to America's lame-duck president:* Lt. Col. Moses N. Thisted, *With the Wisconsin National Guard on the Mexican Border, 1916–1917*, p. 123.

43 *Orozco, returning from his U.S. exile:* Tuck, *Pancho Villa and John Reed*, p. 10.

44 *Carranza made the best of his precarious situation:* Eisenhower, *Intervention!*, pp. 38–43; Clendenin, *Blood on the Border*, pp. 152–53; Tuck, *Pancho Villa and John Reed*, pp. 142–43; Joseph Stout Jr., *Border Conflict: Villistas, Carrancistas and the Punitive Expedition, 1915–1920*, p. 11; Charles Harris III and Louis R. Sadler interviews; Harris and Sadler, *The Texas Rangers and the Mexican Revolution*, p. 118; Katz, *The Life and Times of Pancho Villa*, pp. 195–203; Easterling, *The Mexican Revolution*, pp. 68–71.

45 *Villa had become a popular local figure:* Harris and Sadler interviews.

45 *some of his closest friends affectionately called him "Pancho":* Levario interview.

45 *In a matter of weeks, he recruited five hundred troops:* Tuck, *Pancho Villa and John Reed*, pp. 52–53.

45 *In six months, Villa led several thousand:* Welsome, *The General and the Jaguar*, p. 36. Some estimates range as high as eight thousand.

46 *he eventually operated fifteen different trains:* *Arizona Star*, 5/6/1973.

46 *Villa even paid his soldiers a regular wage:* Ibid.

46 *The American consul based in Nogales:* St. John, *Line in the Sand*, pp. 126–27.

46 *Both held the opinion:* Michael Kazin, *A Godly Hero: The Life of William Jennings Bryan*, pp. 228–30.

47 *Including banning liquor at State Department events:* Ibid., pp. 217–18.

47 *Unlike Taft, President Wilson had grave doubts:* Eisenhower, *Intervention!*, pp. 30–37.

47 *Henry Lane Wilson bombarded:* All additional quotes from and reference to Ambassador Wilson's messages to Secretary Bryan—and Bryan's replies—come from Hanrahan, *Documents on the Mexican Revolution*.

48 *President Wilson, despairing of constructive advice:* Tompkins, *Chasing Villa*, p. 13.

48 *he received a private communication from President Wilson:* Ibid.

49 *The Bureau of Investigation was established:* U.S. Department of Justice, *The FBI: A Centennial History*, pp. 4–8. In 1935, the organization was renamed the Federal Bureau of Investigation. My favorite book about its history is Dr. Willard M. Oliver's *The Birth of the FBI: Teddy Roosevelt, the Secret Service, and the Fight over America's Premier Law Enforcement Agency*.

49 *opening, reading, and reporting suspicious mail:* Harris and Sadler interviews.

49 *In a meeting with an English official:* Thisted, *With the Wisconsin National Guard on the Mexican Border, 1916–1917*, p. 125.

50 *He sent emissaries to sound out Villa:* Eisenhower, *Intervention!*, pp. 50–51.

50 *Wilson made clear in a public announcement:* Tompkins, *Chasing Villa*, p. 12.

51 *In a September letter to his wife:* John F. Chalkley, *Zach Lamar Cobb: El Paso Collector of Customs and Intelligence During the Mexican Revolution, 1913–1918*, pp. 8–9.

51 *Wilson had a plan to compensate:* Ibid., pp. 64–65; Levario and de León interviews.

52 *Villa had just taken Juárez:* Harris and Sadler, *The Secret War in El Paso*, p. 150; Welsome, *The General and the Jaguar*, p. 37; Katz, *The Life and Times of Pancho Villa*, pp. 223–26.

52 *Carranza refused:* John Milton Cooper Jr., *Woodrow Wilson: A Biography*, pp. 241–42; Eisenhower, *Intervention!*, pp. 65–66; Harris and Sadler interviews.

52 *the State Department sent a telegram:* University of Texas at El Paso Special Collections, MS 157, Box 26, Folder 64.

CHAPTER FIVE: FILM CREWS AND
THE REFUGEES NOBODY WANTED

55 *Villa interpreted this as evidence:* Eisenhower, *Intervention!*, p. 57.

55 *Villa paused in Chihuahua City:* Katz, *The Life and Times of Pancho Villa*, pp. 236–40.

56 *Pancho Villa was going to be a movie star:* Mike Dash, "Uncovering the Truth Behind the Myth of Pancho Villa, Movie Star," Smithsonian.com, 11/6/2012.

56 *Other sources indicate Villa sold these rights:* Easterling, *The Mexican Revolution*, p. 78.

57 *The fighting began during the second week in January:* Tuck, *Pancho Villa and John Reed*, p. 55.

57 *Ángeles was an artillery expert:* Katz, *The Life and Times of Pancho Villa*, pp. 272–79.

57 *the federals and refugees abruptly abandoned Ojinaga:* Harris and Sadler, *The Texas Rangers and the Mexican Revolution*, pp. 162–63; Smith, *The Old Army in Texas*, pp. 18–19.

58 *the movie crew was unable to film:* Dash, "Uncovering the Truth Behind the Myth of Pancho Villa, Movie Star."

58 *It was not lost on hardscrabble residents:* Charles H. Harris III and Louis R. Sadler interviews.

59 *there were reports of 1,000 to 1,500 refugees:* Harris and Sadler, *The Texas Rangers and the Mexican Revolution*, p. 163.

59 *The entire U.S. Army comprised:* Smith, *The Old Army in Texas*, p. 3.

60 *Mexican laborers who knew their place:* Miguel Antonio Levario, *Militarizing the Border: When Mexicans Became the Enemy*, pp. 7, 11–12; Juan Manuel Casas, *Federico Villalba's Texas: A Mexican Pioneer's Life in the Big Bend*, p. 18; Miguel Levario and Arnoldo de León interviews.

60 *A U.S. government report:* St. John, *Line in the Sand*, pp. 103–5.

61 *more than 4,600 refugees flooded into Presidio:* My sources for the section describing the temporary care of the refugees in Shafter, their long, terrible walk from Presidio to Marfa, their train ride to El Paso, and their incarceration there and subsequent removal to Fort Wingate are: Interviews with Charles Harris III and Louis R. Sadler; Elam National Archives Military Records, Archives of the Big Bend, Box 3, Folder 5; Frances Faver Cline, Oral History C641cu 1983, Archives of the Big Bend; Sigrid Maitrejean interview; Harris and Sadler, *Texas Rangers and the Mexican Revolution,* pp. 162–63; Harris and Sadler, *The Secret War in El Paso,* p. 157; and Smith, *The Old Army in Texas,* pp. 18–19.

63 *Six months earlier, El Paso had received and housed:* Jessie Peterson and Thelma Cox Knoles, eds., *Pancho Villa: Intimate Recollections by People Who Knew Him,* pp. 170–71.

64 *They were taken to Fort Wingate in New Mexico:* Edith B. Lloyd, Archives of the Big Bend and Edith B. Lloyd letter, The NCO Leadership Center of Excellence NCO Historical Archives, U.S. Army Sergeant Majors Campus, Fort Bliss, Texas.

65 *revolutionaries controlled three-fourths of Mexico:* Mason, *The Great Pursuit,* p. 41.

65 *Germany approved of ongoing strife:* de León interview.

65 *Germany secretly established a War Intelligence Agency:* Heribert von Feilitzsch, *In Plain Sight: Felix A. Sommerfeld, Spymaster in Mexico, 1908 to 1914,* p. 27; Harris and Sadler, *The Archaeologist Was a Spy,* pp. 1–2; Heribert von Feilitzsch, *Felix A. Sommerfeld and the Mexican Front in the Great War,* pp. xxi–xxii; Heribert von Feilitzsch, *The Secret War Council: The German Fight Against the Entente in America in 1914,* pp. 147–48.

66 *Pershing studied the Mexican situation and notified the War Department:* Gen. John J. Pershing, edited by John T. Greenwood, *My Life Before the World War, 1860–1917,* p. 328.

CHAPTER SIX: VERACRUZ

An unexpectedly rich source of information for this chapter is the little known memoir by Edith O'Shaughnessy, wife of American chargé d'affaires Nelson O'Shaughnessy. In 1916, after Villa's attack on Columbus and during America's controversial Punitive Expedition into Mexico to capture and punish him, Harper & Brothers in New York published Mrs. O'Shaughnessy's *A Diplomat's Wife in Mexico.* This was a collection of letters written by her to family and friends back in the U.S., many of them composed during the seizing of and subsequent occupation of Veracruz. Mrs. O'Shaughnessy was particularly diligent in describing her husband's private comments about his meetings and negotiation with Huerta. Though *A Diplomat's Wife in Mexico* was long out of print, it has recently been republished and is now in public domain and available.

Interviews with Miguel Levario, Sigrid Maitrejean, Arnoldo de León, Charles H. Harris III, and Louis R. Sadler contributed to this entire chapter.

67 *On Thursday morning, April 9, 1914:* Robert E. Quirk, *An Affair of Honor: Woodrow Wilson and the Occupation of Veracruz*, pp. 11–69; Eisenhower, *Intervention!*, pp. 82–108; Clendenin, *Blood on the Border*, pp. 154–74.

69 *He spent Friday afternoon fruitlessly hunting:* Edith O'Shaughnessy, *A Diplomat's Wife in Mexico*, pp. 258–60.

70 *Americans learned that a German-registered ship:* Quirk, *An Affair of Honor*, pp. 69–84; Hart, *Empire and Revolution*, p. 307.

70 *President Taft's plan to invade Mexico:* Harris and Sadler, *The Archaeologist Was a Spy*, p. 24.

71 *Wilson wired orders, in all capital letters:* Tuchman, *The Zimmermann Telegram*, pp. 47–48.

71 *Just before 10 a.m. and the Ypiranga's scheduled arrival:* O'Shaughnessy, *A Diplomat's Wife in Mexico*, pp. 285–88; Quirk, *An Affair of Honor*, pp. 94–102; Eisenhower, *Intervention!*, pp. 109–24; Hart, *Empire and Revolution*, p. 308; Mason, *The Great Pursuit*, pp. 47–50; Welsome, *The General and the Jaguar*, pp. 46–47.

73 *they were American arms being legally delivered:* Welsome, *The General and the Jaguar*, pp. 46–47; Tuchman, *The Guns of August*, pp. 45–49; Quirk, *An Affair of Honor*, pp. 98–99.

73 *Wilson and his advisors did not understand:* Welsome, *The General and the Jaguar*, pp. 43–44.

74 *Wilson reimposed a full American arms embargo:* Harris and Sadler, *The Secret War in El Paso*, p. 176.

74 *Mexican newspapers reflected the rage:* O'Shaughnessy, *A Diplomat's Wife in Mexico*, pp. 287–91.

74 *so far as he was concerned:* Katz, *The Life and Times of Pancho Villa*, p. 337.

74 *Huerta privately admitted:* O'Shaughnessy, *A Diplomat's Wife in Mexico*, pp. 285–88.

75 *The American president admitted to a friend:* Eisenhower, *Intervention!*, pp. 131–32.

75 *hadn't he been the only Mexican leader:* Katz, *The Life and Times of Pancho Villa*, p. 355.

75 *he received a threatening message:* George Marvin, "The First Line of Defense in Mexico," *The World's Work*, August 1916.

76 *Funston sent numerous messages to Washington:* Eisenhower, *Intervention!*, pp. 132–33.

76 *Funston turned his energy and personal drive:* Ibid., pp. 136–38.

76 *The three organizing Latin nations wanted to broker:* Ibid., p. 132.

CHAPTER SEVEN: CARRANZA AND VILLA COLLIDE

The story of the Aguascalientes convention is too complex to describe in complete detail. It's worth an entire book on its own. Perhaps that book has yet to be written, because I couldn't find one.

80 *one of Villa's bloody, entirely unnecessary acts:* Peterson and Knoles, eds., *Pancho Villa*, p. 48; Katz, *The Life and Times of Pancho Villa*, pp. 326–30; Horgan, *Great River*, p. 914.

81 *Carranza tried to slow Villa's momentum:* Eisenhower, *Intervention!*, pp. 141–42.

81 *now decided to attack Zacatecas:* Tuck, *Pancho Villa and John Reed*, p. 56; Katz, *The Life and Times of Pancho Villa*, pp. 348–53.

82 *Villa wasn't oblivious to the welfare of his* soldados: Miguel Levario interview.

82 *Carranza was determined that Obregón:* Charles H. Harris III and Louis R. Sadler interviews.

83 *Now Woodrow Wilson communicated again:* Quirk, *An Affair of Honor*, pp. 156–65.

83 *England successfully cut the Atlantic Ocean cables:* Feilitzsch, *The Secret War Council*, p. 150.

84 *the Germans did, and took advantage:* Arnoldo de León interview.

84 *Germany would consider financing:* Tuchman, *The Guns of August*, p. 61.

84 *Pershing passed a private message to Villa:* Eisenhower, *Intervention!*, pp. 154–55.

85 *Messages from Zapata reached him:* Harris and Sadler interviews; Katz, *The Life and Times of Pancho Villa*, pp. 339–40.

85 *In another act of spontaneous fury:* Eisenhower, *Intervention!*, pp. 157–58; Tuck, *Pancho Villa and John Reed*, p. 156.

85 *Anxious for a solution that avoided additional war:* Harris, Sadler, and Levario interviews; Clendenin, *Blood on the Border*, p. 177; Easterling, *The Mexican Revolution*, pp. 93–98; Katz, *The Life and Times of Pancho Villa*, pp. 375–84.

86 *Carranza was ready to discuss terms:* Cooper, *Woodrow Wilson*, p. 244; Quirk, *An Affair of Honor*, pp. 166–71.

87 *welcoming crowds filled every open space:* Katz, *The Life and Times of Pancho Villa*, pp. 433–37; Easterling, *The Mexican Revolution*, pp. 100–104, 114–21; Tuck, *Pancho Villa and John Reed*, p. 128.

88 *Ángeles wanted Villa to take the División del Norte:* Katz, *The Life and Times of Pancho Villa*, pp. 478–83.

88 *proud peons who wouldn't understand:* Harris and Sadler interviews.

88 *Before he left Mexico City:* Katz, *The Life and Times of Pancho Villa*, pp. 460–61.

88 *A Japanese warship unexpectedly sailed:* Tuchman, *The Guns of August*, pp. 54–55.

89 *Villa once again demonstrated his loyalty to America:* Mason, *The Great Pursuit*, pp. 58–60; Gen. Hugh Lenox Scott, *Some Memories of a Soldier*, pp. 516–18.

90 *But that was when his opponents were mostly conscripted soldiers:* Harris and Sadler interviews.

90 *Gutiérrez gathered forces loyal to him:* Katz, *The Life and Times of Pancho Villa*, pp. 462–65.

90 *Carranza was relatively well funded:* Ibid., p. 455.

91 *Villa wore down opponents:* Harris and Sadler interviews.

91 *There were two great battles:* University of Texas at El Paso Special Collections MS 157, Box 45, Folder 33; Easterling, *The Mexican Revolution*, pp. 105–11; Welsome, *The General and the Jaguar*, pp. 52–54; *Arizona Star*, 5/6/1973.

92 *The Villistas dug in outside León:* Katz, *The Life and Times of Pancho Villa*, pp. 494–97; Welsome, *The General and the Jaguar*, pp. 54–55; Feilitzsch, *In Plain Sight*, p. 74.

93 *Constitutionalists controlled seven-eighths of Mexico:* Eisenhower, *Intervention!*, p. 183.

94 *German agents began hiring mercenaries:* Tuchman, *The Zimmermann Telegram*, pp. 75–76.

95 *Cobb learned that Huerta and Orozco were en route:* Chalkley, *Zach Lamar Cobb*, pp. 29–32.

95 *Wilson wasn't convinced:* Katz, *The Life and Times of Pancho Villa*, p. 510.

CHAPTER EIGHT: THE PLAN DE SAN DIEGO

As with the Aguascalientes convention, the *Plan de San Diego* is so complex and so critical to history that entire books could be written about it—and a fine one has: Charles H. Harris III and Louis R. Sadler's *The Plan de San Diego: Tejano Rebellion, Mexican Intrigue*. Several lengthy interviews with Harris and Sadler and their book are the basis for much of this chapter. If you find this chapter intriguing, you should read their book.

97 *Villarreal contacted authorities in McAllen:* William M. Hager, "The Plan of San Diego," *Arizona and the West*, Winter 1963; Harrigan, *Big Wonderful Thing*, pp. 477–80; Mike Cox, *Time of the Rangers: Texas Rangers from 1900 to the Present*, pp. 62–65.

98 *There was nothing original about would-be Mexican revolutionaries:* Harris and Sadler interviews.

99 *After the arrival of the railroad:* Arnoldo de León interview; Harrigan, *Big Wonderful Thing*, pp. 473–74.

99 *Their resentment was natural:* de León interview.

100 *"you meet a bunch of Mexicans":* Levario, *Militarizing the Border*, pp. 24–27.

100 *"Those Tejanos who tried to remain":* de León interview.

100 *on February 20 when nothing happened:* Montejano, *Anglos and Mexicans in the Making of Texas*, pp. 118–19.

101 *"We must presently do":* Tompkins, pp. 34–35.

101 *Texas governor James E. Ferguson asked the president:* Gomez, *A Most Singular Country*, pp. 135–36.

101 *The cause of border raids, Funston declared:* Ibid., p. 136.

102 *There was an ominous sense:* Harris and Sadler, *The Texas Rangers and the Mexican Revolution*, pp. 210–21.

102 *there was finally confrontation:* Ibid, p. 261.

103 *he would require at least fifty thousand soldiers:* Ibid., p. 254.

103 *Carranza, encouraged by Villa's concurrent battlefield defeats:* Miguel Levario interview.

103 *August was worse:* Harris and Sadler, *The Texas Rangers and the Mexican Revolution*, pp. 259–61.

104 *The attackers chose the buildings:* Monica Muñoz Martinez, *The Injustice Never Leaves You: Anti-Mexican Violence in Texas*, p. 21; Arnoldo de León, ed., *War Along the Border: The Mexican Revolution and Tejano Communities*, pp. 73–74.

105 *They were helped in August by the plotters themselves:* Harrigan, *Big Wonderful Thing*, p. 480.

105 *Flores Magón had always included these races:* Harris and Sadler interviews.

105 *South Texas Tejanos began choosing the risks of war:* Harris and Sadler, *The Texas Rangers and the Mexican Revolution*, p. 272.

106 *General Funston acknowledged the emergency was greater:* Ibid., pp. 266–69.

106 *General Pershing took issue with that restriction:* Pershing, *My Life Before the World War*, pp. 334–35.

106 *raiders crossed the river and attacked:* Harris and Sadler, *The Texas Rangers and the Mexican Revolution*, p. 283.

107 *Private Richard Johnson was taken prisoner:* Ibid., pp. 286–87.

107 *Funston informed the War Department:* Ibid., pp. 289–91.

CHAPTER NINE: THE TEXAS RANGERS
AND THEIR BANDIT WAR

The history of the Texas Rangers is long and controversial. This chapter focuses only on their conduct during the Bandit War, and it obviously does not reflect well on them. The facts make it impossible to represent the Rangers otherwise. I owe a special thanks for material in this chapter that was provided to me by historian Doug J. Swanson. Though his *Cult of Glory: The Bold and Brutal History of the Texas Rangers* had not yet been published as I worked on my own book, he generously shared with me not only portions of his manuscript, but copies of key documents pertaining to events we were both writing about.

109 *In a letter written to his mother:* Roy Aldrich Papers, Archives of the Big Bend.

109 *There were never many full-time Rangers:* Charles H. Harris III, Louis R. Sadler, and Doug J. Swanson interviews.

110 *Ranger Captain Leander McNelly sent a message:* Harrigan, *Big Wonderful Thing,* pp. 378–79.

110 *"The two men responsible for this crime":* Aldrich Papers, Archives of the Big Bend.

110 *to the Rangers they all looked alike:* Arnoldo de León and Miguel Levario interviews.

110 *"We were feared as men were never feared":* David J. Weber, ed., *Foreigners in Their Native Land: Historical Roots of the Mexican American,* pp. 188–90.

111 *Rangers were considered:* Carlysle Graham Raht, *The Romance of the Davis Mountains and Big Bend Country: A History,* p. 248.

111 *"there is mighty little to do here":* Aldrich Papers, Archives of the Big Bend.

112 *Henry Lee Ransom was a veteran:* Harris and Sadler, *The Texas Rangers and the Mexican Revolution,* pp. 255–58.

113 *The Rangers had names of suspected raiders:* Swanson interview.

113 *to them, Mexicans lacked the mental acuity:* Levario interview.

113 *Company D encountered Jesús Bazán and Antonio Longoria:* Harrigan, *Big Wonderful Thing,* pp. 472–73.

114 *The Rangers went in shooting:* Harris and Sadler, *The Plan de San Diego,* p. 45.

114 *the corpses of fourteen Mexicans were found:* Ibid., pp. 77–78.

114 *"nothing less than death squads":* Doug J. Swanson interview.

114 *"We can't leave the ranch":* Aldrich Papers, Archives of the Big Bend.

114 *"in my judgment 90 percent of those":* Harris and Sadler, *The Plan de San Diego,* p. 45.

114 *encouraged them to do more:* Ibid., pp. 78–82.

115 *Their term for the Rangers became "los rinches":* de León interview.

115 *Tejanos began sympathizing:* Levario interview.

115 *As many as one to three thousand Tejanos:* Montejano, *Anglos and Mexicans in the Making of Texas,* p. 125.

115 *"Mexicans who had always been tractable":* Ibid., p. 119.

116 *"They will all be killed in the long run":* Aldrich Papers, Archives of the Big Bend.

116 *an organic movement among resentful Mexicans:* It has never been determined who planned, organized, and directed the *Plan de San Diego.* Historians energetically disagree, some blaming Carranza, others Germany, and a few are convinced that it was an organic movement sometimes supported by Carranza

and Germany to further their own ends. I am part of the organic camp. It is always possible for diligent, objective researchers to study the same facts and arrive at different conclusions. I invite readers to make up their own minds.

117 *He wrote in his diary:* Tuchman, *The Zimmermann Telegram*, p. 82.

CHAPTER TEN: WILSON CHOOSES CARRANZA

119 *Villa sensed what was coming:* Katz, *The Life and Times of Pancho Villa,* pp. 499–510.

120 *each "Villa peso" was worth about 30 U.S. cents:* Ibid., pp. 510–13.

120 *Scott was still surprised:* Mason, *The Great Pursuit,* p. 61.

121 *if he could strike out west and take one or two other critical border towns:* Punitive Expedition Report, p. 5.

121 *He believed his own iron will would inspire his troops:* Miguel Levario interview.

122 *his plan was no longer secret:* Eisenhower, *Intervention!,* pp. 189–91.

123 *Villa seemed calm:* Welsome, *The General and the Jaguar,* pp. 58–59.

123 *Carranza made an immediate demand:* Charles H. Harris III and Louis R. Sadler interviews.

124 *the journalist later described:* Katz, *The Life and Times of Pancho Villa,* pp. 526–27. Katz writes that Villa also spoke briefly with General Funston.

124 *He told the physicians:* Eisenhower, *Intervention!,* p. 209.

124 *he posted a manifesto:* Katz, *The Life and Times of Pancho Villa,* pp. 528–30.

125 *When they came to Nogales:* Clendenin, *Blood on the Border,* pp. 189–90; St. John, *Line in the Sand,* p. 134.

125 *A few days later in the hamlet of San Pedro de la Cueva:* John Read and Richard Dean interviews; University of Texas at El Paso Special Collections, MS 157, Box 45, Folder 33; Thomas H. Naylor, "Massacre at San Pedro de la Cueva," *Western Historical Quarterly,* Vol. 8, No. 2.

126 *He declared that Carranza sold out to the U.S.:* Feilitzsch, *Felix A. Sommerfeld and the Mexican Front in the Great War,* p. 161.

126 *The U.S. provost marshal in El Paso:* Fort Bliss Archives.

126 *General Pershing and El Paso mayor Tom Lea announced:* Leon C. Metz, *El Paso Chronicles: A Record of Historical Events in El Paso, Texas,* p. 179.

127 *the Plan-related border raids immediately ceased:* Harris and Sadler interviews.

127 *Ferguson announced that border conditions:* Cox, *Time of the Rangers,* p. 72.

127 *Six days later in Matamoros:* San Antonio Express, 11/29/1915.

127 *Carranza envisioned a rosy future:* Katz, *The Life and Times of Pancho Villa,* pp. 546–50.

CHAPTER ELEVEN: SANTA YSABEL AND THE EL PASO RIOTS

129 *El Paso's civic and business leaders gathered:* Arnoldo de León, Miguel Levario, Charles H. Harris III, and Louis R. Sadler interviews.

130 *Pershing always excelled:* Abundant material regarding John J. Pershing's background and early military career can be found at the University of El Paso's Special Collections MS 157, Box 25, Folder 72. Other sources used in this chapter include Eisenhower, *Intervention!*, pp. 235–36; Mason, *The Great Pursuit*, pp. 76–80; Boot, *The Savage Wars of Peace*, pp. 190–192; and Welsome, *The General and the Jaguar*, pp. 163–67.

132 *Obregón helped his own cause:* Peterson and Knoles, eds., *Pancho Villa*, p. 55; Mason, *The Great Pursuit*, p. 63.

133 *Pancho Villa did not understand:* Levario interview.

134 *ordering all Americans there to leave Mexico or die:* Levario, *Militarizing the Border*, p. 44.

134 *The* El Paso Herald *printed its editorial doubts:* Smith, *The Old Army in the Big Bend of Texas*, p. 25.

134 *if it might not be possible to withdraw most U.S. troops:* Harris and Sadler, *The Plan de San Diego*, p. 117.

135 *he dictated a long message to Emiliano Zapata:* Archives of the Big Bend; Katz, *The Life and Times of Pancho Villa*, pp. 552–57; Welsome, *The General and the Jaguar*, p. 61.

135 *On Saturday, January 8:* This description of the massacre at Santa Ysabel is drawn from multiple sources, including interviews with Miguel Levario and Arnoldo de León; Punitive Expedition Report, pp. 8–9; James A. Sandos, *Rebellion in the Borderlands: Anarchism and the Plan of San Diego, 1904–1923*, p. 300; Katz, *The Life and Times of Pancho Villa*, pp. 557–60; Tompkins, *Chasing Villa*, pp. 38–39; de León, ed., *War Along the Border*, pp. 140–43; Eisenhower, *Intervention!*, pp. 214–16; Welsome, *The General and the Jaguar*, pp. 63–68; Peterson and Knoles, eds., *Pancho Villa*, p. 56.

138 *talk segued into violence:* Levario, *Militarizing the Border*, pp. 48–50; Metz, *El Paso Chronicles*, p. 181; de León, ed., *War Along the Border*, pp. 143–48; Levario interview.

140 *These restrictions remained in place:* Levario interview.

140 *Another incident further alienated:* Levario, *Militarizing the Border*, pp. 57–66, 72.

140 *Villa ordered his officers to begin:* Punitive Expedition Report, p. 114.

140 *That was more problematic for Carranza:* Fort Bliss Archives.

141 *there was a spate of desertions:* Katz, *The Life and Times of Pancho Villa*, pp. 560–61.

141 *Only weeks later, he sent out his officers:* Punitive Expedition Report, pp. 19–24; Katz, *The Life and Times of Pancho Villa*, pp. 561–62.

CHAPTER TWELVE: COLUMBUS

In this and subsequent chapters, considerable information is based on material from The NCO Leadership Center of Excellence, NCO Historical Archives, U.S. Army Sergeants Major Academy Campus, Fort Bliss, Texas. I'm deeply grateful to the Army, and in particular to the outstanding staff there, for allowing access to these important materials. Because of the length of the official title of these archives, they are referred to in individual notes as Fort Bliss Archives. No disrespect is intended.

143 *"bifurcated cities" sprang up:* St. John, *Line in the Sand,* pp. 83–85.

144 *Columbus wasn't entirely without amenities:* John Read interview.

144 *It was their responsibility to guard:* Tompkins, *Chasing Villa,* p. 42.

144 *Substance abuse was rampant:* "Staff Ride AA-07 draft," Fort Bliss Archives.

145 *"It's clear that at least some":* Ibid.

145 *Married officers lived with their families:* Richard Dean interview.

145 *The town was roughly divided:* Welsome, *The General and the Jaguar,* pp. 83–84.

146 *Anglos felt no particular discomfort:* John Read interview.

147 *Zach Lamar Cobb, director of customs for El Paso:* Levario, *Militarizing the Border,* p. 67; Feilitzsch, Felix A. *Sommerfeld and the Mexican Front in the Great War,* p. 178.

147 *the Mexican commander in Juárez:* Welsome, *The General and the Jaguar,* p. 93.

147 *Slocum needed only one sentence:* Elam National Archives Records, Archives of the Big Bend, Slocum folder.

148 *on the afternoon of March 7:* Tompkins, *Chasing Villa,* pp. 43–44; Welsome, *The General and the Jaguar,* p. 95. Some historians believe Munoz met with Slocum on March 7 and Favela on March 8.

148 *Slocum offered Muñoz $20:* Welsome, *The General and the Jaguar,* p. 95.

148 *The colonel was less direct with Favela:* Dean interview.

149 *Columbus merchant Louis Ravel delivered:* Clee Woods, "Night of Fury," *New Mexico,* March 1958. Some belief persists that Villa chose to attack Columbus solely in retaliation for Sam Ravel, Louis Ravel's brother, selling him defective ammunition. That action certainly factored in—during the raid, Villistas targeted Ravel's businesses—but if Villa targeted the hometowns of every American border businessman who sold him defective goods, Columbus would have been only one of hundreds of raids.

149 *Slocum accordingly issued orders:* Levario, *Militarizing the Border,* pp. 71–72; Tompkins, *Chasing Villa,* pp. 44–45.

150 *Slocum received a phone call:* Welsome, *The General and the Jaguar,* p. 104.

150 *Then Slocum left town:* Dean interview; Eisenhower, *Intervention!,* p. 221; Welsome, *The General and the Jaguar,* p. 104; Fort Bliss Archives.

150 *leaving in place the same minimal camp security:* Welcome, *The General and the Jaguar,* p. 104.

150 *First Lieutenant John P. Lucas disembarked:* Tompkins, *Chasing Villa,* pp. 50–51.

CHAPTER THIRTEEN: THE RAID

Above all other sources, information in this chapter is based on "Staff Ride AA-07 draft" from the remarkable NCO Leadership Center of Excellence, NCO Historical Archives, U.S. Army Sergeants Major Academy Campus, Fort Bliss Texas. This meticulously detailed study is the result of Army personnel visiting Columbus, New Mexico, and walking through every location of Pancho Villa's March 9, 1916, raid. With additional inclusion of relevant archival documents and, perhaps most of all, the creation of maps delineating participant movement for each critical moment of the battle, "Staff Ride AA-07 draft" is the most comprehensive account of the Columbus raid I found during my two years of research. I hope that in the future it will be made available to other civilian historians.

153 *Villistas chose victims in the same random way:* Richard Dean interview.

153 *Town veterinarian Harry Hart:* Welcome, *The General and the Jaguar,* p. 118.

154 *obeying orders to kill all the men:* Ibid., p. 116.

154 *Lucas had slept for only a few hours:* Tompkins, *Chasing Villa,* pp. 51–53.

156 *Parks's husband was out of town: Columbus Courier,* 5/26/1916.

157 *Slocum claimed:* Fort Bliss Archives (separate from "Staff Ride AA-07 draft").

157 *Major Frank Tompkins approached Slocum:* Tompkins, *Chasing Villa,* pp. 55–57.

158 *sixty-seven corpses were soaked:* There has always been considerable discrepancy in the number of Villistas killed, and also how many U.S. soldiers and Columbus civilians died. I relied on the information provided in the program for the March 9, 2019, remembrance ceremony in Columbus, and my January and March 2019 interviews with Richard Dean.

159 *Favela said that Slocum:* Peterson and Knoles, eds., *Pancho Villa,* p. 220.

CHAPTER FOURTEEN: "THE MOST SERIOUS SITUATION"

161 *President Wilson personally escorted Baker:* Scott, *Some Memories of a Soldier,* p. 518.

162 *Senator Albert Fall of New Mexico was advocating:* Haldeen Braddy, *Pershing's Mission in Mexico,* p. 8; Welcome, *The General and the Jaguar,* pp. 158–59.

162 *Baker went to his office:* Scott, *Some Memories of a Soldier,* pp. 519–20.

163 *Baker and Scott next sent a wire:* Ibid.

163 *Pershing was a better choice than Funston:* Boot, *The Savage Wars of Peace,* p. 190.

163 *Now, Wilson and Lansing believed:* "Correspondence Between Mexico and the United States Regarding the American Punitive Expedition 1916," *American Journal of International Law*, Vol. 10, No. 3, pp. 180–81; Welsome, *The General and the Jaguar*, pp. 159–60.

164 *he well understood the risk:* Charles H. Harris III and Louis R. Sadler interviews.

165 *the U.S. president acknowledged that he was reluctant:* Cooper, *Woodrow Wilson*, p. 322.

165 *Cobb wired from El Paso:* Chalkley, *Zach Lamar Cobb*, p. 69.

165 *Mexican residents were warned to clear out of town:* Richard Dean interview.

165 *There were rumors of Mexicans being randomly killed:* Ibid.

166 *They responded to Carranza:* "Correspondence Between Mexico and the United States Regarding the American Punitive Expedition 1916," *American Journal of International Law*, pp. 67–68.

166 *He demonstrated that he didn't like it:* Harris and Sadler interviews.

166 *Funston released to the press:* New York Times, 3/10/1916.

167 *he wrote privately to General Scott:* Fort Bliss Archives.

167 *Many civilians in Columbus also believed:* Ibid.

167 *Slocum provided a fuller written report:* Ibid.

168 *his superiors reminded him:* Tompkins, *Chasing Villa*, pp. 70–71; Punitive Expedition Report, p. 3.

168 *Trucks rolled in, but not many:* Smith, *The Old Army in the Big Bend of Texas*, p. 44.

169 *Patton, enthralled, did the same:* Carlo D'Este, *Patton: A Genius for War*, p. 175.

169 *he begged Pershing for a place:* Welsome, *The General and the Jaguar*, pp. 167–68; Mason, *The Great Pursuit*, pp. 184–85; Boot, *The Savage Wars of Peace*, p. 197; Eisenhower, *Intervention!*, p. 238.

170 *the Punitive Expedition totaled:* Mason, *The Great Pursuit*, pp. 83–85.

171 *But on the night of the 13th:* Punitive Expedition Report, p. 7; Tompkins, *Chasing Villa*, p. 71.

171 *The American troops had their guns ready:* Tompkins, *Chasing Villa*, p. 74.

172 *their canteen water was frozen solid:* Ibid. p. 75.

CHAPTER FIFTEEN: ELUSIVE PREY

I found the Punitive Expedition Report cited in this chapter in the Fort Bliss Archives. Some of the information included in that report comes from interrogation of captured Villistas and is the basis for my description of Villa's movements, particularly after he was wounded at Guerrero.

173 *Villa castigated these officers:* Punitive Expedition Report, p. 34.

174 *On March 15, Villa reached El Valle:* Ibid., p. 41.

175 *This portion of the northern Mexican state:* Stout, *Border Conflict,* p. 22; Punitive Expedition Report, p. 40.

175 *His first informants indicated:* Braddy, *Pershing's Mission in Mexico,* p. 11.

175 *Pershing telegraphed Funston:* Punitive Expedition Report, pp. 10–14.

176 *"They were of little use":* Pershing, *My Life Before the World War,* p. 346.

176 *Funston was angry with Pershing:* Fort Bliss Archives.

176 *Lansing received formal notification:* "Correspondence Between Mexico and the United States Regarding the American Punitive Expedition 1916," *American Journal of International Law,* pp. 185–86.

176 *Two days later, Lansing replied:* Ibid.

176 *Mexico City's immediate response:* Ibid., p. 187.

177 *the Villistas rode in to Namiquipa:* Braddy, *Pershing's Mission in Mexico,* p. 13.

178 *Dodd had his forces there the next day:* Tompkins, *Chasing Villa,* pp. 78–84; Welsome, *The General and the Jaguar,* pp. 187–89.

178 *dead horses in particular:* Welsome, *The General and the Jaguar,* p. 188.

179 *Villa divided his forces accordingly:* Braddy, *Pershing's Mission in Mexico,* p. 15; Tompkins, *Chasing Villa,* pp. 161–63; Punitive Expedition Report, p. 47.

179 *into the back of Villa's right leg:* Braddy, *Pershing's Mission in Mexico,* p. 15. Opinions vary among historians whether Villa was struck in the right or left leg. In *The Great Pursuit,* Herbert Malloy Mason Jr. quotes Modesto Nevares, one of the reluctant conscripts, about their efforts to shoot Villa during the first battle at Guerrero. Nevares describes seeing Villa shot in the right leg.

180 *a Mexican alerted Dodd:* Welsome, *The General and the Jaguar,* pp. 190–93; Boot, *The Savage Wars of Peace,* p. 193; Braddy, *Pershing's Mission in Mexico,* pp. 15–16; Punitive Expedition Report, pp. 14–15, 41–47.

181 *Villa's entourage inched their way toward Parral:* Punitive Expedition Report, pp. 63–68; Mason, *The Great Pursuit,* pp. 126–27; Welsome, *The General and the Jaguar,* pp. 189, 193–96; Braddy, *Pershing's Mission in Mexico,* pp. 17–18.

182 *The Punitive Expedition had its own difficulties:* Tompkins, *Chasing Villa,* pp. 93, 106, 147, 151.

182 *Lieutenant Patton especially delighted:* Ibid., pp. 113, 116–18.

183 *Pershing suspected that most of the Villistas:* Welsome, *The General and the Jaguar,* pp. 199–206; Tompkins, *Chasing Villa,* pp. 116–18.

184 *"The history of Villa's bandit days":* Tompkins, pp. 116–18.

184 *Tompkins, homed in on Parral:* Braddy, *Pershing's Mission in Mexico,* pp. 26–27.

185 *a Mexican rode in:* Tompkins, *Chasing Villa,* pp. 135–36; Braddy, *Pershing's Mission in Mexico,* p. 27.

185 *Tompkins was puzzled:* My description of the battle in Parral comes primarily from three sources—Tompkins, *Chasing Villa,* pp. 137–46; Welsome, *The General and the Jaguar,* pp. 213–19; and Eisenhower, *Intervention!,* pp. 260–75.

There is one critical point of contention among historians. Some believe the mob in Parral was agitated into violence by Elisa Griensen Zambrano, a German national married to a Mexican husband and living in Parral. But Tompkins, who was actually there, describes "a small, compactly-built man . . . [who] was well-dressed and looked like a German." Though his guess regarding nationality must be regarded as a hunch, it still seems entirely possible, even probable, as events described in subsequent chapters bear out.

186 *It took more than three hours for the Americans:* Tompkins, *Chasing Villa,* pp. 153–57; Braddy, *Pershing's Mission in Mexico,* pp. 33–35.

187 *the Mexican government dispatched two vehement telegrams:* "Correspondence Between Mexico and the United States Regarding the American Punitive Expedition 1916," *American Journal of International Law,* pp. 192–95.

187 *Lansing . . . replied that the Punitive Expedition's purpose:* Ibid., p. 196.

188 *Pershing urged the opposite:* Pershing, *My Life Before the World War,* pp. 351–52.

188 *Funston wired back:* Welsome, *The General and the Jaguar,* p. 233.

188 *Some Villista officers printed and distributed:* Punitive Expedition Report, p. 61.

189 *U.S. border agent George Carothers had warned:* Fort Bliss Archives.

CHAPTER SIXTEEN: "RESPONSIBILITY FOR THE CONSEQUENCES"

191 *Baker, previously an advocate:* Eisenhower, *Intervention!,* p. 281.

191 *"it seems increasingly probable":* Horgan, *Great River,* p. 928.

192 *they presented three:* Mason, *The Great Pursuit,* pp. 147–48.

192 *Obregón and the two American generals met:* Tompkins, *Chasing Villa,* pp. 197–98; Eisenhower, *Intervention!,* pp. 282–86; Welsome, *The General and the Jaguar,* pp. 227–32; Mason, *The Great Pursuit,* pp. 153–54.

193 *Scott wrote in his memoirs:* Scott, *Some Memories of a Soldier,* pp. 522–23.

194 *Scott informed Washington:* Mason, *The Great Pursuit,* pp. 155–57; Braddy, pp. 49–51; Punitive Expedition Report, p. 27; Tompkins, *Chasing Villa,* pp. 191–92.

195 *A band of about sixty raiders:* Elam National Archives Military Records, Archives of the Big Bend, Box 4; "The Glen Springs Raid," Captain C. D. Wood, *West Texas Historical and Scientific Society,* No. 19 (Wood uses "Glen" rather than "Glenn," the accepted spelling in maps and other works by historians); Smith, *The Old Army in the Big Bend of Texas,* pp. 36–36; Mason, *The Great Pursuit,* pp. 169–72.

196 *The Mexican president informed the U.S.:* Mason, *The Great Pursuit,* pp. 173–74.

196 *they would be overwhelmed with opportunities:* Charles H. Harris III and Louis R. Sadler interviews; Miguel Levario interview; Harris and Sadler, *The Plan de*

San Diego, pp. 182–83; Harris and Sadler, *The Texas Rangers and the Mexican Revolution*, p. 302.

197 *placed more than forty additional agents and informers:* Harris and Sadler interviews; Harris and Sadler, *The Archaeologist Was a Spy*, pp. 7–8.

197 *Ferguson increased the Texas Rangers force:* Harris and Sadler, *The Texas Rangers and the Mexican Revolution*, p. 50.

197 *its self-appointed militiamen:* Casas, *Federico Villaba's Texas*, p. 24.

198 *He urged President Wilson:* Mason, *The Great Pursuit*, p. 174.

198 *There was concern that Germany:* Ibid., pp. 196–200.

198 *Pershing believed that they "were much aroused":* Punitive Expedition Report, p. 29.

199 *Patton was assigned to take ten soldiers:* Braddy, *Pershing's Mission in Mexico*, pp. 41–42; D'Este, *Patton*, pp. 173–77; Punitive Expedition Report, pp. 28–29; Welsome, *The General and the Jaguar*, pp. 261–62; Mason, *The Great Pursuit*, pp. 184–87; Eisenhower, *Intervention!*, p. 288.

200 *the Mexican government sent a formal, lengthy letter:* "Correspondence Between Mexico and the United States Regarding the American Punitive Expedition 1916," *American Journal of International Law*, pp. 197–211.

200 *Both the U.S. and Mexico had in place:* Harris and Sadler interviews.

201 *America held a basic, significant advantage:* Ibid.

201 *Pershing could not understand:* Pershing, *My Life Before the World War*, p. 355.

202 *A small force of American soldiers:* Tompkins, *Chasing Villa*, pp. 202–3; Welsome, *The General and the Jaguar*, pp. 261–66; Mason, *The Great Pursuit*, pp. 188–93.

202 *two thousand destitute refugees:* Metz, *El Paso Chronicles*, p. 183.

202 *An American consul in Mexico reported:* Tuchman, *The Zimmermann Telegram*, p. 88.

202 *Carranza was offering amnesty:* Harris and Sadler, *The Plan de San Diego*, pp. 134–35, 163–65.

202 *Lansing and Baker privately advised Wilson:* Tuchman, *The Zimmermann Telegram*, p. 89.

203 *Lansing still had not made an official reply:* Feilitzsch, *Felix A. Sommerfeld and the Mexican Front in the Great War*, p. 238.

203 *On the night of June 10:* Mason, *The Great Pursuit*, pp. 200–201.

204 *Treviño wired a stark warning:* Punitive Expedition Report, p. 30; Welsome, *The General and the Jaguar*, pp. 271–72.

204 *Brigadier General James Parker sent troops:* Harris and Sadler, *The Plan de San Diego*, pp. 185–89; Harris and Sadler interviews.

205 *Secretary Lansing finally sent an official reply:* "Correspondence Between Mexico and the United States Regarding the American Punitive Expedition 1916," *American Journal of International Law*, pp. 212–213.

CHAPTER SEVENTEEN: CARRIZAL

207 *The U.S. positioned warships:* Welsome, *The General and the Jaguar,* p. 272.

207 *General Obregón made a public plea:* Ibid.

207 *war against the U.S. was imminent:* Mason, *The Great Pursuit,* pp. 203–5.

208 *He summoned Captain Charles T. Boyd:* Braddy, *Pershing's Mission in Mexico,* p. 48.

208 *Pershing explained to Boyd:* Pershing, *My Life Before the World War,* pp. 355–56.

208 *"We are going to test that":* Eisenhower, *Intervention!,* p. 294.

209 *Morey, who did not know:* Ibid.

209 *McCabe agreed to let the U.S. troops spend the night:* Welsome, *The General and the Jaguar,* pp. 274–76; Mason, *The Great Pursuit,* pp. 208–9.

210 *The three American officers:* The description of the battle is drawn from interviews with Charles H. Harris III and Louis R. Sadler; Mason, *The Great Pursuit,* pp. 209–11; Welsome, *The General and the Jaguar,* pp. 276–81; Eisenhower, *Intervention!,* p. 297.

212 *Wilson learned the terrible news:* Mason, *The Great Pursuit,* pp. 212–13.

213 *Pershing was first informed:* Ibid.

213 *he dispatched a blistering message:* Ibid., p. 214.

213 *Pershing was less certain:* Harris and Sadler interviews.

214 *Then Pershing contacted Funston:* Pershing, *My Life Before the World War,* p. 359.

214 *the Mexican government sent a terse note:* Mason, *The Great Pursuit,* p. 215.

214 *Secretary Lansing responded:* Ibid.

215 *Venustiano Carranza was exultant:* Miguel Levario, Harris and Sadler interviews.

215 *any advantages held by his country would not last long:* Harris and Sadler interviews.

215 *the twenty million men in America:* Harris interview (via email).

216 *twenty-four men dressed in rags:* Eisenhower, *Intervention!,* p. 299; Mason, *The Great Pursuit,* p. 217; Welsome, *The General and the Jaguar,* p. 284.

216 *the Mexican government contacted Secretary Lansing:* Mason, *The Great Pursuit,* pp. 216–17.

216 *Wilson selected Secretary of the Interior Franklin K. Lane:* Horgan, *Great River,* p. 935.

216 *Congressional leaders offered an oblivious suggestion:* St. John, *Line in the Sand,* p. 131.

216 *Carranza was convinced:* Harris and Sadler interviews; Clendenen, *Blood on the Border,* p. 312.

216 *The Americans wanted to address:* Mason, *The Great Pursuit,* p. 223.

217 *Wilson couldn't afford:* Ibid.

217 *on orders from Carranza:* Harris and Sadler interviews.

217 *Pancho Villa was back:* Clendenen, *Blood on the Border,* pp. 312–13.

CHAPTER EIGHTEEN: THE RETURN OF VILLA

219 *Care for his injury was primitive:* Punitive Expedition, "Report of Operations of 'General' Francisco Villa Since November 1915," pp. 70–72.

219 *Villa could, if he chose, slip away:* Miguel Levario interview.

221 *Villistas attacked and overran several towns:* Mason, *The Great Pursuit*, pp. 223–24.

221 *There was no sighting of Villa himself:* Punitive Expedition Report on Villa, p. 81.

221 *temporarily capturing the state capital:* Welsome, *The General and the Jaguar*, p. 297.

222 *Mexican officials were stunned:* Punitive Expedition Report on Villa, p. 81.

222 *but not as much as General Pershing:* Charles H. Harris III and Louis R. Sadler interviews.

222 *In April 1916, Pershing assigned "special service officers":* Harris and Sadler interviews form the basis of this section about Pershing's unsuccessful attempt to assassinate Villa. I also drew information from the Punitive Expedition Report on Villa, pp. 70–79; Harris and Sadler, *The Border and the Revolution*, pp. 7–9, 12–15; and Welsome, *The General and the Jaguar*, pp. 294–96.

224 *the rejuvenated Villistas didn't assault:* Mason, *The Great Pursuit*, p. 225.

225 *it was time for the Punitive Expedition:* Ibid.

225 *Funston concurred, but Woodrow Wilson didn't:* Ibid.

225 *On December 24, the delegations jointly announced:* Eisenhower, *Intervention!*, p. 307; Mason, *The Great Pursuit*, pp. 228–29.

226 *In October, Villa published a grand "Manifesto to the Nation":* Mason, *The Great Pursuit*, p. 228.

226 *"Villa has called to his standard like a mad mullah":* Katz, *The Life and Times of Pancho Villa*, p. 587.

226 *There was a drawback:* Ibid.

227 *Carranza countered in early December:* St. John, *Line in the Sand*, pp. 137–38; Eisenhower, *Intervention!*, p. 309.

227 *Villa predicted to a reporter:* Braddy, *Pershing's Mission in Mexico*, p. 60.

227 *Three days after the Joint High Commission announced:* Hart, *Empire and Revolution*, p. 330; Mason, *The Great Pursuit*, p. 230.

CHAPTER NINETEEN: WITHDRAWAL

229 *Pershing and Tompkins believed this so strongly:* Pershing, *My Life Before the World War*, p. 358; Tompkins, *Chasing Villa*, p. 209.

229 *George Patton wrote that the U.S. president:* Katz, *The Life and Times of Pancho Villa*, p. 605.

230 *"the native Mexican is utterly unreliable"*: Punitive Expedition Report, p. 81.

230 *Pershing ordered that everyone participate:* Charles H. Harris III, Louis R. Sadler, and Arnoldo de León interviews; Boot, *The Savage Wars of Peace*, pp. 200–201; Pershing, *My Life Before the World War*, pp. 260–61; Eisenhower, *Intervention!*, pp. 307–8.

230 *"In the matter of fire tactics"*: Fort Bliss Archives.

230 *Slocum was a particular object:* Ibid.

231 *Pershing's concern for his men:* Clendenen, *Blood on the Border*, pp. 328–31; Welsome, *The General and the Jaguar*, pp. 287–89; Mason, *The Great Pursuit*, pp. 218–19.

231 *The commander himself enjoyed:* D'Este, *Patton*, pp. 179–80; Welsome, *The General and the Jaguar*, pp. 288–90.

232 *Carranza was certain that America would always treat Mexico:* de León, Sigrid Maitrejean, and Miguel Levario interviews.

233 *Carranza quietly sent representatives to Tokyo:* Thomas Boghardt, *The Zimmermann Telegram: Intelligence, Diplomacy, and America's Entry into World War I*, pp. 57–58.

233 *Carranza suggested to German officials:* Eisenhower, *Intervention!*, p. 311; Boghardt, *The Zimmermann Telegram*, p. 46.

234 *the Mexican envoy to Berlin followed up:* Boghardt, *The Zimmermann Telegram*, p. 46.

234 *Villa and his troops should attack:* Katz, *The Life and Times of Pancho Villa*, pp. 662–63.

234 *Pershing wired Army chief of staff Scott:* Fort Bliss Archives.

235 *The withdrawal column included:* Metz, *El Paso Chronicles*, p. 189; D'Este, *Patton*, p. 184.

235 *the Chinese were transferred to Fort Bliss:* Boot, *The Savage Wars of Peace*, p. 202; Smith, *The Old Army in the Big Bend of Texas*, p. 50.

236 *281 Villistas were "killed and captured"*: Punitive Expedition "Report of Operations of 'General' Francisco Villa Since November 1915," Appendix, pp. 7–8.

236 *The estimated cost to taxpayers:* Braddy, *Pershing's Mission in Mexico*, p. 66; Sandos, *Rebellion in the Borderlands*, p. 310.

236 *Now it would be Pershing:* D'Este, *Patton*, p. 184.

236 *at almost the same moment:* Tuchman, *The Zimmermann Telegram*, p. 139.

CHAPTER TWENTY: GERMANY MAKES ITS MOVE

There are books about the saga of the Zimmermann Telegram. In this chapter, I focus mostly on those aspects of the story regarding Mexico. For readers who want more complete descriptions, I recommend two books: Barbara W. Tuchman's heralded *The Zimmermann Telegram: America Enters the War, 1917–1918*, and Thomas

Boghardt's brilliantly researched *The Zimmermann Telegram: Intelligence, Diplomacy, and America's Entry into World War I*. As the notes for this chapter indicate, these titles were indispensable to me.

237 German government and military leaders met: Boghardt, *The Zimmermann Telegram*, pp. 62–75; Barbara W. Tuchman, *The Zimmermann Telegram: America Enters the War, 1917–1918*, pp. 125–30; Harrigan, *Big Wonderful Thing*, pp. 937–39.

237 German citizens would soon be reduced: John Toland, *Adolf Hitler*, p. 73.

240 Two missteps, both stemming at least in part: Boghardt, *The Zimmermann Telegram*, pp. 77–79; Tuchman, *The Zimmermann Telegram*, pp. 133–34.

242 Bernstorff's suggestion to the German military: Tuchman, *The Zimmermann Telegram*, pp. 134–35.

242 Eckhardt should take the German alliance proposal: Ibid., p. 144.

242 Had Germany made its offer: Charles H. Harris III and Louis R. Sadler interviews.

243 Aguilar visited Japan's mission: Boghardt, *The Zimmermann Telegram*, p. 217.

243 British intelligence shared the decoded Zimmermann Telegram: Tuchman, *The Zimmermann Telegram*, pp. 148–56; Mason, *The Great Pursuit*, pp. 234–35.

244 Wilson made his Monday address: Tuchman, *The Zimmermann Telegram*, pp. 156–57.

244 Carranza offered no public response: Boghardt, *The Zimmermann Telegram*, p. 218; Tuchman, *The Zimmermann Telegram*, pp. 164–67.

245 the Regular Army was not currently sufficient: Thisted, *With the Wisconsin National Guard on the Mexican Border*, p. 9.

245 Wilson appointed Henry P. Fletcher: Eisenhower, *Intervention!*, p. 310.

245 German U-boats sank three American ships: Tuchman, *The Guns of August*, pp. 178–79.

245 he declared that neutrality was no longer possible: Ibid., pp. 179–80.

245 Four days later, Congress approved: Michael McGerr, *A Fierce Discontent: The Rise and Fall of the Progressive Movement in America, 1870–1920*, pp. 279–81; Boghardt, *The Zimmermann Telegram*, p. 1.

245 Eckhardt pleaded with Carranza: Tuchman, *The Zimmermann Telegram*, pp. 177–78.

246 American troops reached France in three: John Keegan, *The First World War*, p. 372.

246 Prominent among them: Thomas T. Smith interview.

246 many Americans forgot about Mexico: Harris and Sadler interviews.

246 the gathered crowd cheered: Mason, *The Great Pursuit*, p. 235.

246 Texas Rangers responded in savage, indiscriminate fashion: Arnoldo de León and Doug J. Swanson interviews.

CHAPTER TWENTY-ONE: THE RANGERS GO TOO FAR

247 *nineteen-year-old Laird Engle joined:* Rebecca Johnson Collection, letters dated 8/29/1916, 9/2/1916, and 9/10/1916.

247 *"legacy of racial tension":* Harris and Sadler, *The Plan de San Diego,* pp. 259–63.

248 *there were sixty-four Texas Rangers:* Harris and Sadler, *Rangers Revolution,* p. 308.

249 *there were still sufficient arbitrary killings:* Texas State Library and Archives, Adjutant General Correspondence.

249 *Another memo from Austin in November:* Ibid.

249 *the Texas legislature approved:* Harris and Sadler, *The Texas Rangers and the Mexican Revolution,* p. 325.

249 *He promptly appointed a new Ranger adjutant general:* Cox, *Time of the Rangers,* p. 77.

250 *One of Harley's first acts:* Harris and Sadler, *Rangers Revolution,* pp. 381–86.

250 *"the Rangers may have made some mistakes in the past":* Ibid., p. 387.

250 *a band of Mexican raiders attacked:* Cox, *Time of the Rangers,* pp. 77–78.

250 *Ranger Captain J. M. Fox sent a message:* Aldrich Papers, Archives of the Big Bend.

251 *eight Company B Rangers:* Robert Keil, *Bosque Bonito: Violent Times Along the Borderlands During the Mexican Revolution,* pp. 27–34.

252 *Fox sent his account to Ranger headquarters:* Aldrich Papers, Archives of the Big Bend.

253 *Trust Fox rather than Warren:* Harris and Sadler, *Rangers Revolution,* p. 353.

253 *"Insofar as I know":* Texas State Library and Archives, Adjutant General Correspondence.

253 *Hanson, Harley's "special agent," informed his boss:* Ibid.

254 *On May 29 General W. A. Holsworth:* Elam Texas Ranger Force Records, 1901–1919, Folder 8, Archives of the Big Bend.

254 *Harley's assistant admonished the Ranger captain:* Ibid.

255 *J. M. Fox had responded to his Porvenir-related demotion:* Harris and Sadler, *Rangers Revolution,* pp. 400–402.

255 *Many Texans living along or near the border:* Doug J. Swanson interview.

256 *he used political connections:* Harris and Sadler, *Rangers Revolution,* p. 417.

256 *a relative of Canales named Santiago Tijerina:* Cox, *Time of the Rangers,* p. 87.

256 *Canales took the threat seriously enough:* Ibid.

256 *Canales introduced a bill:* Harris, Sadler and Swanson interviews; Harris and Sadler, *Rangers Revolution,* pp. 432–61; Cox, *Time of the Rangers,* pp. 90–97.

258 *There is no way to be certain:* Arnoldo de León, Swanson, Miguel Levario, John Read, Charles H. Harris III, and Louis R. Sadler interviews.

CHAPTER TWENTY-TWO: SHOWDOWN AT NOGALES

My description of Ambos Nogales is based on interviews with Sigrid Maitrejean and Axel Holm, lifelong residents and city historians.

259 *Carranza sought the support:* Katz, *The Life and Times of Pancho Villa*, pp. 616–20.

261 *the Germans approached Villa:* Chalkley, *Zach Lamar Cobb*, p. 83.

262 *So did powerful Americans:* Tuck, *Pancho Villa and John Reed*, pp. 185–86; Katz, *The Life and Times of Pancho Villa*, pp. 666–69.

263 *Villa clashed again with General Murguía:* Katz, *The Life and Times of Pancho Villa*, pp. 632–35.

263 *Villa's rebellion against Carranza was reduced:* Tuck, *Pancho Villa and John Reed*, p. 185.

263 *it was probably the ranch's location:* Cox, *Time of the Rangers*, p. 83.

263 *the same officer who was present:* Elam National Archive Military Records, Archives of the Big Bend, Box 3, Folder 2.

265 *Colonel W. J. Glasgow concluded:* Ibid.

265 *All Army pursuit of Mexican bandits:* Smith, *The Old Army in the Big Bend of Texas*, p. 62.

265 *the problem escalated to the point:* Elam National Archive Military Records, Archives of the Big Bend, Box 2, Folder 2.

266 *American border agents reported rumors of German military advisors:* Sigrid Maitrejean interview; Annita Harlan, "The Battles of Ambos Nogales, 1910–1920," courtesy of the Pima Alta Historical Society, Nogales, Arizona; Elliott Stearns, M.D., "Battle of Ambos Nogales," *Sombrero*, May 1990.

266 *The border itself ran along a main downtown street:* Axel Holm and Maitrejean interviews.

267 *Twice, Ambos Nogales was rocked:* St. John, *Line in the Sand*, p. 134; *Brownsville Daily Sentinel*, 11/27/1915; Clendenen, *Blood on the Border*, pp. 189–90.

267 *American guards shot and killed Mexican nationals:* Stearns, "Battle of Ambos Nogales."

267 *the two cities' mayors agreed to temporarily supplement:* Maitrejean interview.

267 *about 850 American soldiers were stationed on the Arizona side:* Stearns, "Battle of Ambos Nogales."

268 *"everything was war and Germans":* Harlan, "The Battles of Ambos Nogales, 1910–1920."

268 *The unidentified man who shuffled toward the downtown crossing:* Maitrejean and Holm interviews; Stearns, "Battle of Ambos Nogales"; St. John, *Line in the Sand*, pp. 143–44; Clendenen, *Blood on the Border*, pp. 346–49; *Tombstone Prospector*, 8/29/1915; *Washington Post*, 1/10/2019; *Nogales International*, 8/24/2018.

270 *Their solution was to replace:* Nogales International, 8/24/2018; St. John, *Line in the Sand,* pp. 144–49.

CHAPTER TWENTY-THREE: VILLA'S LAST ATTACK

271 *Villa hatched a plan:* Katz, *The Life and Times of Pancho Villa,* pp. 639–40.

272 *He was despondent enough to write:* Ibid., pp. 640–41.

273 *assuring everyone that he shared their outrage:* Miguel Levario interview.

274 *The numbers were still against him:* Katz, *The Life and Times of Pancho Villa,* p. 704.

274 *To raise the necessary money:* Charles H. Harris III and Louis R. Sadler interviews.

274 *Carranza, determined to no longer depend:* Katz, *The Life and Times of Pancho Villa,* pp. 681–704.

274 *Villa attacked and occupied key rail hub:* Harris and Sadler, *The Secret War in El Paso,* p. 313.

274 *Zapata had been lured into an ambush:* Easterling, *The Mexican Revolution,* p. 133.

275 *Now he was back:* Katz, *The Life and Times of Pancho Villa,* pp. 698–99.

275 *whose chief characteristic as a commander:* Ibid., pp. 706–7.

275 *So did General James B. Erwin:* Elam National Archives Military Records, Archives of the Big Bend, Box 2, Folder 5. General Erwin's remarkable six-page "Report of Action Against Villistas, June 15th and 16th, 1919" is the source for my description of the battle at Juárez. It includes the coded text of his instructions in the event of threat to American citizens in El Paso. As was the custom at that time among American military officers stationed along the border, he refers to federal soldiers as "Carranzistas."

277 *Snead, a veteran of the Punitive Expedition, recalled:* Peterson and Knoles, eds., *Pancho Villa,* pp. 239–40.

277 *General González insisted:* Harris and Sadler, *The Secret War in El Paso,* p. 365.

278 *Villistas would have taken the city:* Ibid., p. 365.

278 *A railroad manager in Chihuahua reported:* Katz, *The Life and Times of Pancho Villa,* p. 719.

278 *his reputation was tarnished further:* Ibid., pp. 719–20.

278 *General Joaquín Amaro, experienced and aggressive:* Ibid., p. 720.

279 *By spring 1920, it seemed inevitable:* Miguel Levario interview.

279 *Álvaro Obregón announced his intention:* Eisenhower, *Intervention!,* pp. 316–17.

CHAPTER TWENTY-FOUR: AFTERWARD

281 *agreed in July to lay down his arms:* Eisenhower, *Intervention!*, p. 322.

281 *Even the twenty-one* Villista *prisoners: Deming Headlight,* 4/29/1921.

282 *But some of the great landowners began breaking:* Hart, *Empire and Revolution,* p. 344.

282 *In early 1923, he mused to reporters:* Katz, *The Life and Times of Pancho Villa,* p. 756.

284 *offered "a return to normalcy":* Jeff Guinn, *The Vagabonds: The Story of Henry Ford and Thomas Edison's Ten-Year Road Trip,* p. 157.

285 *Pershing did not share this distinguished postwar career:* D'Este, *Patton,* p. 272.

285 *"there were irradicable hard feelings on both sides":* Arnoldo de León interview.

285 *"whatever [these] officials discovered:"* Miguel Levario interview.

285 *Only about seventy-five U.S. border agents:* St. John, *Line in the Sand,* p. 186.

285 *Congress appropriated $1 million:* Ibid.

286 *During the first nine months of 1929:* St. John, *Line in the Sand,* pp. 187–93.

287 *5.8 miles of chain link fence:* Ibid., pp. 203–4.

Bibliography

Books

Anderson, Mark Gronlund. *Pancho Villa's Revolution by Headline*. Red River Books/University of Oklahoma Press, 2000.

Bailey, Lynn R. *The "Unwashed Crowd": Stockmen and Ranches of the San Simon and Sulphur Spring Valleys, Arizona Territory, 1878–1900*. Westernlore Press, 2014.

Banks, Stephen A. *Doing My Duty: Corporal Elmer Dewey—One National Guard Doughboy's Experiences During the Pancho Villa Campaign and World War I*. Signature Book Printing, 2011.

Barry, John M. *The Great Influenza*. Penguin, 2009.

Beschloss, Michael. *Presidents of War: The Epic Story, from 1807 to Modern Times*. Crown, 2018.

Boghardt, Thomas. *The Zimmermann Telegram: Intelligence, Diplomacy, and America's Entry into World War I*. Naval Institute Press, 2012.

Boot, Max. *The Savage Wars of Peace: Small Wars and the Rise of American Power*. Basic Books, 2014, revised edition.

Braddy, Haldeen. *The Paradox of Pancho Villa*. Texas Western Press, 1978.

———. *Pershing's Mission in Mexico*. Texas Western Press, 1966.

Casas, Juan Manuel. *Federico Villalba's Texas: A Mexican Pioneer's Life in the Big Bend*. Iron Mountain Press, 2008.

Casteñeda, Jorge G. *Mañana Forever? Mexico and the Mexicans*. Alfred A. Knopf, 2011.

Cervantes, Federico. *Francisco Villa y la Revolución*. Ediciones Alonso, 1960.

Chalkley, John F. *Zach Lamar Cobb: El Paso Collector of Customs and Intelligence During the Mexican Revolution, 1913–1918*. Texas Western Press/University of Texas at El Paso, 1998.

Chang, Iris. *The Chinese in America*. Viking, 2003.

Clendenen, Clarence C. *Blood on the Border: The United States Army and the Mexican Irregulars*. Macmillan, 1969.

Coerver, Don M., and Linda B. Hall. *Texas and the Mexican Revolution: A Study in State and National Border Policy, 1910–1920*. Trinity University Press, 1984.

Cooper, John Milton Jr. *Woodrow Wilson: A Biography*. Alfred A. Knopf, 2009.

Cox, Mike. *Time of the Rangers: Texas Rangers from 1900 to the Present*. Forge, 2009.

Dalton, Kathleen. *Theodore Roosevelt: A Strenuous Life*. Alfred A. Knopf, 2002.

Daudistel, Marcia Hatfield, and Mimi R. Gladstein. *The Women of Smeltertown*. TCU Press, 2018.

Dean, Richard. *Pancho Villa Raids Columbus: March 9, 1916*. Self-published, 1986.

de León, Arnoldo. *They Called Them Greasers: Anglo Attitudes Toward Mexicans in Texas, 1821–1900*. University of Texas Press, 1983.

de León, Arnoldo, ed. *War Along the Border: The Mexican Revolution and Tejano Communities*. Texas A&M University Press, 2012.

de Quesada, Alejandro: *The Hunt for Pancho Villa: The Columbus Raid and Pershing's Punitive Expedition 1916–1917*. Osprey, 2012.

D'Este, Carlo. *Patton: A Genius for War*. HarperCollins, 1995.

de Varona, Frank. *Benito Juarez: President of Mexico*. Millbrook Press, 1994.

Diamond, Jared. *Guns, Germs, and Steel*. W. W. Norton, 1999.

Easterling, Stuart. *The Mexican Revolution: A Short History, 1910–1920*. Haymarket Books, 2012.

Eisenhower, John S. D. *Intervention! The United States and the Mexican Revolution, 1913–1917*. W. W. Norton, 1993.

Enoch, C. Reginald. *Mexico: Its Ancient and Modern Civilization, History and Political Conditions, Topography and Natural Resources, Industries and General Development*. T. F. Unwin, 1925.

Eppinga, Jane. *Nogales: Life and Times on the Frontier*. Arcadia Publishing, 2002.

Fehrenbach, T. R. *Fire and Blood: A History of Mexico*. Da Capo Press, 1995.

Ganster, Paul, with David E. Lorey. *The U.S.-Mexican Border Today: Conflict and Cooperation in Historical Perspective*. Rowman & Littlefield, 2016.

Gomez, Arthur R. *A Most Singular Country: A History of Occupation in the Big Bend*. Charles Redd Center for Western Studies/Brigham Young University, 1990.

Goodwin, Doris Kearns. *No Ordinary Time: Franklin and Eleanor Roosevelt: The Homefront in World War II*. Simon & Schuster/Touchstone, 1995.

Grandin, Greg. *The End of the Myth: From the Frontier to the Border Wall in the Mind of America*. Metropolitan Books, 2019.

Guinn, Jeff. *The Last Gunfight: The Real Story of the Shootout at the O.K. Corral—And How It Changed the American West*. Simon & Schuster, 2011.

———. *The Vagabonds: The Story of Henry Ford and Thomas Edison's Ten-Year Road Trip*. Simon & Schuster, 2019.

Guzman, Martin Louis, with translation by Virginia H. Taylor. *Memoirs of Pancho Villa*. University of Texas Press, 1975.

Harrigan, Stephen. *Big Wonderful Thing: A History of Texas*. University of Texas Press, 2019.

Harris, Charles H. III, and Louis R. Sadler. *The Archaeologist Was a Spy*. University of New Mexico Press, 2003.

———. *The Border and the Revolution: Clandestine Activities of the Mexican Revolution, 1910–1920*. High-Lonesome Books, 1988.

———. *The Great Call-Up: The Guard, the Border, and the Mexican Revolution*. University of Oklahoma Press, 2015.

———. *The Plan de San Diego: Tejano Rebellion, Mexican Intrigue*. University of Nebraska Press, 2013.

———. *The Secret War in El Paso: Mexican Revolutionary Intrigue, 1906–1920*. University of New Mexico Press, 2009.

———. *The Texas Rangers and the Mexican Revolution: The Bloodiest Decade, 1910–1920*. University of New Mexico Press, 2004.

Hart, John Mason. *Empire and Revolution: The Americans in Mexico Since the Civil War*. University of California Press, 2002.

Henderson, Timothy J. *The Mexican Wars for Independence*. Hill & Wang, 2009.

Horgan, Paul. *Great River: The Rio Grande in North American History*. Wesleyan University Press, 1984.

Hurst, James W. *Pancho Villa and Black Jack Pershing: The Punitive Expedition in Mexico*. Praeger, 2008.

———. *The Villista Prisoners of 1916–1917*. Yucca Tree Press, 2000.

Johnson, Benjamin Heber. *Revolution in Texas: How a Forgotten Revolution and Its Bloody Suppression Turned Mexicans into Americans*. Yale University Press, 2003.

Katz, Friedrich. *The Life and Times of Pancho Villa*. Stanford University Press, 1998.

———. *The Secret War in Mexico: Europe, the United States and the Mexican Revolution*. University of Chicago Press, 1981.

Kazin, Michael. *A Godly Hero: The Life of William Jennings Bryan*. Alfred A. Knopf, 2006.

Keegan, John. *The First World War*. Alfred A. Knopf, 1999.

Keil, Robert. *Bosque Bonito: Violent Times Along the Borderlands During the Mexican Revolution*. Center for Big Bend Studies, 2002.

Krauze, Enrique. *Mexico: Biography of Power, 1810–1996*. HarperCollins, 1997.

Levario, Miguel Antonio. *Militarizing the Border: When Mexicans Became the Enemy*. Texas A&M University Press, 2012.

Lorey, David E. *The U.S.-Mexican Border in the Twentieth Century*. SR Books, 1999.

Luján, Esteban, translation by Jonathan Van Coops. *El Rondín: Campañas del Coro-*

nel Toribio Ortega y del Coronel José de la Cruz Sánchez en la Revolución de 1912. Originally published 1912; Regent Press edition, 2019.

Martinez, Monica Muñoz. *The Injustice Never Leaves You: Anti-Mexican Violence in Texas*. Harvard University Press, 2018.

Mason, Herbert Molloy Jr. *The Great Pursuit*. Smithmark, 1970.

McGerr, Michael. *A Fierce Discontent: The Rise and Fall of the Progressive Movement in America, 1870–1920*. Free Press, 2003.

McLynn, Frank. *Villa and Zapata: A History of the Mexican Revolution*. Basic Books, 2000.

Merry, Robert W. *A Country of Vast Designs: James K. Polk, the Mexican War, and the Conquest of the American Continent*. Simon & Schuster, 2009.

Metz, Leon C. *The Border*. TCU Press, 2008.

———. *El Paso Chronicles: A Record of Historical Events in El Paso, Texas*. Mangan Books, 1993.

Miller, Roger G. *A Preliminary to War: The 1st Aero Squadron and the Mexican Punitive Expedition of 1916*. University Press of the Pacific, 2005.

Montejano, David. *Anglos and Mexicans in the Making of Texas, 1836–1986*. University of Texas Press, 1987.

Oliver, Willard M. *The Birth of the FBI: Teddy Roosevelt, the Secret Service, and the Fight over America's Premier Law Enforcement Agency*. Rowman & Littlefield, 2019.

O'Shaughnessy, Edith. *A Diplomat's Wife in Mexico*. Harper & Brothers, 1916.

Pershing, Gen. John J., edited by John T. Greenwood. *My Life Before the World War, 1860–1917*. University Press of Kentucky, 2013.

Peterson, Jessie, and Thelma Cox Knoles, eds. *Pancho Villa: Intimate Recollections by People Who Knew Him*. Hastings House, 1977.

Pletcher, David M. *The Diplomacy of Annexation: Texas, Oregon, and the Mexican War*. University of Missouri Press, 1973.

Quirk, Robert E. *An Affair of Honor: Woodrow Wilson and the Occupation of Veracruz*. University Press of Kentucky, 1962.

Ragsdale, Kenneth Baxter. *Quicksilver: Terlingua and the Chisos Mining Company*. Texas A&M University Press, 1976.

Raht, Carlysle Graham. *The Romance of the Davis Mountains and Big Bend Country: A History*. Rahtbooks Company, 1919; reprinted by Forgotten Books, 2012.

Reed, John. *Insurgent Mexico: With Pancho Villa in the Mexican Revolution*. Appleton, 1911.

Rodríguez, Juan Barragán. *Historia del Ejército y de la Revolución Constitucionalista*. Mexico, D.F.: Antigua Librería Robredo, 1946.

Ruiz, Ramón Eduardo. *Triumphs and Tragedy: A History of the Mexican People*. W. W. Norton, 1992.

Russell, Francis: *The Shadow of Blooming Grove: Warren G. Harding in His Times.* McGraw-Hill, 1968.

Russell, Thomas Herbert. *Mexico in Peace and War.* Reilly & Britton, 1914.

Sandos, James A. *Rebellion in the Borderlands: Anarchism and the Plan of San Diego, 1904–1923.* University of Oklahoma Press, 1992.

Scott, Gen. Hugh Lenox. *Some Memories of a Soldier.* The Century Co., 1928.

Smith, Thomas T. *The Old Army in Texas: A Research Guide to the U.S. Army in Nineteenth-Century Texas.* Texas State Historical Association, 2000.

———. *The Old Army in the Big Bend of Texas: The Last Cavalry Frontier, 1911–1921.* Texas State Historical Association, 2018.

St. John, Rachel. *Line in the Sand: A History of the Western U.S.-Mexican Border.* Princeton University Press, 2011.

Stout, Joseph Jr. *Border Conflict: Villistas, Carrancistas and the Punitive Expedition, 1915–1920.* TCU Press, 1999.

Swanson, Doug J. *Cult of Glory: The Bold and Brutal History of the Texas Rangers.* Viking, 2020.

Thisted, Lt. Col. Moses N. *With the Wisconsin National Guard on the Mexican Border, 1916–1917.* Self-published, 1966.

Toland, John. *Adolf Hitler.* Doubleday, 1976.

Tompkins, Col. Frank. *Chasing Villa: The Last Campaign of the U.S. Cavalry.* High-Lonesome Books, 1916; originally published by Military Service Publishing Company, 1934.

Torrans, Thomas. *Forging the Tortilla Curtain: Cultural Drift and Change Along the United States–Mexico Border from the Spanish Era to the Present.* TCU Press, 2000.

Tuchman, Barbara W. *The Guns of August: The Outbreak of World War I.* Random House, 1962; Random House trade paperback edition, 2014.

———. *The Zimmermann Telegram: America Enters the War, 1917–1918.* Macmillan, 1958; Random House trade paperback edition, 2014.

Tuck, Jim. *Pancho Villa and John Reed: Two Faces of Romantic Revolution.* University of Arizona Press, 1984.

Turner, John Kenneth. *Barbarous Mexico.* Charles H. Kerr & Company, 1911.

Utley, Robert M. *Lone Star Lawmen: The Second Century of the Texas Rangers.* Berkley Books, 2007.

von Feilitzsch, Heribert. *Felix A. Sommerfeld and the Mexican Front in the Great War.* Henselstone Verlag, 2014.

———. *In Plain Sight: Felix A. Sommerfeld, Spymaster in Mexico, 1908 to 1914.* Henselstone Verlag, 2012.

———. *The Secret War Council: The German Fight Against the Entente in America in 1914.* Henselstone Verlag, 2015.

Weber, David J., ed. *Foreigners in Their Native Land: Historical Roots of the Mexican American*. University of New Mexico Press, 1973.

Welsome, Eileen. *The General and the Jaguar: Pershing's Hunt for Pancho Villa*. Little, Brown, 2006.

Werne, John Richard. *The Imaginary Line: A History of the United States and Mexican Boundary Survey, 1848–1857*. TCU Press, 2007.

Wilson, Henry Lane. *Diplomatic Episodes in Mexico, Belgium and Chile*. Doubleday, Page & Co., 1927.

Witcover, Julius. *Marathon: The Pursuit of the Presidency, 1972–1976*. Viking, 1977.

Wright, Bill. *The Whole Damn Cheese: Maggie Smith, Border Legend*. TCU Press, 2018.

Magazines

American Historical Review, "The Treaty of Guadalupe-Hidalgo," by Jesse S. Reeves, Vol. 10, No. 2, January 1905.

American Journal of International Law, "Correspondence Between Mexico and the United States Regarding the American Punitive Expedition 1916," Vol. 10, No. 3.

Arizona and the West, "The Plan of San Diego: War and Diplomacy on the Texas Border," by James A. Sandos, Vol. 14, No. 1, Spring 1962; "The Plan of San Diego: Unrest on the Texas Border in 1915," by William M. Hager, Vol. 15, No. 4, Winter 1963.

Automobile Quarterly, "Charge of the Brigadier's Dodge," by Karla A. Rosenbusch, Vol. 39, No. 1, 1999.

Collier's, "What Happened in Columbus," by James Hopper, April 15, 1920.

El Paso Magazine, "El Paso and the American Revolution," by Leon Metz, September 1983; "The Saga of Pancho Villa, Pt. 1," by Leon Metz, September 1987; "The Saga of Pancho Villa, Pt. 2," by Leon Metz, October 1967; "The Saga of Pancho Villa, Pt. 3," by Leon Metz, November 1987; "The Texas Rangers" by Leon Metz, March 1988.

Grain Producers News, "La Senora Diablo," by Ray Bourbon as told to Carlton Stowers, April 1975.

Hispanic American Historical Review, "Precursors of the Mexican Revolution of 1910," by Charles C. Cumberland, Vol. 22, No. 2, May 1942.

Huachuca Illustrated, "The 10th Cavalry to the Rescue," Vol. 1, 1993.

Journal of Big Bend Studies, "J. J. Kilpatrick versus the Army: Strife in Candelaria, Texas, 1919–1921," by Lonn Taylor; and "The Secret Book of Francisco I. Madero, Leader of Mexico's 1910 Revolution," by C. M. Mayo, Vol. 29, 2017.

Journal of Latin American Studies, "Pancho Villa and American Security: Woodrow

Wilson's Mexican Diplomacy Reconsidered," by James A. Sandos, Vol. 13, No. 2, November 1981.

Journal of Popular Culture: "The Legacy of the Treaty of Guadalupe Hidalgo on Tejanos' Land," by Sonia Hernandez, Vol. 35, No. 2, September 2001.

Journal of the United States Cavalry Association, "Cavalry Work of the Punitive Expedition," by First Lieutenant George S. Patton Jr., Vol. 27, No. 111, January 1917.

New Mexico, "Night of Fury," by Clee Woods, March 1958.

New Mexico Historical Review, "Conditions Along the Border 1915—The Plan de San Diego," by Allen Gerlach, Vol. 43, No. 3, July 1968.

Policeman's News, "Along the Mexican Border," by Jack Rodolph, October 1919.

Prologue Magazine, "The United States Armed Forces and the Mexican Punitive Expedition, Pt. 1," by Mitchell Yockelson, Vol. 29, No. 3, Fall 1997.

The Quarterly Journal of Military History, "Greatest Unsung American General of World War I," by Edward M. Coffman, Summer 2006, Vol. 18, No. 4.

Sombrero, "Battle of Ambos Nogales" by Elliott Stearns, M.D., May 1990.

Southwestern Historical Quarterly, "Border Raids in the Lower Rio Grande Valley—1915," by Charles C. Cumberland, January 1954.

Texas Municipalities, "A State Police Force for Texas," by Paul E. Fidler, Vol. 22, March 1935.

True West, "Nine Days to Columbus," by Gerry Hawk, January 1998.

West Texas Historical and Scientific Society, "The Glen Springs Raid," by Captain C. D. Wood, Vol. 19.

Western Historical Quarterly, "Massacre at San Pedro de la Cueva: The Significance of Pancho Villa's Disastrous Sonora Campaign," by Thomas H. Naylor, Vol. 8, No. 2, April 1977.

The World's Work, "The First Line of Defense in Mexico," by George Marvin, August 1916.

Newspapers

Arizona Daily Star—5/6/1973
Arizona Republic—6/15/1911; 12/8/1924
Boston Daily Globe—9/5/1910
Brownsville Daily Sentinel—10/27/1915; 11/27/1915
Brownsville Herald—12/6/1942
Buffalo Morning Express—2/12/1891
Calexico Chronicle—9/13/1919; 9/27/1923
Columbus (New Mexico) *Courier*—11/5/1915; 5/26/1916
Corpus Christi Caller and Daily Herald—3/31/1916
Deming (New Mexico) *Headlight*—4/29/1921

El Paso Herald—11/1/1910; 1/14/1916; 3/11/1916; 3/27/1916
El Paso Times—11/4/1903; 1/29/1912; 1/11/1916; 1/12/1916; 3/11/1916; 3/20/1916; 3/24/1916; 3/25/1916; 4/1/1916; 4/4/1916; 7/22/1923
Fort Worth Star-Telegram—2/9/1920
Houston Chronicle—9/3/1915
Los Angeles Herald—10/25/1910; 8/24/1915
Los Angeles Times—10/11/1903; 8/9/1906; 9/16/1908; 3/30/1916
Marathon (Texas) Hustler—5/13/1916
New York Times—2/9/1902; 12/23/1902; 12/24/1912; 3/12/1913; 1/7/1914; 1/14/1914; 3/10/1916; 3/22/1916; 3/23/1916; 3/24/1916; 4/1/1916; 4/17/1916; 3/3/2019; 11/9/2019
Nogales International—8/24/1918; 3/21/1952
Omaha Daily Bee—7/22/1910
Philadelphia Inquirer—3/12/1916
Rapid City Daily Journal—4/4/1924
San Antonio Express—10/20/1915; 11/27/1915; 5/16/1916; 5/17/1916; 5/27/1916
San Antonio Light—5/17/1916; 5/18/1916
San Francisco Examiner—3/14/1916; 3/28/1916
San Luis Obispo Daily Telegram—2/4/1920
Tombstone Prospector—8/29/1918
Tucson Citizen—9/1/1911
Washington Post—1/10/2019

U.S. Government Publications

45th Congress Committee on Foreign Affairs, "Relations of the United States with Mexico," 1878.
63rd Congress, Second Session, Senate Doc. 566, Washington, D.C., 1914.
The FBI: A Centennial History, 1908–2008, U.S. Department of Justice.
Historical Sketch of the Diplomatic Post at Mexico City, Historical Studies Division, U.S. Department of State, August 1975.

U.S. Military Records

The NCO Leadership Center of Excellence, NCO Historical Archives, U.S. Army Sergeants Major Academy Campus, Fort Bliss, Texas.
Report of Operations of "General" Francisco Villa Since November 1915, by Headquarters, Punitive Expedition in the Field, Mexico (July 31, 1916).
Report of the Punitive Expedition by Maj. Gen. John J. Pershing, Commanding the Expedition (October 10, 1916).

Report of the War Department, 1915–16.

Report on Mobilization of the Organized Militia and National Guard of the United States, 1916 (published January 15, 1917).

The U.S. Army on the Mexican Border: A Historical Perspective, by Matt M. Matthews (The Long War Series Occasional Paper 22, Combat Studies Institute Press, Fort Leavenworth, Kansas, 2007).

U.S. Army Campaigns of World War I: The Mexican Expedition, 1916–1917 (U.S. Army Center of Military History, 2016; written by Julie Irene Prieto).

State Government Records

Arizona Historical Society, Tucson.

Sul Ross State University, Alpine, Texas—Archives of the Big Bend.

Texas State Library and Archives, Texas Adjutant General Correspondence.

University of Texas at El Paso Special Collections.

University of Texas at El Paso Special Collections Institute of Oral History: Col. H. Crampton Jones (ret.), Transcript No. 125, "Personalities and Events of the Pershing Expedition into Mexico."

Websites

The Anarchist Library, "Flores Magón and the Mexican Liberal Party," by Brian Morris, https://theanarchistlibrary.org/library/brian-morris-flores-magon-and -the-mexican-liberal-party/bbselect?selected=pre-post.

Fort Sam Houston Museum, http://ameddregiment.amedd.army.mil/Fshmuse/funston .htm.

Smithsonian.com, "Uncovering the Truth Behind the Myth of Pancho Villa, Movie Star," by Mike Dash, November 6, 2012.

Texas State Historical Association, *The Handbook of Texas Online,* https://tshaonline .org/handbook/online/articles/apk01.

United States Customs and Border Protection, https://www.cbp.gov/border-security /border-wall/border-wall-system.

Personal Papers

Ada Jones, "Battle of Nogales," an eyewitness account of the clash between federal and Constitutionalist troops on March 13, 1913. First published in *The Nogales International,* March 21, 1952. Cited here with permission of Pimeria Alta Historical Society, Nogales, Arizona.

Private Collection

Rebecca Johnson, Granbury, Texas: Letters from Laird Frierson Engle to Rosa Pauline Taylor—8/28/1916; 9/2/1916; 9/10/1916.

Transcript of Public Presentation

"Manifest Opportunity and the Gadsden Purchase," Louis Bernard Schmidt at the First Annual Arizona Historical Convention in Tucson, March 26, 1960.

Dissertation

John Busby McClung, "Texas Rangers Along the Rio Grande: 1910–1919," Diss., Texas Christian University, 1972.

Acknowledgments

Thanks as always to the tremendously talented Bob Bender, Johanna Li, Stephen Bedford, and Christine Calella at Simon & Schuster, and to literary agent Jim Donovan. Copy editor Fred Chase remains an unsung hero. I'm grateful to Andrea Ahles Koos, Jim Fuquay, Ralph Lauer, Anne E. Collier, Brooklee Han, Zetta Hamersley, and Yelena Koos for their work on research, photography, acquisition of photo rights, and scheduling. Carlton Stowers, James Ward Lee, Rebecca Moore, and Fielding McGehee read along as I wrote and offered advice and constructive criticism.

Thanks are also owed to these particularly knowledgeable historians and authors who generously spent so many hours answering my questions: the late Richard Dean, Arnoldo de León, Charles Harris III, Alex Holm, Rebecca Johnson, Miguel Levario, C. Sigrid Maitrejean, Louis R. Sadler, Doug J. Swanson, and John Read.

I especially want to recognize and commend the archivists and staff at several outstanding research institutions: everyone at the Pimeria Alta Historical Society in Nogales, Arizona; Claudia A. Rivers and Abbie Weiser at Special Collections, University of Texas at El Paso; Melleta Bell at the Archives of the Big Bend, Sul Ross State University; and Everett Dague, Sergeant Major Haywood Leon Vines, and Tabatha Bowen at the NCO Leadership Center of Excellence, NCO Historical Archives, U.S. Army Sergeants Major Academy Campus,

Fort Bliss, Texas. Their expertise informs every page. Without the guidance and assistance of such dedicated professionals, books like this one simply could not be written.

Everything I write is always for Nora, Adam, Grant, and Harrison. As usual, Cash kept me company as I worked.

Index

Photo Credits

Photo 1: City of Bisbee, Courtesy of the Bisbee Mining & Historical Museum

Photo 2: Arizona Historical Society, U.S. Army-Punitive Expedition: 1 (#28337)

Photo 3: Arizona Historical Society, Portraits-Carranza, Pres. V: 16 (#48110)

Photo 4: Arizona Historical Society, Portraits-Villa, Pancho: 102 (#29945)

Photos 5, 15, 17: University of Texas at El Paso Library, Special Collections Department

Photo 6: Arizona Historical Society, Portraits-Villa, Pancho: 102 (#46445)

Photo 7: Arizona Historical Society, Portraits-Villa, Pancho: 102 (#29942)

Photo 8: Courtesy of the El Paso Public Library, Border Heritage Center, Aultman Collection

Photo 9: Arizona Historical Society, U.S. Army-Punitive Expedition: 1 (#28351)

Photo 10: Arizona Historical Society, Douglas, AZ Photos ca. 1915-1917: 2 (#A7H)

Photo 11: Arizona Historical Society, Places-Out of State-Mexico-Soldiers, Wars and Revolutions: 2 (#44204)

Photo 12: Arizona Historical Society, Douglas, AZ Photos ca. 1915-1917: 3 (#AV)

Photo 13: Arizona Historical Society, U.S. Army-Punitive Expedition: 1 (#28358)

Photo 14: Arizona Historical Society, U.S. Army-Punitive Expedition: 1 (#28360)

Photo 16: Courtesy of Robert Runyon Collection, the Dolph Briscoe Center for American History, University of Texas at Austin

Photo 18: Arizona Historical Society, U.S. Army-Punitive Expedition: 1 (#28343)

Photo 19: Arizona Historical Society, U.S. Army-Punitive Expedition: 1 (#28370)

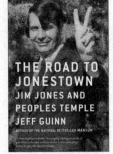

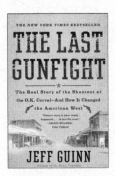